THE ECLIPSE OF BIBLICAL NARRATIVE

The Eclipse of Biblical Narrative

A Study in Eighteenth and Nineteenth Century Hermeneutics

Hans W. Frei

New Haven and London, Yale University Press

Library of Congress catalog card number: 73–86893
ISBN: 0–300–01623–9
         0–300–02602–1 pbk.

Designed by John O. C. McCrillis
and set in Baskerville type.
Printed in the United States of America by
BookCrafters, Inc., Chelsea, Michigan.

12   11   10   9   8   7

Contents

Preface

This essay falls into the almost legendary category of analysis of analyses of the Bible in which not a single text is examined, not a single exegesis undertaken. Faced with certain puzzles that demanded historical, philosophical, and theological explanations, I tried to provide them as best I could; but there is no denying the odd result of a book about the Bible in which the Bible itself is never looked at. Nonetheless, I am confident that the essay may have significant implications for the study of the Bible. In making that claim I have to put myself in the awkward position of advertising my own wares. Those who might want to know how I would put my thoughts to an exegetical test 1 refer to sections 10–13 in a brief theological experiment I tried some time ago, to be published by Fortress Press in the fall of 1974 under the title, *The Identity of Jesus Christ: An Inquiry into the Hermeneutical Bases of Dogmatic Theology*.

My debts in the present work are innumerable. Among authors who have been particularly influential on my thought I want to mention Erich Auerbach, Karl Barth, and Gilbert Ryle. The impact of Auerbach's classic study, *Mimesis: The Representation of Reality in Western Literature*, is evident throughout the essay. This great book has inevitably undergone increasingly severe scrutiny as the years have gone by. But to the best of my knowledge no student of the Bible has ever denied the power and aptness of the analysis of biblical passages and early Christian biblical interpretations in the first three chapters of *Mimesis*. And yet the reasons for the remarkable strength of these explorations have remained more or less and exasperatingly unexplored. I have tried in some measure to put his suggestions to use.

In the case of Karl Barth, I am most deeply indebted not to the famous commentary on Romans, nor to *The Doctrine of the Word of*

God, the methodological introduction to his *Church Dogmatics*, but to the later volumes of that monumental enterprise, beginning approximately with vol. II, 2, on the doctrine of divine election. It seems to me that Barth's biblical exegesis is a model of the kind of narrative reading that can be done in the wake of the changes I describe in this book. He distinguishes historical from realistic reading of the theologically most significant biblical narratives, without falling into the trap of instantly making history the test of the *meaning* of the realistic form of the stories. Simply as good instances of this procedure I want to cite, from a vast number of other examples, Barth's remarkable use of figural interpretation of the Old Testament in *Church Dogmatics* II, 2, pp. 340–409, and his narrative treatment of the gospel story in IV, 1, pp. 224–28. I must add that Barth would probably not have been very happy to receive this praise. In his hands theology becomes an imperious and allegiance-demanding discipline, and he might well have rejected out of hand the external treatment it receives in the present essay.

Gilbert Ryle's *The Concept of Mind* has been subjected to severe critical examination, much of it sound, in a discussion given the collective title of "The Philosophy of Mind." Nevertheless, anybody interested in hermeneutics has special reason to be grateful to the book for its demystification of the concept of intentional personal action, and the author's steady refusal to divide intelligent activity into separate mental and external components. It is a lesson well applied to the way one views written statements and hence also how to read them. It is best not to be dogmatic on these complex matters, but at the very least Ryle's work (although not directly about hermeneutics and whether or not finally successful) is a marvelous antidote to the contorted and to my mind unsuccessful efforts of certain phenomenologists and philosophers of "Existence" or "Being" to tackle a similar dualism. And therefore it serves to explain better than they do how it is that we can read written discourse with the expectation of doing it reasonably intelligently.

Anyone writing as slowly as I is particularly fortunate to have friends and colleagues with whom he can discuss matters he finds difficult, not only once or twice but through the years. There have been many such indispensable conversational partners while this book was in the making. Four of them not only aided in that capacity but read the manuscript and gave me penetrating advice. Without their encouragement and criticism I would not have finished, and that is the measure of my debt as well as my gratitude to them. They are William A. Clebsch, Stephen D. Crites, David H. Kelsey, and Claude Welch. Similarly indispensable was the patient, expert help of Jane Isay, Yale University Press editor, and of Anne Wilde, copyeditor. George Hunsinger aided greatly in the preparation of the index.

H. W. F.

Ezra Stiles College
Yale University
October 22, 1973

1 Introduction

Western Christian reading of the Bible in the days before the rise of historical criticism in the eighteenth century was usually strongly realistic, i.e. at once literal and historical, and not only doctrinal or edifying. The words and sentences meant what they said, and because they did so they accurately described real events and real truths that were rightly put only in those terms and no others. Other ways of reading portions of the Bible, for example, in a spiritual or allegorical sense, were permissible, but they must not offend against a literal reading of those parts which seemed most obviously to demand it. Most eminent among them were all those stories which together went into the making of a single storied or historical sequence. Long before a minor modern school of thought made the biblical "history of salvation" a special spiritual and historical sequence for historiographical and theological inquiry, Christian preachers and theological commentators, Augustine the most notable among them, had envisioned the real world as formed by the sequence told by the biblical stories. That temporal world covered the span of ages from creation to the final consummation to come, and included the governance both of man's natural environment and of that secondary environment which we often think of as provided for man by himself and call "history" or "culture."

The preeminence of a literal and historical reading of the most important biblical stories was never wholly lost in western Christendom. It actually received new impetus in the era of the Renaissance and the Reformation when it became the regnant mode of biblical reading. From it, modern biblical interpretation began its quest, in continuity as well as rebellion. Most important were three elements in the traditional realistic interpretation of the biblical stories, which also served as the foci for the rebellion against it.

First, if it seemed clear that a biblical story was to be read literally, it followed automatically that it referred to and described actual historical occurrences. The true historical reference of a story was a direct and natural concomitant of its making literal sense. This is a far cry from taking the fact that a passage or text makes best sense at a literal level as *evidence* that it is a reliable historical report. When commentators turned from the former to the latter interpretive use of literal meaning or used the two confusedly (as happened frequently in the later eighteenth century), it marked a new stage in the history of interpretation—a stage for which deistic convictions, empirical philosophy, and historical criticism form part of the technical intellectual background.

The second element in precritical realistic reading was that if the real historical world described by the several biblical stories is a single world of one temporal sequence, there must in principle be one cumulative story to depict it. Consequently, the several biblical stories narrating sequential segments in time must fit together into one narrative. The interpretive means for joining them was to make earlier biblical stories figures or types of later stories and of their events and patterns of meaning. Without loss to its own literal meaning or specific temporal reference, an earlier story (or occurrence) was a figure of a later one.[1] The customary use of figuration was to show that Old Testament persons, events, and prophecies were fulfilled in the New Testament. It was a way of turning the variety of biblical books into a single, unitary canon, one that embraced in particular the differences between Old and New Testaments.

Far from being in conflict with the literal sense of biblical stories, figuration or typology was a natural extension of literal interpretation. It was literalism at the level of the whole biblical story and thus of the depiction of the whole of historical reality. Figuration was at once a literary and a historical procedure, an interpretation of stories and their meanings by weaving them together into a common narrative referring to a single history and its patterns of meaning.

In the third place, since the world truly rendered by combining biblical narratives into one was indeed the one and only real world, it must in principle embrace the experience of any present age and reader. Not only was it possible for him, it was also his duty to fit himself into that world in which he was in any case a member, and he too did so in part by figural interpretation and in part of course by his mode of life. He was to see his disposition, his actions and passions, the shape of his own life as well as that of his era's events as figures of that storied world.

A story such as that of man's creation and "fall" (Genesis 1-3) made sense in its own right and as part of the larger story into which it was incorporated by Christian interpreters, beginning with St. Paul. But in addition, figuration made sense of the general extra-biblical structure of human experience, and of one's own experience, as well as of general concepts of good and evil drawn from experience. The point is that such experiences, events, concepts were all ranged figurally into the smaller as well as the overarching story. Biblical interpretation became an imperative need, but its direction was that of incorporating extra-biblical thought, experience, and reality into the one real world detailed and made accessible by the biblical story—not the reverse. As Auerbach suggests, in a striking contrast of Homer's *Odyssey* and Old Testament narrative:[2]

> Far from seeking, like Homer, merely to make us forget our own reality for a few hours, it seeks to overcome our reality: we are to fit our own life into its world, feel ourselves to be elements in its structure of universal history . . . Everything else that happens in the world can only be conceived as an element in this sequence; into it everything that is known about the world . . . must be fitted as an ingredient of the divine plan.

In the process of interpretation the story itself, constantly adapted to new situations and ways of thinking, underwent ceaseless revision; but in steadily revised form it still remained the adequate depiction of the common and inclusive world until the coming of modernity. As the eighteenth century went on, this mode of interpretation and the outlook it represented broke down with increasing rapidity. The seeds of disintegration were already there in the seventeenth century, not only among radical thinkers like Spinoza but also among conservatives. Johannes Cocceius in the seventeenth century and Johann Albrecht Bengel in the eighteenth, devout Christians both, signal a subtle transformation made more obvious in retrospect by the Deists' discussions in England and the subsequent rise of historical criticism. Both Cocceius and Bengel, the former using typology far more heavily than the latter, tried to locate the events of their day vis-à-vis the narrative framework of biblical story and history, and to locate by means of biblical sayings the present stage of the actual events we experience and predict future stages as well as the end of actual history. It was hardly an unprecedented preoccupation among Christian writers. But in the fuller context of that particular era it was a sign, though obviously not noticeable to devout minds at the time, of the breakup of the cohesion between the literal meaning of the biblical narratives and their reference to actual events. This kind of prophecy, rather than an anachronism, was the sign of a new cultural development, for its emphasis was on the events, on their likely course and on the hidden signs and references to this "real" world of past and future history, spread through the Bible. The mysterious signs and number schemes to be worked out from biblical verbal configurations represent a kind of proleptic verification of the shape of events not yet come to pass. Ironically—in view of the biblicism of these two men—it was a kind of detachment of the "real" historical world from its biblical description. The real events of history constitute an autonomous temporal framework of their own under God's providential design. Instead of rendering them accessible, the narratives, heretofore indispensable as means of access to the events, now simply verify them, thus affirming their autonomy and the fact that they are in principle accessible through any kind of description that can manage to be accurate either predictively or after the event. It simply happens that, again under God's providence, it is the Bible that contains the accurate descriptions. There is now a logical distinction and a reflective distance between the stories and the "reality" they depict. The depicted biblical world and the real historical world began to be separated at once in thought and in sensibility, no matter whether the depiction was thought to agree with reality (Cocceius and Bengel) or disagree with it (Spinoza).

This logical and reflective distance between narrative and reality increased steadily, naturally enough provoking a host of endeavors to bridge the gap. Not only did an enormous amount of inquiry into the factual truth (or falsity) of the biblical stories develop, but an intense concentration as well on their meaning and religious significance, whether factual or of some other sort. Many of those inquiring into the basic religious meaning of the biblical stories were determined to show that they harmonized with and illuminated extra-biblical experiences and concepts, as well as independent apprehensions of reality, even if many of these same commentators were equally determined that such inquiry must not involve their complete reduction to another framework of fact and meaning.

The point is that the direction of interpretation now became the reverse of earlier days. Do the stories and whatever concepts may be drawn from them describe what we apprehend as the real world? Do they fit a more general framework of meaning than that of a single story? Dr. Conyers Middleton, an English commentator of latitudinarian and skeptical leanings, thought that it didn't matter whether Genesis 1-3 was allegory or fact, since its meaning was the same in either case: "that this world had a beginning and creation from God; and that its principal inhabitant man, was originally formed to a state of happiness and perfection which he lost and forfeited, by following his lusts and passions, in opposition to the will of his Creator." [3] Belief in a creator—the foundation of any and all religion—and the supposition of man's fall—the basis of the need for revealed religion—are the meaning of the story, whether the version of it given in this particular narrative is taken literally or allegorically. In other words, whether or not the story is true history, its *meaning* is detachable from the specific story that sets it forth. Middleton was characteristic of many commentators, even some (like Locke) who had no doubt of the historicity of the narrated events: their meaning is nonetheless referable to an external more general context, and the story now has to be interpreted into it, rather than that external pattern of meaning being incorporated—figurally or in some other way—into the story.

If one sign of the breakdown of literal-realistic interpretation of the biblical stories was the reversal in the direction of interpretation that accompanied the distancing between the narratively depicted and the "real" world, the other and related indication was the collapse of figural interpretation. Typology or figuration simply could not cope with this reversal. It had been credible as an extension of literal reading, but once literal and historical reading began to break apart, figural interpretation became discredited both as a literary device and as a historical argument. As a literary or (more basically) logical device, figuration offended against the elementary assumption that a propositional statement has only one meaning. As a historical argument (i.e. that the Old Testament contained prophecies specifically referring to and fulfilled in Jesus Christ), it strained credulity beyond the breaking point by the suggestion that sayings and events of one day referred predictively to specific persons and events hundreds of years later. Simultaneously of course it faded into oblivion as a means for relating the world of biblical narrative to present experience and to the world of extra-biblical events, experiences, and concepts. Once again, the interpretive demand now became reversed, and figuration found successors in such mirror-image categories of interpretation as allegory and, somewhat later, myth. These and other notions served for the technical classification of biblical stories and also for their meaningful incorporation into an independent sense of a world of experience and of rational interpretation.

As the realistic narrative reading of the biblical stories broke down, literal or verbal and historical meaning were severed and literal and figural interpretation, hitherto naturally affiliated procedures, also came apart. Figural reading had been literalism extended to the whole story or the unitary canon containing it. But now figural sense came to be something like the opposite of literal sense. In the first place, verbal or literal sense was now equated with the single meaning of statements, a logical and grammatical rule prevalent everywhere so that figural reading of the Bible seemed a senseless exception to it. Secondly, the very attempt to read unity out of (or into) the Bible now appeared different from, if not incompatible with, the self-confinement of literal reading to specific texts.

Furthermore, figural reading was no longer a persuasive instrument for unifying the canon. Literal reading came increasingly to mean two things: grammatical and lexical exactness in estimating what the original sense of a text was to its original audience, and the coincidence of the description with how the facts really occurred. Realistic reading came in effect to be identical with the latter; it consisted of matching the written description against the reconstruction of the probable historical sequence to which it referred. Increasingly, historical-critical reading became the heir of the older type of realistic reading. Unlike figural reading, both were not only about history but also about specific historical sequences, so that they were not concerned with the unity of the canon.

Figural reading, to the degree that it had been an extension of literal interpretation in the older kind of realistic, narrative reading, was now bound to look to historical-critical eyes like a rather preposterous historical argument, and it rapidly lost credibility. In the past, one of its chief uses had been as a means for unifying the canon; it had not simply been an awkward historical proof-text. Its breakdown upon being introduced into the arena of historical argument and demonstration was accompanied by a similar failure as an instrument for uniting the Bible. Historical critics were concerned with specific texts and specific historical circumstances. The unity of the Bible across millennia of differing cultural levels and conditions in any case seemed a tenuous, indeed a dubious hypothesis to them. But if it were to be demonstrated, it would have to be done by an argument other than a historical claim to specific miraculous fulfillment of Old Testament sayings and events in the New Testament. In sum, figural reading broke down not only as a means of locating oneself and one's world vis-à-vis the biblical narratives; in addition, it was forced to become a historical-factual argument in favor of the unity of the canon—and a poor one at that. But like its former partner, literal-realistic interpretation, it had to have a successor, for the unity of the Bible was as important to Christian theologians as its reliability.

Realistic, literal reading of the biblical narratives found its closest successor in the historical-critical reconstruction of specific events and texts of the Bible. The question was: How reliable are the texts? Figural reading, concerned as it was with the unity of the Bible, found its closest successor in an enterprise called biblical theology, which sought to establish the unity of religious meaning across the gap of historical and cultural differences. This could be done in a variety of ways. One might try to demonstrate the identity or similarity of the chief religious *concepts* in the whole range of the Bible, or one could try to show that the whole Bible reflects a single, gradually developing and cumulative *history*. This is a history at once of the distinctive or unique events affecting the people of Israel and of the developing and yet unitary as well as unique "Hebrew mind." The distinctiveness of both events and "mind" together constitutes the unity, both natural-historical and divinely guided, of the Bible.

Literal and figural reading of the biblical narratives, once natural allies, not only came apart, but the successors looked with great unease at each other—historical criticism and biblical theology were different enterprises and made for decidedly strained company. Yet each in its own way became crucial for the assertion of the religious and doctrinal authority of the Bible which Protestantism had always maintained. For that authority was bound to be gravely weakened if the Bible was neither reliable nor unitary.

The pages that follow are an investigation of the breakdown of realistic and figural interpretation of the biblical stories, and the reversal in the direction of interpretation. This is not a book about historical criticism of the Bible and its history, even though that procedure became part heir to the older kind of interpretation. Historical criticism will be a pertinent topic at many points, but the question of how to interpret obviously involved more than that topic. To be sure, once that method became standard scholarly practice, the stories were often tested against specific factual occurrence, or identified with a reconstruction of the process by which they originated and of their cultural setting.

But interpretation, and thus hermeneutics—the study of the principles and rules of interpretation and understanding—meant more. Attention continued to be paid to the verbal sense of the stories. In the course of the eighteenth century it came to signify not so much a literary depiction which was literal rather than metaphorical, allegorical, or symbolic, but rather the single meaning of a grammatically and logically sound propositional statement. The basic context for the investigation of verbal meaning often became single words in addition to full statements. In any case, "verbal sense" was philological or "grammatical-historical" (a common technical designation in the later eighteenth century, indicating the lexical in addition to the grammatical study of the words of a text) more than literary.

Beyond the verbal sense of texts was their religious significance, ideational meaning, or subject matter as it was sometimes called to distinguish it from the "merely" verbal sense. Just what that was, and whether it was intrinsic to the text or merely a particular use or application to which a text was put by some readers, became matters of vigorous disagreement. But commentators all agreed that something more than understanding a text's verbal sense was involved in understanding the text. The interpretation of texts and hermeneutics trenched on historical-critical analysis, and some scholars thought that critical reconstruction of the reported events constituted the subject matter of narrative texts. Nevertheless, interpretation, and therefore its theory, also included inquiry into verbal sense and ideational meaning or religious significance, so that despite some confusion about "subject matter" it was not unequivocally or universally reduced to the text's "true" historical occasion or setting.

This book, then, is about one segment of the history of the theory of biblical interpretation rather than the history of biblical criticism, even though one cannot draw a neat or complete distinction between the two enterprises. In particular, its topic is the eighteenth- and early nineteenth-century discussion about the proper rules and principles to guide interpretation of the history-like stories of the Old and New Testaments. It is not a full history of the hermeneutics of biblical narratives during that period but rather a historical study under a thesis and includes preeminently a description and explanation of the ways in which the older realistic and figural approaches to these stories broke down.

To state the thesis: a realistic or history-like (though not necessarily historical) element is a feature, as obvious as it is important, of many of the biblical narratives that went into the making of Christian belief. It is a feature that can be highlighted by the appropriate analytical procedure and by no other, even if it may be difficult to describe the procedure—in contrast to the element itself. It is fascinating that the realistic character of the crucial biblical stories was actually acknowledged and agreed upon by most of the significant eighteenth-century commentators. But since the precritical analytical or interpretive procedure for isolating it had irretrievably broken down in the opinion of most commentators, this specifically realistic characteristic, though acknowledged by all hands to be there, finally came to be ignored, or—even more fascinating—its presence or distinctiveness came to be denied for lack of a "method" to isolate it. And this despite the common agreement that the specific feature was there!

Biblical commentators again and again emphasized the simplicity of style, the life-likeness of depiction, the lack of artificiality or heroic elevation in theme in such stories as the first three chapters of Genesis, the story of Abraham's willingness to sacrifice Isaac, and the synoptic gospels. In other words, they believed that

representation and depiction and what they represented, had a
great deal to do with each other and came very close in these
stories. Meaning and narrative shape bear significantly on each
other. Even if one was convinced that the history-like or realistic
character of the narratives finally bespoke an illusion, so that
their true history either had to be reconstructed historically or
their true sense explained as allegory or myth, the realistic
character was still there. This led to the odd situation described
above. Some commentators explained the realistic feature by
claiming that the stories are reliably or unreliably reported
history. Others insisted that they are not, or only incidentally,
history and that their real meaning is unconnected with historical
reporting. In either case, history or else allegory or myth, the
meaning of the stories was finally something different from the
stories or depictions themselves, despite the fact that this is
contrary to the character of a realistic story.

In the days before empirical philosophy, Deism, and historical
criticism, the realistic feature had naturally been identified with
the literal sense which in turn was automatically identical with
reference to historical truth. But once these thought currents had
had their effect, and the "literal sense" of the stories came to be
governed with a heavy hand by, and logically subordinated to,
probable and language-neutral historical veracity, the reverse
would have had to be the case: in order to recognize the realistic
narrative feature as a significant element in its own right (viz. as a
story's making literal rather than allegorical or mythical or some
other nonliteral sense regardless of whether the literal sense is also
a reliable factual report) one would have had to distinguish
sharply between literal sense and historical reference. And then
one would have had to allow the literal sense to stand as the
meaning, even if one believed that the story does not refer
historically. But commentators, especially those influenced by
historical criticism, virtually to a man failed to understand what
they had seen when they had recognized the realistic character of
biblical narratives, because every time they acknowledged it they
thought this was identical with affirming not only the history-

likeness but also a degree of historical likelihood of the stories. Those who wanted to affirm their historical factuality used the realistic character or history-likeness as evidence in favor of this claim, while those who denied the factuality also finally denied that the history-likeness was a cutting feature—thus in effect denying that they had seen what they had seen because (once again) they thought history-likeness identical with at least potentially true history.

In both affirmative and negative cases, the confusion of history-likeness (literal meaning) and history (ostensive reference), and the hermeneutical reduction of the former to an aspect of the latter, meant that one lacked the distinctive category and the appropriate interpretive procedure for understanding what one had actually recognized: the high significance of the literal, narrative shape of the stories for their meaning. And so, one might add, it has by and large remained ever since.

It is well to go a little more closely into the realistic and narrative character of biblical stories and the sort of analytical procedure appropriate to it, in order to bring into proper relief the extraordinary situation at the end of the eighteenth century.

The synoptic gospels (for example) are partly narrative in character. They may also be other things, such as *kerygma*, i.e. the proclamatory rather than didactic shape of the faith of the early Christian community or, to put the matter another way, written forms of self-committing statements which make sense by evoking similar dispositions on the part of the reader. In addition of course they are documents of their culture and community, with analogues in the structure of the religious and mythological literature of the Near East and of mankind in general, and not, except perhaps incidentally, records reporting some things that may have happened amidst many that undoubtedly did not. All of this is to say that there are many ways of making sense of these stories. But in part they *are* distinctive narratives, a fact agreed upon by most commentators, including many who did not know what to make of it. The distinctiveness is simply indelible and a significant feature the synoptic gospels share with large sections of the Old Testament. We must keep in mind that it was the stories of Genesis and the gospels which provided the main topics for the development of biblical hermeneutics in this period.

By speaking of the narrative shape of these accounts, I suggest that what they are about and how they make sense are functions of the depiction or narrative rendering of the events constituting them—including their being rendered, at least partially, by the device of chronological sequence. The claim, for example, that the gospel story is about Jesus of Nazareth as the Messiah means that it narrates the way his status came to be enacted. There are, of course, other kinds of stories that merely illustrate something we already know; and there are other stories yet that function in such a way as to express or conjure up an insight or an affective state that is beyond any and all depiction so that stories, though inadequate, are best fitted for the purpose because they are evocations, if not invocations, of a common archetypal conscious-ness or a common faith. In both of these latter cases the particular rendering is not indispensable, though it may be helpful to the point being made. Part of what I want to suggest is that the hermeneutical option espied but not really examined and thus cast aside in the eighteenth and early nineteenth centuries was that many biblical narratives, especially the synoptic gospels, may belong to the first kind, for which their narrative rendering, in effect a cumulative account of the theme, is indispensable.

This is one of the chief characteristics of a narrative that is "realistic." In that term I include more than the indispensability of the narrative shape, including chronological sequence, to the meaning, theme, or subject matter of the story. The term realistic I take also to imply that the narrative depiction is of that peculiar sort in which characters or individual persons, in their internal depth or subjectivity as well as in their capacity as doers and sufferers of actions or events, are firmly and significantly set in the context of the external environment, natural but more particu-larly social. Realistic narrative is that kind in which subject and social setting belong together, and characters and external circumstances fitly render each other. Neither character nor

circumstance separately, nor yet their interaction, is a shadow of
something else more real or more significant. Nor is the one more
important than the other in the story. "What is character but the
determination of incident? What is incident but the illustration of
character?" asked Henry James.[4]

In all these respects—inseparability of subject matter from its
depiction or cumulative rendering, literal rather than symbolic
quality of the human subject and his social context, mutual
rendering of character, circumstance, and their interaction—a
realistic narrative is like a historical account.[5] This, of course,
does not preclude differences between the two kinds of account.
For example, it is taken for granted that modern historians will
look with a jaundiced eye on appeal to miracle as an explanatory
account of events. Historical accounting, by almost universal
modern consent, involves that the narrative satisfactorily rendering a sequence believed to have taken place must consist of
events, and reasons for their occurrence, whose connections may
be rendered without recourse to supernatural agency. By contrast
in the biblical stories, of course, nonmiraculous and miraculous
accounts and explanations are constantly intermingled. But in
accordance with our definition, even the miraculous accounts are
realistic or history-like (but not therefore historical and in that
sense factually true) if they do not in effect symbolize something
else instead of the action portrayed. That is to say, even such
miraculous accounts are history-like or realistic if the depicted
action is indispensable to the rendering of a particular character,
divine or human, or a particular story. (And, in fact, biblical
miracles are frequently and strikingly nonsymbolic.)

Finally, realistic narrative, if it is really seriously undertaken
and not merely a pleasurable or hortatory exercise, is a sort in
which in style as well as content in the setting forth of didactic
material, and in the depiction of characters and action, the
sublime or at least serious effect mingles inextricably with the
quality of what is casual, random, ordinary, and everyday.[6] The
intercourse and destinies of ordinary and credible individuals
rather than stylized or mythical hero figures, flawed or otherwise,

are rendered in realistic narratives. Furthermore, they are usually rendered in ordinary language (mixed style, so called by Auerbach as the language shaping together ordinary intercourse and serious effect). Style and account go together: for example, the parabolic mode of Jesus' teaching integrates extraordinary themes with analogies drawn from workaday occurrences; and it does so in pithy, ordinary talk. Action and passion in realistic narrative illustrate the same principle. Believable individuals and their credible destinies are rendered in ordinary language and through concatenations of ordinary events which cumulatively constitute the serious, sublime, and even tragic impact of powerful historical forces. These forces in turn allow the ordinary, "random," lifelike individual persons, who become their bearers in the crucial intersection of character and particular event-laden circumstance, to become recognizable realistic "types," without thereby inducing a loss of their distinctively contingent or random individuality. (Type, unsurprisingly, is a designation of which Marxist literary critics like to make use, though it is a good question whether they do not, in their interpretive procedure, reduce the randomness of the individual completely to his historical typicality. The suspicion, finally warranted or not, is at least in order when one deals with literary interpretations that are governed by extrinsic ideological considerations. Obviously, however, the notion is not confined to them. The resort to human "type" as a necessary device for making literature convincing is shared by men as different as Aristotle and S. T. Coleridge.[7])

Erich Auerbach suggests that the realistic tradition has persisted through the ebb and flow of its own fortunes in Western literature. But he also sees three historical high points in its development: the Bible, Dante's *Divine Comedy*, and the nineteenth-century novel, especially in France. Biblical commentators have generally agreed that this cumulative, realistic, or history-like narrative feature is characteristic of the Bible, though they have obviously had to deny that it pervades the whole Bible or that it is the sole literary feature even of some of the stories that do indeed exhibit it. Obviously the Psalms, Proverbs, Job, and the

Pauline epistles are not realistic narratives. Also, there are highly stylized rather than realistic features in the description of Jesus and in the sequence chain in the Fourth Gospel. They are not even absent from the more nearly realistic synoptic gospels, where the only immediately evident (but obviously important) chronological continuity is the story of the passion, crucifixion, and resurrection of Jesus. But with all of this conceded, there is still general agreement that cumulative realistic narrative of a very serious rather than low, comical, or idyllic sort is characteristic of the Bible, especially if one compares it to other ancient literature of either sacred or profane character.

Explicitly or implicitly, all of this has long been conceded by commentators, including those of the eighteenth and early nineteenth centuries when, coincidentally, there was at least in England a strong resurgence of serious realistic literature and criticism. But in effect, the realistic or history-like quality of biblical narratives, acknowledged by all, instead of being examined for the bearing it had in its own right on meaning and interpretation was immediately transposed into the quite different issue of whether or not the realistic narrative was historical.

This simple transposition and logical confusion between two categories or contexts of meaning and interpretation constitutes a story that has remained unresolved in the history of biblical interpretation ever since. Were we to pursue our theme into the biblical hermeneutics of the twentieth century, I believe we would find that with regard to the recognition of the distinctiveness of realistic biblical narrative and its implications for interpretation, historical criticism, and theology, the story has remained much the same.

2 Precritical Interpretation
of Biblical Narrative

Biblical interpretation since the eighteenth century has always proceeded in two directions which sometimes have appeared to be on collision course. On the one hand there has been the question of the origin and, in some respects, the reliability of biblical writings. On the other there has been inquiry into the proper ways of learning what abiding meaning or value these writings might have. Collision threatened whenever the answer to the second question seemed to be partially or wholly dependent on the answer to the first. The task of interpretation has frequently been taken to be that of plotting a chart for the narrows between these two shoals.

The origins of modern biblical-historical criticism and its slightly younger cousin, historical-critical theology, are a subject of continuing discussion and argument. The method owes much to the seventeenth century, for instance to Spinoza's reflections in the first twelve chapters of the *Tractatus theologico-politicus*, to the conviction of the Socinians that the veracity of scripture would and should be attested by independent rational judgment rather than dogmatic authority, and to the pioneering critical exegesis of men like Hugo Grotius and Richard Simon.[1] But there is no doubt that as concerted practice, building into a continuing tradition and literature, it started in the second half of the eighteenth century, chiefly among German scholars.

The earlier parts of the Pentateuch, especially what scholars were pleased to call the biblical cosmogony, together with the original literary shape of the gospels, were topics of particular critical concern. Hermeneutical theory in this period, also deeply engrossed in these two portions of the Bible, was thus constantly looking over its shoulder at the intense wrestling going on, sometimes clearly, sometimes obscurely, between conservatives

17

and liberals on the place and the fruits of historical investigation in biblical exegesis. Conservatives argued the factuality of the events narrated in these stories and the authoritative (because inspired) truth of the written texts. Liberal critics argued that the accuracy and truth of the sacred books have to be subjected to the same criteria of evaluation as all other writings, and that ancient writings containing miracle reports as well as reports of unexperienceable happenings have to be reconstructed in the light of natural experience and explanatory theory.

Historical-critical method meant that putative claims of fact in the Bible were subjected to independent investigation to test their veracity and that it was not guaranteed by the authority of the Bible itself. It meant explaining the thoughts of the biblical authors and the origin and shape of the writings on the basis of the most likely, natural, and specific conditions of history, culture, and individual life out of which they arose. It meant applying these explanatory principles without supplementary appeal to (though also without necessary prejudice against) divine causation either of the biblical history or the biblical writings.

Disentangling and relating hermeneutics and historical criticism was no easy matter then or now. Some commentators tended to think that the interpretive job was finished once historical criticism had done its work on a text; others distinguished sharply between the historical analysis and garnering a text's meaning. Still others saw a large if not complete coincidence between explicative and historical-critical interpretation, which left only the job of normative application above and beyond this "scientific" task: What religious lessons are to be learned from the text?

THE PROTESTANT REFORMERS

In earlier days, when principles of exegesis had been firmly united to dogmatically formulated religion, it was easier to set forth the principles of interpretation, including their relation to historical judgment—such as it was. The Protestant Reformers had said that the Bible is self-interpreting, the literal sense of its words being their true meaning, its more obscure passages to be read in the light of those that are clear. This tradition was expressed typically in Luther's oft-quoted remark that scripture is "through itself most certain, most easily accessible, comprehensible, interpreting itself, proving, judging all the words of all men." [2] Luther said many other things about the scripture as Word of God to be heard and trusted for the comfort of the faith which it engenders. He warned against a merely historical reading of the text and consequently against a merely historical faith. He insisted on an internal and not only a formal external reading, paying heed to the true subject matter rather than the mere word, so that one would find Christ at the center of the Bible; for Christ is the meaning not only of the New but also of the Old Testament.

But Luther's quoted words remained his typical view on the crucial technical issue of scriptural interpretation on which so much of the claim to the direct authority of the Bible, unmediated by the teaching office of the Church and her tradition, depended. They represent his drastic alternative to the complex and long development of traditional theory of scriptural interpretation which had come to distinguish among literal, allegorical, anagogical, and tropical senses of the text. Against that multiplex view Luther's simplification meant drastic relief, affirming as it did that the literal or, as he preferred to call it, the grammatical or historical sense is the true sense.[3]

The Lutheran and Calvinistic traditions came to diverge over a wide spectrum of issues, ranging all the way from clear and precise doctrinal disagreement to basic differences in religious, moral, and political ethos. But on procedure in biblical interpretation they differed in emphasis rather than substance, though one observes divergences between them as one moves from their technical treatment of texts to the larger contexts of their exegesis. On the primacy of the grammatical sense they were as one, an agreement that went back to the two Reformers themselves. In addition, however, both Luther and Calvin supplemented a close grammatical reading of the text with figural or typological interpretation, and this in turn allowed them to relate texts and teachings as well as earlier and later incidents to each other, so that they gained that view of the Bible as a unified canon for which their theology called. Calvin, like Luther, saw Christ as the subject matter of the whole Bible, and despite differing accents they held largely similar views about the way this unity was exhibited throughout the two testaments which constituted the very Word of God himself, directly spoken to men for their salvation. For Calvin, not all texts referred either directly or indirectly to Christ, but by and large the Old Testament either predicted or else prefigured Christ and the salvation as well as the form of life he was to institute.

The Reformers' procedure, not their thought on the theology and authority of scripture, is the primary focus of these pages, so that it is more important to note their agreement in the way one goes about extracting meaning from the Bible than either their agreement or divergence in the meanings extracted. Nonetheless, process and result are not always easy to disentangle. Luther was deeply persuaded that the law, God's severe and unbending demand for human righteousness and obedience to his commands, which was embedded both in scripture and in the common life on this earth, was the essential yet negative and terrifying guide driving men to rely on the heart of God's Word, the gospel of free divine grace bestowed in faith apart from all the works of the law, and made palpable in Christ. It was our inability to be righteous in the sight of God which left us no recourse but to throw ourselves, meritless, on his mercy. And in the coming of Christ, as told in scripture, we have the assurance of that mercy made effective.

So strong was Luther's conviction that this is the basic relation between God and man that he regarded only those portions of scripture as genuinely true and authoritative which proclaimed or clearly implied this awesome tension between law and gospel— between an absolute and unflinching divine demand before which every man was a hopelessly lost sinner, and an equally full and unconditional gift of divine forgiveness which bestowed free mercy solely from the prompting of its own divine graciousness. Calvin agreed emphatically. But unlike Luther he tended to see God's Word equally pervading all scriptural texts, even those that did not substantiate the sternly condemnatory role of the law. He had a more positive estimate of the constructive part the law played in the community of men in general and in the Christian life in particular.[4] This in turn helped him think of the law as virtually synonymous with the whole Old Testament. In this way the law itself became the equivalent of the promise which Calvin, like most orthodox Christians in the Western tradition, espied in the Old Testament and regarded as fulfilled or ratified in the New. The substance of law and gospel, and thus of the two Testaments, is the same: a covenant of spiritual rather than material salvation, for the implementation of which Christ served as the mediator between God and men.[5] More schematically inclined than Luther, Calvin saw a correlation even broader than that of the progression from law to gospel with that from Old to New Testament and from promise of salvation to its fulfillment. History, doctrine, description of shape of life, all converged for him and were held together by their common ingredience in the storied text of the scriptural word, and by the Holy Spirit's internal testimony to that text through his awakening of the reader's and hearer's faithful beholding.

Calvin's doctrine of the Spirit's internal testimony points toward a frequently held modern theological conviction that a fruitful paradoxical tension must be maintained between a close reading of the biblical text and a logically independent spiritual or existential appropriation of the Divine Word within the text. But Calvin sees no impediment at all where nineteenth- and twentieth-century theologians find the heaviest thickets. A modern commentator on Calvin's principles of exegesis, H. J. Kraus, rightly says that the Bible is, for Calvin, not inspired and hence does not itself in the first place inspire, but communicates and informs.[6] The reader, not the text, is to be illumined by the internal or inspiring testimony of the Spirit[7] so that he may discern the written biblical word to be God's own Word, intended for his own and the Church's edification. The text is God's Word in its own right and communicates the truth quite clearly. This intrinsic clarity, however, does not make the internal testimony of the Spirit exegetically peripheral. Kraus rightly goes on to emphasize that the Spirit's internal testimony and the resultant religious attitude by which alone the reader learns the right use of the text, God himself speaking in it, is not for Calvin a kind of secondary or ancillary principle to proper, expert exegesis.[8] The religious bearing is rather part and parcel of what Calvin believes to be the unified web involved in a proper interpretive stance.

On the other hand there is no warrant from Calvin for going to the opposite extreme and turning what is for him a fitting, unproblematic correlation between the text's perspicuity and the Spirit's internal testimony into a powerful, high-level theory of a "paradoxical" or "dialectical" relation between the "objective" Divine Word or the "objective" "saving facts" and the believer's personal trust. Calvin has no systematic scheme for correlating faith as a proposition to be believed and faith as personal life stance, or "historical knowledge" of "saving facts" and a "present faith event," after the fashion of many systematic Christian theologians of the nineteenth and twentieth centuries who hoped with the aid of some such theory to argue the coherent intelligibility of a divine revelation which is riveted to a unique and indispensable occurrence of past history and yet is equally an occasion and exercise in the present personal commerce between God and man.

Both moves, the one denigrating the inward testimony of the Spirit to a secondary, "merely edifying" status in interpretive procedure, the other raising it to a crucial ingredient in a complex theory of religious knowledge or understanding, including biblical understanding, are foreign to Calvin's thought. For Calvin, the coherence of the internal testimony of the Spirit with the meaning of the text was simply part of the same correlation in which promise and fulfillment, law and gospel, Old and New Testaments go together; in which history, doctrine, and life description cohere by virtue of the common or joint depiction they receive in the biblical text. This coherence had no need of a special explicatory or justifying theory in any of its parts. Thus a proper explication of the text is at the same time reference to its subject matter and instruction in its religious application. Calvin simply did not separate in principle the literal or for that matter the figural meaning of a text from its historical reference or its religious use, not even for purposes of arguing that they belong together. Here, as on so many other matters, he and Luther agreed, although the coherence between explicative reading, religious use, and historical as well as other subject matter reference was even closer for Calvin than Luther.

Both men would have agreed that *if* one has to choose between the subject matter and the words of a biblical text, one obviously opts for the former. However, the choice presented itself more frequently to Luther than to Calvin. For Luther, certain contrasts and their resolution—such as that between law and gospel, or between the realm or kingdom in which God's love dominates and the realm of God's preserving justice in the midst of the perduringly sinful order of this world—were a large part of the subject matter of scripture. Calvin, on the other hand, had a stronger sense of the subject matter of scripture being constituted by or identical with its narrative. But for both the important fact was that the choice between subject matter and text was in effect secondary and a matter of edifying corrective rather than distinction in principle. Calvin insisted that a merely correct historical or doctrinal faith, obedient to the literal belief set forth in a text, would not do. The proper knowledge of God must be personal (as we would put the matter today); it must be correlated to self-knowledge, and it has to be of a religious or pious nature.[9] In that sense among others it is true to say that the letter kills while the spirit brings life. But far more significant in the use of scripture is the fact that spirit and letter cohere fitly and do not contradict each other. The literal or grammatical meaning, primary for Luther and Calvin, was for both men usually identical with the text's subject matter, i.e. its historical reference, its doctrinal content, and its meaningfulness as life description and prescription.

The correlation of text with internal testimony of the Spirit in turn belongs to this general pattern of natural or naturally appropriate coherence. It is therefore fair to say that the text fitly rendered what it talked about in two ways for Calvin. It was in the first place a proper (literal or figurative) rather than allegorical depiction of the world or reality it narrated. But in the second place it rendered that reality itself to the reader, making the reality accessible to him through its narrative web. He could therefore both comprehend it and shape his life in accordance with it. The identity between the explicative sense and the historical reference of texts rested largely on the narrative rendering constituting that identity and not on a linguistic theory of reference, that is, of nouns naming and thereby standing in the conceptual place of the things they refer to, things of which one would have an independent, language-neutral apprehension.

Through the coincidence or even identity between a world being depicted and its reality being rendered to the reader (always under the form of the depiction), the reader or hearer in turn becomes part of that depicted reality and thus has to take a personal or life stance toward it. For Calvin, more clearly than for Luther, not the *act of recital or preaching* of a text, but the cumulative *pattern constituting the biblical narrative* (the identification of God's dealing with the world in the peculiar way depicted in the promise of the law and its fulfillment in the gospel) is the setting forth of the reality which simultaneously constitutes its effective rendering to the reader by the Spirit. And this harmony of depiction, world, and religious appropriation should occasion no surprise: for He who moves the world in particular ways moves the human heart also. The internal testimony of the Spirit, then, is neither a peripheral edifying appendage to the actual reading of the biblical text nor an explanatory theory that alone would warrant the unity of the objective claims made in the text with the personal life stance of Christian faith. It is the effective rendering of God and his real world to the reader by way of the text's appropriate depiction of the intercourse of that God and that world, engaging the reader's mind, heart, and activity.

Calvin's rejection of allegorical and anagogical readings of the biblical texts was, if anything, even more pronounced than Luther's. He was persuaded that the grammatical sense was the genuine sense, except where the writer's intention or the larger context indicated otherwise. But even these two criteria for gathering the meaning of a passage were not independent explanatory factors, as they were to become for later commentators. Rather than superseding, they enhanced the grammatical or "genuine" reading of a text.

And even where Calvin found it impossible to read a seemingly nonallegorical text literally, as in Christ's words instituting the Lord's Supper,[10] he gave it an analogical reading that is closer to figuration than to allegory. One concept stands for another with similar though not identical features, bread for body and wine for blood, indicating a similar and significant resemblance between physical reality and the spiritual reality of which it is the figure. From what I have said about the verbal, narrative rendering of reality, and given Calvin's own stress on the importance of preaching and action specifically connected with the words of institution, it is evident that for him the linguistic performance of celebrating the Lord's Supper not only fitly signifies but verbally embodies the spiritual reality it represents.

If verbal sense and real reference or the rendering of reality cohere so closely where the web of meaning is analogical, so that allegorical or anagogical interpretation is excluded even here, the relation is obviously even closer where the literal meaning alone is enough to present a text's sense. Two instances will suffice to indicate the fact, both of them examples of a reading at once literal and ostensive or historical, though of apparently opposite tendency in their bearing on the all-important matter of the christological unity of both Testaments. Genesis 3:15 has God speaking to the serpent, after his temptation of Eve: "I will put enmity between you and the woman, and between your seed and

her seed; he shall bruise your head, and you shall bruise his heel."
Traditionally this saying, often referred to as the *protevangelium*,
had been taken as the veiled first prophecy and figure of Christ's
triumph over sin and the devil. Calvin, always wary of hidden
specific reference to Christ in the Old Testament, denies this
interpretation on logical and grammatical grounds:[11]

> Other interpreters take the seed for Christ, without contro-
> versy; as if it were said, that some one would arise from the
> seed of the woman who should wound the serpent's head.
> Gladly would I give my suffrage in support of their opinion,
> but that I regard the word "seed" as too violently distorted
> by them; for who will concede that a collective noun is to be
> understood of one man only? Further, as the perpetuity of
> the contest is noted, so victory is promised to the human race
> through a continual succession of ages. I explain, therefore,
> the seed to mean the posterity of the woman generally.

If a literal reading leads him to a general rather than specific
prophecy of the course of events as the meaning of this verse, the
same kind of reading of Isaiah 7:14 brings him to the opposite
conclusion. "Therefore the Lord himself will give you a sign.
Behold, a virgin [Calvin opts for this disputed translation] shall
conceive and bear a son, and shall call his name Immanuel."
Calvin rejects, among other referential interpretations of this
prophecy, its merely figural application to Christ, as if "the
Prophet spoke of some child who was born at that time, by whom,
as by an obscure picture, Christ was foreshadowed." His interpretive claim once again is literal, though this time to the opposite
effect: "This name Immanuel could not be literally applied to a
mere man; and, therefore, there can be no doubt that the Prophet
referred to Christ." [12]

Calvin would not have worried in the slightest about the
contrasting conclusions of the literal reading of these two Old
Testament passages, rejecting a reference to Christ in the first
instance but affirming it in the second. He would have denied

that either this primacy of grammatical or literal procedure or any specific outcome of its application in any way softens the claim that the canon is one because the meaning of all of it is salvation in Jesus Christ. The reason for his confidence in the harmony of grammatical with pervasive christological interpretation is his unquestioned assumption of a natural coherence between literal and figural reading, and of the need of each for supplementation by the other. That one reads specific passages in one way rather than another in no sense denies their mutual enhancement. They supplement each other because there is a family resemblance between them. They belong together, though they are on the one hand not identical nor, on the other, a substitute for each other.

This family resemblance, which permits a kind of extension of literal into figural interpretation, especially when one comes to work out a common meaning among a number of diverse texts, involves a difference, though not a contradiction, in the aspect of narrative emphasized by the two procedures. Literal depiction constitutes and does not merely illustrate or point to the meaning of the narrative and theme it cumulatively renders; and simultaneously it depicts and renders the reality (if any) of what it talks about. A realistic story is not necessarily history; but the difference between the two is that of reference or lack of reference, and not that of a different kind of account being appropriate in each case. On the contrary, in respect of descriptive or depictive form, history and realistic story are identical.[13] This coherence between narrative depiction and the reality rendered by it allows a shift in emphasis from depiction or story form to the reality depicted, without a disruption of the conviction that the narrative tissue is what they have inseparably in common. Now if literal reading tends to focus on the narrative shape, implying rather than explicitly making historical references, the reverse tends to be true of figuration or typology. It tends to undertake the shift to an emphasis on the reality depicted, so that its interest in the two or more formally similar narratives included is really that of adjusting them to the one real, temporal sequence involved. (In both literal and figural reading one can speak of no more than a tendency in the specified direction.)

The emphasis in figural interpretation of the Bible is on the whole putatively temporal sequence narrated, and on the fact that inclusion in it shapes into one story the whole set of independent biblical stories covering its chronological subsequences. They become linked as segments of the same sequence by being placed in one chronological order and by being referred to one another. In the service of the one temporally sequential reality the stories become figures one of another without losing their independent or self-contained status. With regard to its own depicted time span, each narrative is literally descriptive; of the whole sequence and its coherence in theme as well as time, all of them together form one literal narrative, by means of earlier and later stories becoming figures one of the other.

In a precritical era, in which literal explicative sense was identical with actual historical reference, literal and figurative reading, far from contradicting each other, belonged together by family resemblance and by need for mutual supplementation. Later on, when explication and reference became separated, the two kinds of readings would not only separate but clash.

Erich Auerbach, who has made the most searching analysis of figural procedure and its fate in the course of time, describes it as follows:[14]

> Figural interpretation establishes a connection between two events or persons in such a way that the first signifies not only itself but also the second, while the second involves or fulfills the first. The two poles of a figure are separated in time, but both, being real events or persons, are within temporality. They are both contained in the flowing stream which is historical life, and only the comprehension, the *intellectus spiritualis*, of their interdependence is a spiritual act.
>
> In this conception, an occurrence on earth signifies not only itself but at the same time another, which it predicts or

confirms, without prejudice to the power of its concrete reality here and now. The connection between occurrences is not regarded as primarily a chronological or causal development but as a oneness within the divine plan, of which all occurrences are parts and reflections. Their direct earthly connection is of secondary importance, and often their interpretation can altogether dispense with any knowledge of it.

Clearly, if figural or typological interpretation was to be successful, it required a delicate balance between the temporally separated occasions, a firm connection with literal or realistic procedure, and a clear rooting in the order of temporal sequence. For one thing, the juxtaposition of type and antitype, or figure and fulfillment, could result in strain and a depreciation of the one in favor of the other. For a person, an event, a body of laws, a rite, etc., to be both itself and real in its own right, and yet stand for something else later in time and equally real which is to fulfill it, imposes a strain especially on the earlier moment.

Similarly, as Auerbach noted (on p. 48), the delicate cohesion between an earlier occasion and its meaning pattern could be easily strained, if not fractured, if this total complex prefigures what comes later only through its meaning structure. "The total content of the sacred writings was placed in an exegetic context which often removed the thing told very far from its sensory base, in that the reader was forced to turn his attention away from the sensory occurrence and toward its meaning. This implied the danger that the visual element of the occurrences might succumb under the dense texture of meanings." Allegory, the attachment of a temporally free-floating meaning pattern to any temporal occasion whatever, without any intrinsic connection between sensuous time-bound picture and the meaning represented by it, was in any case a common interpretive device in early Christianity, including the New Testament. The line between allegory and typological or figural interpretation was often very fine, when the temporal reality of an earlier instance was dissolved in favor of its meaning, but the application of that meaning remained riveted to a temporal occurrence. Christ was always the specific person he was presented to be; but the meaning of manna in the wilderness could be a symbol under a story representation and not the specific depiction it purports to be; and as that symbol of divine help in time of spiritual starvation it could then be applied allegorically to the redeeming activity of Christ.

Figuration faced the further danger (again noted by Auerbach) that it was often both difficult and of secondary significance to state the nature of the temporal or causal connection between two realities quite distant in time, both equally real and ordered in a single teleological sequence, say, God's gift of the promised land to his people and Christ's salvation of his flock, of which the former occasion is a figure. Against rival interpretations of either occasion or both together, figural interpretation had to convince less by a statement of an operative principle establishing a connection and more by sheer juxtaposition of the two occasions, noting the similarities in their constituent features and the order of ascending climax between them. In effect this juxtaposition in itself exhibited—it was hoped in convincing fashion—the divine purpose that constituted the bond between the two occasions. In other words, the "method" of figural procedure was better exhibited in application than stated in the abstract, a fact which cost the figural procedure dearly in the days of deist controversy. Its governing rules had to remain largely implicit and are bound to look arbitrary if not nonexistent to those who are used to the statement of field-encompassing rules for the meaningful use of literary or historical congruence and comparison.

Calvin, who was somewhat inclined toward Platonism in formal philosophy, tended to discern figural order in identical meaning patterns across distinct temporal eras or dispensations within the Bible, rather than in the occurrences in which these meanings are set forth. Parallel to this, he sometimes equated the relation between salvation figurally set forth and its later fulfillment with the change from apprehension of spiritual truth under its material representation to a direct grasp of its spiritual nature. Nonetheless, his sense of figural interpretation remained firmly rooted in the order of temporal sequence and the depiction of temporal occurrences, the links between which can be established only by narration and under the conviction of the primacy of the literal, grammatical sense. As a result, his application of figural interpretation never lost its connection with literal reading of individual texts, and he was never tempted into allegorizing. The family resemblance between the literal and figural interpretations, as well as their mutual supplementation, allowed him to view the two testaments as one canon, the unitary subject of which was the story of man's fall and the salvation wrought by Jesus Christ.

The narrative structure of reality and text as wrought in literal and figural interpretation, and the coherence of explicative sense with real reference allowed him to move naturally and easily (in the midst of the second book of the *Institutes*) from detailing the doctrine and form of life arising out of the history of God's dealing with man to an examination of the canon which presents that history, and back again to the history itself. Appropriate to the cumulative pattern of a narrative framework, Calvin exhibits his figural scheme of the unitary meaning of both Testaments by keeping the similarity and the difference of the two books firmly together within a context of temporal sequence (2.9–11). The law excited in the saints of the Old Testament an expectation of the Messiah that was to come. He came, and in the light of that fact it is obvious that they had indeed participated in the "understanding and light which shine in the person of Christ." But if this single pattern establishes the unity of the two Testaments, the fact that it is strictly bound to the temporal framework in which it appears also dictates the difference between them: compared to the condition of the Old Testament saints, we who come later "have a clear manifestation of the mysteries, of which they had only an obscure prospect through the medium of shadows" (2.9.1). The gospel is "a new and unusual kind of legation, in which God has performed those things that he had promised." Those things are not only "the gracious remission of sins, by which God reconciles men to himself" and bestows immortality and the knowledge of spiritual truth upon them, but the occurrence or story from which this single, encompassing pattern of meaning cannot be abstracted: "the truth of the promises [appeared] in the person of his Son" (2.9.2).

The covenant God made with the Old Testament saints varies from ours not in substance but administration. Thus, the temporal felicity held before the eyes of the Jews was not to be their ultimate goal but a mark that they were "adopted to the hope of immortality, and that the truth of this adoption was certified to them by oracles, by the law, and by the prophets" (2.10.2). Calvin argues that the Old Testament fathers were well aware that "God rarely or never in this world gives his servants those things which he promises them" (2.10.7) so that they are instead signs or figures of the state which fulfills them: "in order to the better elucidation of the Divine goodness, the prophets represented it to the people in a figurative manner; but . . . they gave such a representation of it as would withdraw the mind from earth and time . . . and would necessarily excite to a contemplation of the felicity of the future spiritual life" (2.10.20). The unity of the two books is further demonstrated because the fathers' covenant, identical with ours, was founded not on their merits but on God's mercy. Also, "they both possessed and knew Christ as the Mediator, by whom they were united to God and became partakers of his promises" (2.10.12).

As for the differences between Old and New Testaments, they are real without detracting from the unity of the canon. In fact, under the heading of difference, Calvin reiterates much of what he had said earlier about unity but in the process changes the emphasis. In the Old Testament the celestial inheritance is exhibited "under the figures of terrestrial blessings," whereas in the New Testament, "the Lord directs our minds to the immediate contemplation of it" (2.11.1). In this context he tends to emphasize the incompleteness rather than the frustration of earthly hopes and blessings. The Israelites were indeed promised and given the land of Canaan in which they were to dwell; but it is nonetheless, under a figure, the promise of a celestial city and of everlasting life. The terrestrial blessings are not so much false as incomplete, so that they do not terminate in themselves but lead on to the spiritual hope instead (2.11.2). Calvin does not simply downgrade the truth and reality of the earthly occasion and its blessings in their own place and time (though he does indeed often tend in that direction), but takes them up into another context where they no longer have a meaning in their own right and instead prefigure what is to come.

In addition, however, there are aspects of the Old Testament (e.g. the ceremonial law) which are abrogated because they were nothing more than temporary manifestations or shadows of what was later given to us to know substantially (2.11.4). The figural relation in this respect is between shadow and reality, the evanescent and the permanent, in the meaning of historically grounded symbols and institutions. Specifically, the ceremonial and sacrificial law is a symbol of the confirmation and ratification of the covenant through the blood of Christ. By relative contrast to this pattern of a shadow–substance relation, the first kind of figuration was that of an earthly, historical promise and occasion anticipating and prefiguring a later historical as well as eternal state of affairs. The family resemblance between the two kinds of figural interpretation is evident.

Calvin adds another difference between the testaments that involves the figuration of the later by the earlier state of affairs at once in relative contrast and similarity, because both are ordered within one temporal framework: the law is a literal, the gospel a spiritual doctrine, though both teach the same substance. The first is engraved on tablets of stone, the second is inscribed on the heart. Again, the common order at once depending on and shaping a unitary temporal sequence is figural: "The law having an image of things that were at a distance, it was necessary that in time it should be abolished and disappear. The gospel, exhibiting the body itself, retains a firm and perpetual stability" (2.11.8).

Figural interpretation, then, sets forth the unity of the canon as a single cumulative and complex pattern of meaning. This pattern is ingredient in the unitary temporal sequence and its stages, and it depends on the successive narrative rendering of the sequence. Once again, given the reality and cumulative unity of that temporal sequence, literal and figural readings, each indispensable to the other, form its appropriate narrative rendering. Only by their joint operation is the sequence accessible. Literal, realistic interpretation tends to set forth the sense of single stories within the Bible, naturally holding in one their explicative meaning and, where appropriate, their real reference. Figural interpretation, on the other hand, still holding together explication and reference, is a grasp of a common pattern of occurrence and meaning together, the pattern being dependent on the reality of the unitary temporal sequence which allows all the single narrations within it to become parts of a single narration.

But it was not only the coherence between explicative sense and real reference that allowed the unity of literal and figural meaning. Equally indispensable was the firm sense which Calvin shared with the large majority of the Western Christian tradition up to his time that (in Auerbach's words) the two poles of a figure, being real, "both are contained in the flowing stream which is historical life, and only the comprehension, the *intellectus spiritualis,* of their interdependence is a spiritual act." [15] The pattern of meaning glimpsed in a historical event, or within two or more occasions figurally and thus meaningfully related, cannot be stated apart from the depiction or narration of the occasion(s). The occurrence character and the theme or teleological pattern of a historical or history-like narrative belong together. Interpretation or the gathering of meaning is in no sense a material contribution on the part of the interpreter or a unique perspective he might represent. Without this conviction to govern the figural reading of a sequence, it becomes a totally arbitrary forcing together of discontinuous events and patterns of meaning.

Calvin, we noted, speaks about the internal testimony of the Spirit as enlightening the heart and mind to see what the text says in any case. It does not add a new dimension to the text itself. The meaning, pattern, or theme, whether upon literal or figural reading or, most likely, upon a combination of both, emerges solely as a function of the narrative itself. It is not imprinted on the text by the interpreter or by a multifarious interpretive and religious "tradition," a collective noun standing for the story as a product of the storyteller's own mind together with subsequent interpretations of it down to the present and latest reader, for any of whom this interpretive mental accretion itself, and not the text, becomes the cumulative story which is taken to be the text's real subject matter. Whatever Calvin might have thought about the latter possibility ("tradition") as a coherent framework for analyzing biblical texts, he was firm in declining it as a substitute for an actual reading of the narrative text in which literal and, by extension, figural reading render chronological sequence together with the teleological pattern that is a function of the cumulative story.

If Calvin does not speak to the precise issue separating these two views he indicates his stand clearly enough in a nearly identical controversy: there are some, he says, who, upon seeing that God never advances beyond terrestrial rewards and punishments in his dealings with the Hebrews, conclude confidently that "the Jews were separated from other nations, not for their own sakes, but for ours, that the Christian Church might have an image, in whose external form they could discern examples of spiritual things." He defines the point at issue "between us and these persons" as follows:

> They maintain that the possession of the land of Canaan was accounted by the Israelites their supreme and ultimate blessedness, but that to us, since the revelation of Christ, it is a figure of the heavenly inheritance. We, on the contrary, contend, that in the earthly possession which they enjoyed, they contemplated, as in a mirror, the future inheritance which they believed to be prepared for them in heaven.[16]

Did they know what it was they enjoyed? Calvin does not say, and the enjoyment is not necessarily the same thing as the direct knowledge that this is what they were enjoying. The point is not really that the land of Canaan was a figure of the future inheritance at the time if, and only if, "the Israelites" knew it to be such. More important is the fact that they enjoyed the land as a figure of the eternal city, and thus it *was* a figure at the time. It is not a figure solely in later retrospective interpretive stance. Calvin is clearly contending that figural reading is a reading forward of the sequence. The meaning pattern of reality is inseparable from its forward motion; it is not the product of the wedding of that forward motion with a separate backward perspective upon it, i.e. of history and interpretation joined as two logically independent factors. Rather, the meaning of the full sequence emerges in the narration of the sequence, and therefore interpretation for Calvin must be, as Auerbach suggests it is for the tradition at large, part of the flowing stream which is historical life. The only spiritual act is that of comprehension—an act of mimesis, following the way things really are—rather than of creation, if it is to be faithful interpretation.

For Calvin, we have reality only under a description or, since reality is identical with the sequential dealing of God with men, under the narrative depiction which renders it, and not directly or without temporal narrative sequence. The reason for this is obvious. We are, as interpreters as well as religious and moral persons, part of the same sequence. We are not independent observers of it from outside the temporal framework in which we have been cast. We have no more external vantage point for thought than for action. To say that the land of Canaan is a figure only to us, since the revelation of Christ, is to deny the coherence of narrative sequence, the effective rendering of reality with the pattern of meaning that is dependent upon it. It is also to deny that the interpreter's situation is that of having to range himself into the same real sequence by participating intellectually in it as a forward motion, a direction it still maintains even though we, unlike those of the Old Testament, know its goal without figuration. The task of interpretation is to garner the sense of the narrative, and not interfere with it by uniting historical and/or narrative sequence with a logically distinct meaning that may be either the interpreter's own perspective or an amalgam of narrative event and interpretation, in which it is impossible to decide how much "meaning" belongs to the event, and how much to the interpretive perspective upon it.

The unity of literal and figural reading depended, in the first place, on the coherence of literal or grammatical sense with historical reference. Secondly, it depended on the conviction that the narrative renders temporal reality in such a way that interpretive thought can and need only comprehend the meaning that is, or emerges from, the cumulative sequence and its teleological pattern, because the interpreter himself is part of that real sequence. When the identity of literal sense and historical reference is severed, literal and figural reading likewise no longer belong together. Similarly, when the pattern of meaning is no longer firmly ingredient in the story and the occurrence character of the text but becomes a function of a quasi-independent interpretive stance, literal and figural reading draw apart, the latter gradually looking like a forced, arbitrary imposition of unity on a group of very diverse texts. No longer an extension of literal reading, figural interpretation instead becomes a bad historical argument or an arbitrary allegorizing of texts in the service of preconceived dogma.

POST-REFORMATION PROTESTANTISM

The affirmation that the literal or grammatical sense is the Bible's true sense became programmatic for the traditions of Lutheran and Calvinistic interpretation. Additionally, the Bible's inspiration came to mean the inspiration of the individual written words and thus the identity of the Word of God with the text. Among the Lutherans, this stark literalism, which had its roots in Luther but was by no means Luther's full position, dominated from the first writing on hermeneutics, the *Clavis scripturae sacrae* (1567) of Matthias Flacius Illyricus, to the dogmatic theologies of such later orthodox writers as J. A. Quenstedt, D. Hollaz, and A. Calov. Not surprisingly these writers, long after they were dead and the doctrinal winds had changed, became the focus of sharp criticism by the neological and rationalist scholars of the later eighteenth century. They were accused of having subjected textual interpretation to the requirements of orthodox dogma.

But equally if not more unwelcome to the more liberal scholars of the eighteenth century was another view, more recent than that of Protestant scholastic orthodoxy—the Pietist tradition chiefly among Lutherans, with its subjection of hermeneutics to dogmatic theology. Pietist commentators were not nearly so completely wedded to the grammatical sense of the biblical texts as their more orthodox and scholastically minded counterparts. While they affirmed a literal grammatical reading they also sought to transcend it. Indeed, the accusation of a plural sense given to single statements, leveled against figural reading, actually found its proper target instead in pietistic interpretation. A typical pietist work on hermeneutics, highly regarded when it was published, was the *Institutiones hermeneuticae sacrae* (1724)[17] of Johann Jacob Rambach (1693–1735), a professor in Giessen and follower of the great Pietist August Hermann Francke, preacher and professor in Halle. Rambach emphasized the indispensability of such spiritual gifts as the illumination of the intellect, the love of Jesus, and of God's Word for the exegete of scripture, along with the expert training and knowledge he must possess. The inspiring activity of the Spirit is clearly distributed equally and evenly over the sacred pages and the hearts and minds of those who attend them properly. However, unlike the Reformers, who had made similar though not identical claims, Rambach found that the congruence between these two repositories of the Spirit's work demands that one be able to discern a spiritual sense above the ordinary grammatical and logical senses in at least some of the sacred words. Moreover, the spiritual sense of such individual words lends them an expanded force or emphasis, so that they have as much meaning and resonance attributed to them as they can possibly bear. "Emphasis" becomes a technical term. It stands for a doctrine or a way of seeing a meaning of scriptural words quite beyond what they appear to have in ordinary usage or in their immediate context.

If in these respects Rambach differed drastically from orthodox theologians like Calov, who pursued the literal sense tenaciously and exclusively, he followed them in regarding as a fundamental clue to the interpretation of important passages the "analogy of faith," a device which sought to harmonize all other meanings in biblical texts, especially those that are obscure, by conforming them to the saving doctrines to be found in the Bible as a whole. And these doctrines were of course soundly Lutheran, conforming to the Augsburg Confession, even if among Pietists they were held with a personal fervor that transformed them from the status of didactic truths which they had among the more scholastically inclined Lutheran theologians.

The difference between these two guardian traditions of the Bible's supremacy was more than temperamental. The difference between an exclusively literal reading and one that supplements it with a spiritual interpretation of veiled meanings, open only to the devout in spirit, left its mark not only on contemporary religious quarrels but also on the later liberal scholars who opposed both views. No matter how much they disliked orthodox literalism they detested even more the ungovernable claims of a variety of layers of meaning in the same text and the search for hidden emphases and meanings in individual words. The neological and rationalist scholars of the later eighteenth century insisted that there is only one meaning to a biblical as to any other proposition, and all interpretation ought to begin with as strict or faithfully reconstructed reading of the original text as possible. To this extent they were closer to their orthodox than their Pietist antagonists. Ernesti, for example, a pioneer in a New Testament hermeneutics based on general and natural principles of interpretation, was quite conservative in his theological views. He could reject pietistic hermeneutical views with an alacrity he did not muster against the more orthodox dogmatic tradition.

Yet such are the perverse ways of history that Pietism despite itself had a fair share in the inception of biblical criticism. The passion for the discovery of the same saving truth in all the biblical texts and their precise wording made not only for such endeavors as the many harmonies of the gospels composed in the eighteenth century but also motivated such great textual scholars of pietist persuasion as the distinguished Swabian Johann Albrecht Bengel in their endeavors to determine the original Greek text of the New Testament from the earliest available manuscripts.

On our central topic, orthodox and pietist traditions agreed. They followed the Reformers and a large consensus of Western Christendom from earliest times in their interpretation of biblical narratives. To them all, literal and historical readings of these narratives were in effect the same thing. Luther, we noted, quite naturally identified the grammatical and the historical sense of the words of the Bible. If a biblical text was obviously literal rather than allegorical or tropical, and if it was a narrative, then it was historical. Moreover, neither Luther nor Calvin saw any contradiction between a literal reading and the claim that the whole Bible, both Old and New Testaments, preached Christ. To solve any such tension was the service rendered by figural reading. But figural reading underwent a transition as the logical relation between literal or grammatical and historical reading changed. It became a historical argument of doubtful value, instead of an extension of the literal sense. Among Pietists the latter function came instead to be performed by the mystical or spiritual sense of words, by virtue of which any of them could have an "emphasis" through which the Holy Spirit referred them to Christ—or, for that matter, to present and future history.

The logical identification of the explicative interpretation of biblical narratives with their historical factuality came apart gradually and then with increasing speed during the course of the eighteenth century, although we shall see that it left some important residual confusions. Furthermore, figurative and typological reading of Old Testament passages, which had gained a more than tacit acknowledgment among many Protestant interpreters (Cocceius as an outstanding example), as time went by met with even greater scorn than biblical literalism among more advanced eighteenth-century scholars.

The split between the explicative meaning and the historical estimation of biblical narratives had crucial consequences for the principles of interpretation. It was mended after a fashion, but the very work of repair actually finalized the rift: the earlier situation was now exactly reversed. Then, historical judgment had been no more than a function of the literal (or sometimes figurative) sense of a narrative passage; now, on the contrary, the sense of such a passage came to depend on the estimate of its historical claims, character, and origin. The only other alternative was to leave historical interpretation and the explication of the sense of narratives totally separate and without so much as a resemblance in type. Each alternative won some adherents, and some tried to rest on very uncertain middle ground. But the position of the earlier day receded ever more rapidly into the past.

Both the split and the beginning of reintegration between historical claims and the explicative sense may be observed incipiently in the seventeenth century and then overtly quite early in the eighteenth century in a controversy between certain Deists and their orthodox opponents about the veracity of the assertions made in the New Testament and the Christian tradition that certain Old Testament prophecies had been fulfilled in the New Testament story. At stake was the correctness or incorrectness of a later interpretation of the words of earlier texts. Did the earlier texts actually mean what at a later stage they had been said to mean? But the criterion that governed the disagreement over this question was the answer to another question: Were the New Testament writers correct or not when they used the Old Testament texts as evidence for the New Testament's own historical truth claims? Is the meaning of a given Old Testament text such that it can be applied (whether by the New Testament writers or later commentators) to the events reported in the New Testament? In other words, the *meaning* of the earlier texts is their *reference*. Do they fit the particular later events they are interpreted to fit, or do they refer to some other occurrence? In either case, their meaning is determined by their reference or failure to refer beyond themselves to certain events.

Spinoza

In the seventeenth century one can note the beginnings of the split between explicative sense and historical reference, and between narrative depiction or form and its meaning or subject matter, in two very dissimilar views of the Bible, those of Benedict de Spinoza (1634–77) and Johannes Cocceius (1603–69), a Dutch theologian of German origin. Spinoza's brilliant and prophetic *Tractatus theologico-politicus* (1670) sets forth most of the important principles of an interpretation at once rationalistic and historical-critical which were to be developed over the course of the eighteenth century. The nature and standards of truth and true virtue, he tells us, are not to be deduced from scripture which is in any case not primarily a source of natural or speculative or historical knowledge but seeks only to inculcate piety and obedience to God.

Whether or not scripture teaches true piety (its sole claim to a divine origin) can be found out only by examining the meaning of biblical statements and the intention of the authors themselves: "Our knowledge of Scripture must . . . be looked for in Scripture only," and again, "Scriptural interpretation proceeds by the examination of Scripture, and inferring the intention of its authors as a legitimate conclusion from its fundamental principles." [18] This principle must be applied, no matter which way the chips fall, even in the unlikely event that the deliverances of scripture turn out not merely to differ from but to disagree with those of reason.

For the main Protestant tradition the (apparently) identical principle meant the coherence if not the identity of the letter and the spirit in the biblical writings, not only of the literal sense with the real historical reference of the historical narratives, but also of the religious meaning of biblical statements with religious truth. Not so for Spinoza, who sternly admonishes his readers (*Works,* p. 101) that in interpreting scripture "we are at work not on the truth of passages, but solely on their meaning," examining them "solely by means of the signification of the words, or by a reason acknowledging no foundation but Scripture."

Scripture teaches in a way that necessitates careful distinctions between verbal or literal sense and the actual meaning or teaching that is conveyed by it. This is certainly true of the faith or matters to be believed, which it inculcates, but it is true also of the spirit of piety which is its chief aim to nurture:

> Scripture does not explain things by their secondary causes, but only narrates them in the order and the style which has most power to move men, and especially uneducated men, to devotion; and therefore it speaks inaccurately of God and of events, seeing that its object is not to convince the reason, but to attract and lay hold of the imagination [*Works*, p. 91].

Obviously, the real subject matter of biblical narratives is not the events they narrate but the quite separable religious lessons they convey, a separation in principle made all the clearer by the fact that the manner of conveying the lesson is as important as the lesson itself. The purpose of scripture is not only to teach the right kind of religion but to move men's hearts to its practice. To move their minds is an easier task, for in principle men know universal and right religion from their own nature and from general ideas, and not merely from scripture, which agrees with this faith. The universal religion, identical with the Divine Law, is "universal and common to all men" and deducible from universal human nature and therefore "does not depend on the truth of any historical narrative whatsoever" (*Works*, p. 61). It tends to one doctrine only: "that there exists a God, that is, a Supreme Being, Who loves justice and charity, and Who must be obeyed by whosoever would be saved; that the worship of this Being consists in the practice of justice and love towards one's neighbour." [19]

Since this universal and naturally knowable religion is also the pervasive content of the Bible, the meaning of its narratives does not lie in their historical truth. Not only are they historically questionable, scriptural reports being notoriously unreliable so

that their literal meaning and their historical reference do not
necessarily coincide (and must therefore be separate matters), but
even where they do agree, this is not necessarily their real content
or subject matter. The latter is of a distinctively religious kind and
therefore only secondarily or peripherally historical:

> The truth of a historical narrative, however assured, cannot
> give us the knowledge nor consequently the love of God, for
> love of God springs from knowledge of Him, and knowledge
> of Him should be derived from general ideas, in themselves
> certain and known, so that the truth of a historical narrative
> is very far from being requisite for our attaining our highest
> good [*Works*, p. 61].

Even these distinctions between literal, historical, and religious
meaning are not exhaustive. For while one may hope that the
religious meaning of a biblical passage is identical with its truth,
i.e. with God's true meaning in it, it is not to be taken for granted
but becomes a matter of demonstration in which, presumably,
scriptural ideas are measured for their agreement or disagreement
with the universal faith by means of general ideas drawn from
human nature: "it is one thing to understand the meaning of
Scripture and the prophets, and quite another thing to understand the meaning of God, or the actual truth." [20]

   In view of this complex series of uses (and distinctions between
uses) of meaning, and especially in view of the last distinction
between meaning and truth, one can understand Spinoza's stern
injunction to trace the meaning of a biblical passage solely from
itself and not from its agreement with "reason" or truth. Thus it is
indeed the case that the literal sense of a miraculous tale is
incompatible with any historical reference because either nothing
or in any case something other than what was described
happened. But even more important, at the more nearly speculative end of the meaning spectrum, if the literal sense of a passage
seems to clash with reason and yet its language is not metaphorical, we are not to resort to metaphorical interpretation, nor to the
claim that the passage "admits of various, nay, contrary mean-

ings" (*Works,* p. 115) in order then to opt for the interpretation most conformable to reason. We will simply have to accept the clash between the verbal sense and reason or truth, hoping to iron out the difficulty in some other way, e.g. that it is on a fine, metaphysically speculative and therefore religiously peripheral point, or that the content of a biblical passage is different from its verbal form (rather than being the conclusion drawn from a variety of different readings of its verbal form).

What, then, counts for an explanation of a biblical passage? We must understand the meaning of the words by means of the passage's historical context—linguistic use at the time, the author's general opinions, the relation of the passage to the general historical environment. Having thus first established the sense of the passage, and never in contravention to it, we can go on to investigate "the minds of the prophets and of the Holy Spirit." And the chief point here is that "we seek first for that which is most universal, and serves for the basis and foundation of all Scripture" (*Works,* p. 104). This turns out to be the universal faith which is the fruit of general ideas reflecting on universal human nature. It is both the general meaning of scripture and the foundation of the "particular external manifestations of true virtue" set forth in it. It turns out therefore that the perilous cleavage between scriptural meaning (founded purely upon itself, regardless of its compatibility or incompatibility with reason or truth) and reason is not so dangerous after all. All such asseverations notwithstanding, the ultimate meaning of scripture is without question identical with what we know in any case to be religious truth.

Even though we must not "confound the mind of a prophet with the mind of the Holy Spirit and the truth of the matter" and some passages of the Bible remain obscure, nonetheless "it is most plain that we can follow with certainty the intention of Scripture in matters relating to salvation and necessary to blessedness" (*Works,* pp. 106, 113). Not only can we follow the scripture on these matters, but because it is without question based on a universal true faith which it presents persuasively to the hearts of men, we may be persuaded also of the harmony between its meaning and God's truth.

The sum of the matter is that literal meaning and historical reference in the Bible are distinct from each other and frequently in opposition; but its religious meaning (in effect equivalent to religious truth), while logically distinct from both of the others, is in no way in opposition to either. Finally, the religious force (distinct from the meaning or truth) of scripture cuts athwart all these ways of meaning because it appeals to the heart rather than the head, to the evocation of piety and virtue rather than to the mind through deduction or intellectual apprehension. Though based on the soundness of the universal faith, this use of scripture is neither identical with it (or with the significations of biblical statements) nor opposed to it.

The distinction between the literal meaning and the historical reference of texts, we may note, is neither the only nor even the most important distinction Spinoza makes in this process of setting forth the right procedures of biblical interpretation. But he does make it, firmly and deliberately.

Cocceius

Johannes Cocceius, a professor of theology in the University of Leyden and a determined follower of John Calvin, succeeded almost despite himself in pointing in various ways into the theological future. He certainly did not intend to be an innovator. The first to work out with thematic clarity the scheme of a "federal theology," he took the traditional reformed concept of a covenant between God and man and worked it into a notion of distinctive temporal stages operative in the history portrayed in scripture. Thus he became the remote progenitor of the so-called *heilsgeschichtliche Schule* of the nineteenth century, for which the unitary meaning of scripture is its reference to one special sequence of real events, from creation to the end of history, with their center in Christ's incarnation, the whole sequence ambiguously related to other historical events.

Joined to the basic contrast of a covenant of works before the fall and a covenant of grace afterward (which in turn Cocceius believed to be grounded in a pretemporal compact between the Father and the Son) is the subdivision of the latter into the stages of a temporally differentiated divine economy. Scripture is thus the depiction of a historical continuum which, viewed from a later perspective (though of course not to Cocceius himself), has an organic shape. Not that one stage of the covenant of grace develops or flows imperceptibly into the next, but each is joined to the next in such a way that there are no gaps or missing links in the divine economy. The work of God described in scripture is a history of salvation through the covenant of grace governing both testaments but climaxing in the New Testament and in the Kingdom of God promised and established by Jesus Christ. Cocceius suggests such characteristic contrasts and developments between the earlier and later stages of the covenant of grace as that between a mere divine overlooking of sin in the earlier stage and genuine forgiveness of sin later, a servile fear of God under the law and a freely rendered love toward him under the gospel.[21]

But now it turns out that this temporally and also psychologically or religiously differentiated character of the one divine economy is not the only theme of the Bible. Cocceius also affirms that Christ is the object of saving faith in both dispensations of the covenant of grace, in the Old Testament as well as the New. Cocceius' contribution to our topic lies in the unsteadiness of focus he has on the relation between history and depiction in his thoroughly conservative interpretation of scripture.

To view Christ as the subject matter of both testaments is quite a different matter from discerning this unity in the temporally distinct and ordered stages of the history of salvation. The two views may be held together, and so may the unity and difference between the two Testaments, through figural interpretation, as Calvin had done. This was the instrument by which the literal, narrative reading of single stories was extended into one overarching story which at the same time renders accessible the real temporal sequence to which it refers. In this fashion the literary unity of the two Testaments in a common theme such as that of salvation through Jesus Christ is not a contradiction of the *sequential, temporally differentiated* character of the events they render.

For Cocceius on the other hand the two things, literal or narrative reading and historical reference, were beginning to come apart. He was, despite his Christian orthodoxy, not so far in this respect from his contemporary and adopted fellow-countryman Spinoza, the forerunner of Deism and historical criticism in his principles of biblical interpretation, who had differentiated far more deliberately than Cocceius between literal and historical interpretation. Once this threat is even vaguely in the air, the biblical narratives' literary unity is in unadjustable tension with the depiction of temporally sequential reality: if Christ is already present as the theme of the Old Testament, then nothing new and real in the history of salvation or revelation happens when he becomes incarnate. On the other hand, if one stresses real novelty in time, then the Old Testament's participation through promise in Christ's fulfillment of the covenant of grace becomes a very dubious matter. For all that one really indicates in that case is the difference between the two dispensations, and consequently the completely anachronistic nature of the earlier, once the new has arrived. In a protracted quarrel over the keeping of sabbatarian laws of the Old Testament, Cocceius's Puritan enemies in effect accused him of holding precisely this view.

Cocceius's stress on the temporally differentiated sequence in the economy of salvation was one more indication of the approaching dissolution of the traditional unity of literal explicative sense and historical reference. The story itself no longer rendered the reality of the history it depicted. Cocceius's case is interesting because it shows what could happen to a conservative whose theology was strongly biblical and who was a forerunner of a new endeavor to set forth the unity of the Bible. Despite his biblicism he was beginning to work with interpretive principles similar to those that were to reign in the deist debate over the fulfillment of prophecy. Even a Cocceius, fully as committed as the Reformers to a narrative view of scriptural unity, was beginning to illustrate the shift in hermeneutical principles that takes place once the narrative as historical reference and as literary and literal sense of the text pull apart, with figural interpretation no longer able to mediate convincingly or naturally between them.

Beyond any technical change, a transition in sensibility is evident here to the historian's retrospective glance. Perhaps the best confirmation for it is Cocceius's extraordinary and baroque proliferation of figural reading. It has all the prodigality and extravagance of a late, decadent growth. Not only did he regard every occasion and ceremony in the Old Testament as a figure of the New Testament, but he also found figure after figure in the Old Testament fulfilled in the events of post-biblical history and in those of his own day, for example, the death of Sweden's ardently Protestant warrior king, Gustavus Adolphus.[22] It was a striking contrast to the Reformers' economy and restraint in this kind of speculation. Their own experience and their sense of present location vis-à-vis the real world and its shape, narrated in the Bible, did indeed require that the heart and head be illumined by the spirit; but granted that gift they knew themselves easily and naturally included in that total narration and by means of it in the world it rendered faithfully. They had therefore no need for the constant and cramped recourse to a kind of figuration that would assure either the inclusion of the present life-location in that total story and history, or, conversely, the inclusion of biblical history in the larger sequence of salvation history which embraced church history, one's own time, and the end-time to come.

But Cocceius's situation was different, and his sensibility and imagination seemed to demand a constant positioning, not so much of his single self as of his sense of his historical era in juxtaposition to the narrated world into whose sequence his present time seemed to fit only by the force of constant figural proliferation. And the same was true of the location of the Old Testament with respect to the novelty of the later dispensation: constant positioning through figures was required to ensure that the continuity between them was as real as the difference. Beyond the technical shift in principles of interpretation, we see here the gradual change to the sense of another temporal reality than the biblical. The self might or might not claim this new historical world as its appropriate home, but in any case the true narrative by which its reality is rendered is no longer identical with the Bible's overarching story. And so, in circular fashion, the Bible's own story becomes increasingly dependent on its relation to other temporal frames of reference to render it illuminating and even real. Its meaning is derived from its fitting the history by which God saved mankind, beginning with the *protevangelium,* through all the biblical-historical narration, the economy of salvation in sacred and secular happenings since then, and from now to Christ's thousand-year reign.

The biblical story begins to be included in a larger framework as its operative world. "Salvation history" comes to be the meaning of the Bible. Like the world of "real" events to which Deists and historical critics had the Bible refer for meaning, the *heilsgeschichtliche Schule,* of whom Cocceius was a forerunner, also had the Bible mean or make explicative sense by ostensive reference, even though their world was far more conservative and biblically derived. In its own right and by itself the biblical story began to fade as the inclusive world whose depiction allowed the reader at the same time to locate himself and his era in the real world rendered by the depiction. Historical hindsight indicates that Cocceius stood at a point of transition, technically and as a matter of cultural sensibility, which the Deists will have left well behind them three generations later.

3 Change in Interpretation: The Eighteenth Century

The full force of the change in outlook and argument concerning the narrative biblical texts came in the eighteenth century. First in England and then in Germany the narrative became distinguished from a separable subject matter—whether historical, ideal, or both at once—which was now taken to be its true meaning. Not only was this view held more self-consciously than it had been in the previous century (a few thinkers like Spinoza excepted) but it also became embroiled in the wider theological controversies so typical of the eighteenth century. It is therefore appropriate to put the hermeneutical issue in the broader theological setting.

ENGLAND

If historical periods may be said to have a single chronological and geographical starting point, modern theology began in England at the turn from the seventeenth to the eighteenth century. Its history has not yet been fully told,[1] and perhaps won't be, because it would demand the confluence of many things, some quite intangible, some not yet well studied, some worked over in too great detail—the history of morals, of piety, of the imagination, of the intellect. It was a point in time when the metaphysical poets had vanished from the scene of cultured discussion in England and Bunyan's more sober mode of allegorical representation, presaging the rise of the modern novel, had begun to capture the imagination of a different but increasingly important stratum of the population. Joseph Addison found it necessary to defend— even while praising—the use and pleasures of the imagination,[2] whereas Bishop Butler severely condemned its intervention in the quest for religious truth, calling it "that forward delusive faculty."[3] (Ironically enough, it was one of his rare well-chosen phrases.) The substance of thought as well as style was increasingly modeled on the precision and sobriety, if not always the economy, of scientific discourse divorced from immediate appeal to sensibility.[4]

From the welter of impressions and issues, certain technical problems stand out, which have rightly been discussed over and over. The chief of these for the study of the history of theology is the inception, coincident with these developments, of the concept of revelation as the central technical concept in theology, a position of eminence to which it has clung through various changes in its own content, brought about by such shifts as that from rationalist to romantic sensibility. There are signs that the day of its decline has arrived.[5] But no matter what its future, it has had more than two and a half centuries of preeminence. All this time is has borne something of the sign of its intellectualistic birthmark, and of the change in the climate of opinion that helped beget it.

The deistic controversy, at once reacting to, shaping, and testing the notion of revelation, began a series of arguments about the credibility of special divine communication and (later on) of divine self-presentation through the medium of historical occurrences.[6] Two issues were at stake from the beginning. The first was of a predominantly philosophical nature. It concerned the inherent rationality or credibility of the very idea of a historical revelation. Was it conceivable or intelligible? Is it likely, it was asked, that a perfectly good God should have left mankind without decisive guidance for so long, only to grant the privilege finally to a tiny, rude, and isolated fraction of the human race? Or is what is called revelation nothing more than a specific instantiation of what God had made known everywhere and all along, concerning truth and human happiness? Furthermore, is the appeal to the "mystery" of revelation anything other than an admission that the idea itself is unintelligible, a token of that unwarranted intrusion of imagination or, worse yet, sheer ignorant superstition into matters religious which the new intellectual rigor must repel?

The second question was: Even granted the rationality or inherent possibility of revelation, how likely is it that such a thing has actually taken place? This is no longer an issue of theoretical but of factual inquiry. The immediate question was whether there are good grounds for believing in the actual occurrence of the miraculous events constituting the indispensable evidence for historical revelation. How authoritative, in short, how well attested are biblical accounts, especially those of miracles, since the natural presumption in a "scientific age" is obviously against them? And closely associated with miracle as the cognate "external evidence" for Christian truth was the argument from the fulfillment of Old Testament prophecies in the events of the New Testament.

Many other problems, such as locating authoritative backing for religious beliefs, and the problems of theodicy and of original sin, obviously played their part in the disagreements of the era, but these were the two main technical theological questions, both of them centering on the viability of the notion of revelation. From its very beginning revelation was a christocentric notion. If you asked just what had been revealed, the typical English latitudinarian answer (echoed later by the "Neologians" in Germany) would be that Jesus was the Messiah, and that this belief is the only one the New Testament demands of Christians, together with the insistence that they firmly resolve to lead a pure, altruistic life.[7] Obviously then, the second or fact question would eventually center on miracles done by Jesus Christ himself, or those which had taken place in connection with his person, including the fulfillment of prophecy in his coming, his deeds, and his fate.

This debate, in turn, could and did have two different emphases. First there was a debate over the general credibility of miracles in a physical and historical world which was increasingly believed to be governed in accordance with natural law, conceived either prescriptively or descriptively.[8] Second, there was a debate over the credibility of the specific miracle accounts of the Bible, especially those of the New Testament including the claims to the fulfillment of prophecy, which involved as one of its chief criteria the reliability of the New Testament writers as reporters. Again, one could go about the latter discussion in several ways. One could argue their moral integrity and veracity or lack of it. This question achieved the unlikely status of a serious debate in England.[9] There were other ways, one of which extended well into the nineteenth century, again mainly in England. The plausibility or implausibility of biblical miracles was argued on the basis of external and independent evidence. For instance, one examined the countryside for geological evidence of a sudden catastrophe, immanently inexplicable and extending, one hoped, over a large portion of the earth or all of it, and dating from the same time (presumably) as the origin of the story of Noah's flood.[10] The remarkable durability of this way of handling the issue of the credibility of the Bible (together with uneasiness over man's place in the universe) goes a long way toward explaining the storm which the publication of Darwin's *Origin of Species* unleashed in England.

GERMANY

In Germany such external procedures in investigating the credibility of miracle accounts in the Bible never played a large role, though the twin issues of the factuality of revelation and the credibility of the Bible in connection with it were fully as important to German as to English writers. But the discussion in the German-speaking lands was shaped by a different tradition of biblical study. It was an Englishman who wrote: "the Bible, I say, the Bible only is the religion of Protestants," [11] but the claim was worked out with great intensity as a theological position in Switzerland, Holland, and Germany. The Bible was taken as the exclusive source specifying the content of Christian belief as well as the norms for Christian conduct. Seventeenth-century debate over the place of tradition in understanding the sacred canon had pretty well settled the issue in the eyes of most Protestants: the contents of the Bible are for the most part luminously perspicuous in their own right, and their meaning must not be tampered with by mere human tradition. This particular inquiry—how and with the aid of what authority one settles the principles of biblical interpretation—had been at the heart of Catholic–Protestant polemics ever since the Reformation. Its technical deposition on the Protestant side could be found in the works of the so-called Protestant scholastics. While the mainspring of Reformation discussion over the Bible had been the questions of its authority and unity, the Protestant interpreters from the post-Reformation era through the seventeenth century additionally focused more narrowly on detailing the principles of textual interpretation, the hermeneutical question proper, hoping thereby to make good on the claim that scripture is indeed directly perspicuous.

Not very much of Protestant orthodoxy passed over into rationalist religious thought, but this one thing surely did: the antitraditionalism in scriptural interpretation of the one bolstered the antiauthoritarian stance in matters of religious meaning and truth of the other. Not only unbroken ecclesiastical tradition, but the contextual and looser authority of confessional formulae, such as the Thirty-Nine Articles and the Formula of Concord, also gradually lost their place of influence in interpretation of scripture. Moreover, the remnants of orthodox belief joined with rationalist interpretation to combat any understanding of scripture claiming to rest on the direct influence of the Holy Spirit on the reader, in lieu of settling for its plain meaning. Despite the influence of Pietism, the fate of "spiritual" reading and thus of double meaning in the interpretation of scripture in the later eighteenth century was finally as dim as that of the principle of interpretation through tradition, evaporating the remnants of whatever mystical-allegorical reading on the part of Protestants had survived the seventeenth century. The eighteenth century was the period of the direct reading of the "plain" text, the one common ground among all the differing hermeneutical schools. Indeed, it was this common position that made *general* hermeneutics possible. No matter what the privileged, singular truth of the Bible, the meaning of the texts as such could be understood by following the rules of interpretation common to all written documents. The consequence of unity and universality in method of interpretation ensured unity of textual meaning also. By the end of the century, belief in layers of meaning in a single text—literal, typological, and spiritual or mystical had virtually disappeared as a major force.

In the latter half of the eighteenth century this tradition of inquiry into the meaning of the biblical texts combined with the factual question about the historical accuracy of the Bible, originating in the wake of Deism. In ways that have still not been fully worked out, this confluence also changed the hermeneutical issue as such. In the earlier Protestant interpretive tradition, we have noted, the literal and religious meaning of texts and the judgment about their factual accuracy had been wholly united. The point to realize is not that they had been conceived to be in harmony with each other but that they had not even been generically distinct issues. As the eighteenth century wears on, this situation is increasingly a thing of the past, simply by virtue of the question of the factuality of revelation as an independent, critical inquiry. From now on, the harmony of historical fact, literal sense, and religious truth will at best have to be demonstrated; at worst, some explanation of the religious truth of the fact-like description will have to be given in the face of a negative verdict on its factual accuracy or veracity.

The relation between historical criticism and hermeneutics has remained an unresolved issue ever since its inception in the eighteenth century. But one thing remained constant: when the German biblical scholars of the later eighteenth century investigated the fact or credibility issue, their own scriptural tradition made certain that it was raised for them in connection with the broader hermeneutical issue of the meaning of biblical texts. Unlike the English discussion of the fact issue, which had by this time become completely mired in the external evidence question, the German scholars' procedure was therefore almost exclusively internal, i.e. literary-historical. And accompanying this literary-historical quest was a flood of essays and books on the principles of interpretation.

So far as the estimate of the factual reliability of biblical accounts was concerned, the subjects for investigation were the internal evidence for or against the claims made in them, for example, their internal and mutual coherence and inherent credibility; the kind of writing an account might be, compared to others of a similar genre within or outside the Bible; the circumstances and outlook of which a particular account might be the product. The fact that the Bible continued to be held in high respect by people with the most diverse theological views, as well as by some with none at all, heightened the interest in the meaning-and-fact issue. No set of questions was more thoroughly aired in late eighteenth-century German biblical scholarship, and it was instrumental in raising German theological work to a level of eminence in the Western Protestant world.[12]

It is well to keep in mind that this literary-historical debate over the trustworthiness of history-like biblical accounts both arose and abode over the claims about unique historical revelation, in particular that Jesus was the Messiah. One ought therefore to make a distinction between two connected "fact" issues, in theology as well as in biblical exegesis. There is first the question, of the reliability of accounts involving physical miracles —events flying in the face of natural law or uniform experience, or at least seemingly inexplicable through them. But secondly, the much more important issue is one that may or may not depend on the answer to the first: Is it really the meaning of the pertinent biblical texts that the salvation of man depends not only on *what* Jesus taught and did, but on all this as an expression of the presumably indispensable fact, given by divine fiat and authority, *that* he existed, and existed as the Son of God incarnate? The latter is the exegetical and theological issue of "positivity" for Christian belief which has nagged theology ever since the latter part of the eighteenth century. (It was also at stake in the earlier English discussion but did not get focused in nearly such specific form.[13])

"Positivity" is not identical with "miracle" conceived as disruption of natural law or uniform experience. But there are obvious parallels between them. For positivity is the affirmation of a direct or unmediated intervention of the Godhead in the finite realm, even though not necessarily one to be known directly in the chain of physical events. Increasingly, Christian theologians, who continued to affirm that the New Testament claimed the historical positivity of revelation by virtue of the unique status of Jesus' being and dignity, located the claim in the moral and personal qualities that bespoke his being. They insisted on these qualities as the description of an authentic, factual history. For these men, miracle did not mean seemingly or really contranatural physical events in connection with Jesus, but rather the qualitative, immanently inexplicable uniqueness of his being, on which an equally mysteriously originated faith in him was totally dependent. Positivity thus became anchored in "miracles" not of a physical but of a peculiarly historical, inward, or moral sort, perhaps one should say miracles of character, and in this way one would hopefully avoid some of the more awkward questions about miracles.

Moreover, in the eyes of these men, positivity did indeed involve the affirmation of the cruciality for human salvation of these historical events as actual transpirings—but not merely that. For quite obviously positivity also involved for them the religious truth content given with and through the occurrences, in particular the quality of life and teaching manifesting the unique being of Jesus. The tension between these two aspects of what theologians have barbarically come to call "the event Jesus Christ" has occupied theological reflection ever since. Is positivity best got at by describing the occurrence character of the event, or its qualitative content? If both, how are they related or unified, or to which does one give priority? This issue, then, has gone hand in hand with the question whether inward or historical miracle is a notion that avoids all the difficulties of the more external kind.

These were obviously issues both of theological argument and biblical interpretation. At both levels theologians, biblical scholars, and others were hard pressed. Most of them, by the end of the eighteenth century, had a due sense of the autonomy and integrity of historical inquiry: it must not be shaped by any extraneous convictions. This was as true of inquiry into the Bible as into any other subject matter. On the other hand, many of them also wanted to affirm to the fullest that the Christian faith, set forth in scripture, is the true religion. And in that era, whether rightly or wrongly, the positivity of revelation was the issue that joined these two perspectives of faith and historical inquiry, be it in harmony or battle, for positivity seemed on the face of it to be the central meaning of the biblical narratives. Everyone agreed on their "history-likeness." (The German term was *Geschichtsähnlichkeit,* and everybody used it.[14]) If positivity wasn't their central meaning, it was up to those demurring against it to demonstrate their case. The biblical question, then, centered on the meaning of the miracle-tinged narrative texts. Were the gospels, for example, to be taken literally? If so, which sections? The narration of events, such as Jesus' birth or passion? The description of Jesus' teachings and being? In either case, or both, one was affirming that positivity is the accounts' meaning.

Thereafter one faced the theological issue of affirming or denying the centrality of positivity for the Christian religion. One chose whether Christianity was a rational-moral, experiential, or historical religion, or a combination of these three.

Locating the positivity of revelation obviously involved disagreement in interpretation as well as emphasizing some texts rather than others. The more pressing the problem, the more concentrated the attention paid to the narrative portions of the Bible, chiefly Genesis and, of course, the gospel story. I have already stressed the divergence between two groups of interpreters: those who sought the meaning of positivity in their event-sequence or narrative character, and those who sought it in connection with the religious truth content and therefore (in the case of the gospels) in the quality of Jesus' teaching, ministry, and life, which they sought to connect with his actual historical being. For the latter interpreters it was increasingly the notion of "the

Kingdom of God" which provided that connection, being at once the content of his preaching and embodied in his bearing and action.

MEDIATING INTERPRETATION

This group of interpreters was actually spread over a fairly wide hermeneutical spectrum, as we shall see, but all of them represented a "mediating" position between two hermeneutical and theological extremes. In both theology and hermeneutics their task was arduous, just as that of their more or less linear successors has been ever since. In theology itself, these early mediators were the Latitudinarians in England and the Neologians in Germany. The pull of the two extremes between which they were caught was illustrated by the instability of their positions.

The Neologians would stress the significance of Jesus' personal bearing, character, and virtue as the expression of his unique being. They would therefore regard the external events, especially his suffering and death, as direct and climactic manifestations of his qualitative being. For the doctrine of salvation it would follow that we are saved by the love of God whose initiative becomes historically implemented in this climactic bearing of Jesus, which is at the same time also the work or disposition of God toward us in and through him. By contrast, they would regard the qualitative aspect or suggestions of meaning emerging from the stress on the sheer occurrences, the narrated events of Jesus' career, as time-conditioned and, therefore, not binding conceptions into which the authors had cast the contents of religious truth. The events of Jesus' life portrayed as a struggle against a really existing, personal, supernatural evil being; his death as a substitutionary blood atonement, appeasing the wrath of God against the guilty through the sacrifice of an innocent man; the eschatological cast of Jesus' own teaching, as well as the writers' eschatological and Jewish-messianic description of his career and second coming—these are all typical instances of such time-conditioned conceptions, explicable from the cultural circumstances and views of the day, to which the writers had "accommodated" themselves. The genuine meaning of such passages, the authors' actual intention in them, is not identical with the words and descriptions of the text. Several of the Neologians, including the greatest among them, J. S. Semler, had recourse to the accommodation theory,[15] bespeaking at the hermeneutical level their inclination toward the notion of positivity as "character" rather than physical miracle, expressed most adequately in its truth content rather than its sheer occurrence character.

Yet when men like Semler were confronted by a flat denial of the factuality of the events narrated (the position of Reimarus on the resurrection), or a denial of their religious significance as supernaturally caused occurrences (the position of rationalists like K. F. Bahrdt and J. B. Basedow), they drew back in the direction of the importance of positivity as factual happening, and therefore of the texts' meaning as deriving from the miraculous-occurrence character of the narrated events. And this included, specifically, the resurrection of Jesus.[16]

It was evident, even at the time, that the Neologians' position was unstable between the rigorous affirmations and denials of the historical positivity of revelation. In locating the importance and revelatory quality of the "fact" in its religious truth content, they had at once raised and left suspended the theological issue whether saving knowledge and faith really depend wholly on the historical occasion. For presumably the truth content is timeless and therefore known at least to some extent naturally and universally, and merely recognized because reexemplified in the historic event. The issue was the same as that raised by the original deistic controversy, for instance by the very title of Matthew Tindal's *Christianity as Old as the Creation: Or, The Gospel, A Republication of the Religion of Nature.* There was only one seemingly watertight device for protecting the theological indispensability of historical revelation against deistic insinuations of a natural, nonpositive saving knowledge of God. This was a root-and-branch affirmation of the specific historical event of original, inherited, and naturally inexpungeable guilt, the fatal moral, metaphysical, and noetic flaw which could be wiped out only by a similarly factual saving occurrence. This would have been a return to the notion of a single overarching story, now held to be factual history, as providing the encompassing interpretive context both for biblical hermeneutics and theology. But all the Neologians, like the Latitudinarians before them, were united in their abhorrence of this doctrine. The Neologians' dilemma between positive revelation and natural religion was a typical instance of the ancient recurring puzzle whether the liberal, poised between the consistent extremes of orthodox dogmatism and radical skepticism about revelation, has a position with an integrity of its own.

Hermeneutically, their problem was shared by several other perspectives. On what grounds or by what criteria does one judge that a given text, whether fact-like description or development of a religious notion, means something other than what an author says (as the accommodation theory, for one, claimed about Jesus, the evangelists, and Paul at certain points), unless he gives us a special hint to that effect or uses obviously figurative language? In other words, a writer may be taken literally and either accepted as an oracle of truth, argued with, or rejected as wrong or deluded. Or else he may be understood in historicist fashion so that his mind is seen to be just as time-conditioned as that of his readers and everybody else. But why assume his capacity to transcend historical relativity (a difficult assumption in any case) just at those points where he seems to manifest this limitation most clearly and does not indicate that he is doing it deliberately? It is difficult, given these alternatives (their correctness or exhaustiveness for the estimate of textual meaning is another question), to avoid the conclusion that those who were in favor of such devices as the notion of accommodation saw in it "the sought-for means for bringing into harmony with reason those biblical concepts which no longer corresponded with the theological views of their day, without touching the authority of the Bible itself directly." [17]

Theologically, the centrifugal pressure of modernity in the late eighteenth century (when outright religious skepticism was still a rare thing) was toward complete polarization between those who, equating revelation with unique, salvific, miraculous occurrence *qua* occurrence, affirmed it, and those who denied positive revelation altogether and opted instead for something else, such as a straightforward theism or "natural religion." The hermeneutical equivalent of this choice was not quite so straightforward. It involved the agreement of those who affirmed theological positivity that the intended and real meaning of the ancient narrative writers was literal, and that they rendered reliable historical accounts. On the other hand, those who denied theological positivity denied not only the reliability of the accounts but (since they usually did not want to dishonor the Bible) also that the real meaning of the accounts is literal (or literally ostensive). The latter move in turn conjured up a Hobson's choice, for while it may have rescued the religious pertinence or status of the Bible for the deniers of revelation, it did so at the expense of its writers' integrity or intelligence. Either they had carefully hidden their actual intentions in writing the narratives, to the point of dissemblance, or they hadn't even realized what they were writing about. Since neither of these assumptions, particularly the first, seemed palatable to the deniers of positivity, they opted instead for an explanation of the narratives which claimed that their real meaning is indeed not the same as their literal meaning, though the authors had intended them to be taken literally. Having rescued the author's integrity, one then went on to salvage their intelligence by explaining that they simply did what everybody in their day and time did: they believed in miracles. In order to do them justice, then, they must be understood from within their own cultural context, and not that of modernity. The understanding appropriate to the authors and their writing is therefore historical, in a relatively new sense of the word. Rather than inquiring simply into what had taken place (though this was also involved), "historical understanding" sought to understand how the ancient writers had experienced and thought, in their own distinctive, culturally or historically conditioned consciousness. The dominance of this way of explaining biblical texts began with the writings of Semler; but in its purest form it was not he but the so-called mythical school (I shall call them mythophiles for the sake of convenience) that advocated it.

Polarization between hermeneutical extremes, corresponding to the theological affirmation and denial of the positivity of revelation, went like this then: on the one side stood those who affirmed the identity of the real and the intended meanings of the narratives, i.e. their literal meanings and also their historical reliability. On the other side stood those who claimed that the narratives, though literally intended, were as fully historically conditioned as other ancient manuscripts, and that their real meaning, therefore, is not the same as the authors' (literal) intention. Their historical reliability must then be judged by the same criteria as those to which we subject all other putatively factual descriptions: it has nothing to do with the authors' integrity or, for that matter, with the real meaning of these writings.

This polarization in hermeneutics, as distinct from the somewhat earlier polarization in theology, came to a head at the end of the eighteenth and beginning of the nineteenth century. Since the ultimate issue involved was that of positivity, the crucial texts were those apparently claiming to be reports of actual though inexperienceable or miraculous historical occurrences. Inexperienceable though these events were, they formed a pattern that was in a certain sense intelligible, because constituted by a sequential order, in contrast to single and wholly portentous miracles. In other words, the crucial texts for the hermeneutical question in theology toward the end of the eighteenth century were the supposedly revelatory salvific narratives, "sacred history" (*die heilige Geschichte*)[18] as it was called. Now the rise of historical criticism and of general (rather than special) principles of meaning in biblical hermeneutics had effectively sundered the dogmatic unity and authority of the canon. Each narrative therefore had now to be examined in its own historical context and its own right. This, in addition to theological and diplomatic reticence about the central figure in revelation, as well as the fact that Jesus and his story were apparently historical (in contrast to the biblical cosmogony), helps to explain why of the two narratives chiefly under debate, the Mosaic creation account was discussed radically and frankly at a slightly earlier date, while the climax of the conflict over the gospel story did not come until the publication of D. F. Strauss's *Life of Jesus* in 1835.

4 Anthony Collins: Meaning, Reference, and Prophecy

The shift in the interpretation of the biblical narratives which came to a climax in the eighteenth century had been gradual and complex. Even in Spinoza's thought the "fact" question, though clearly distinct from the literal sense of the narratives, did not have the centrality it was to assume in the next century. And Cocceius obviously did not realize that he was on his way toward a separation of history and story. But the general situation in eighteenth-century theology, just summarized, meant that the issue of the interpretation of the biblical stories would become central, dramatic, and conscious.

More strikingly than in Spinoza's and Cocceius's writings, a new interpretive situation was illustrated in the early eighteenth-century argument over the fulfillment of Old Testament prophecy in the New Testament, a controversy that ranged Anthony Collins, a friend and philosophical disciple of John Locke and a man of vigorous deistic convictions, against the established ecclesiastical gentry. Just before then a debate had raged in England over the content of Christian doctrine, particularly the intelligibility of the idea of a historical revelation supposedly necessary to rectify the human situation which had gone badly awry at the beginning of history. But now the fact claims of the gospel stories rather than the intelligibility of Christian belief were to be scrutinized. A short time later, a longer and even more acrimonious battle would rage over the credibility of miracles, those of the New Testament in particular. But in the present instance the argument over the supposed fulfillment of prophecy was important for the claim that Jesus was in fact the Messiah. The question was: Are the prophecies cited in evidence really applicable to the event they are supposed to demonstrate, and, if not, is there any reason to believe the Christian claim about

Jesus? For the development of the interpretation of biblical narratives in particular, this controversy was obviously more important than the quarrel about miracles.

TYPOLOGY AND THE CRITERIA OF MEANINGFULNESS

In 1724 Collins published *A Discourse of the Grounds and Reasons of the Christian Religion* in response to a curious argument advanced by William Whiston in *An Essay towards restoring the true Text of the Old Testament, and for vindicating the Citations thence made in the New Testament*. Whiston had reasoned that Jesus and his disciples had meant those Old Testament texts to which they had referred as prophecies to apply literally to Jesus himself as the promised Messiah. But Whiston also conceded that given the shape of the Old Testament text as we presently have it, the prophecies don't seem to jibe with this application. His remedy for the situation was to plead for a restoration of the original text which had obviously been blemished by hostile Jewish sources during the early Christian era in order to destroy the evidence it would constitute in favor of Christianity. Whiston was a literalist indeed, even if he did take his stand firmly in thin air.

This farfetched bit of speculation was itself a sign that the struggle between Deists and orthodox defenders had moved to the arena of fact claims, although a question of meaning was also involved. The bone of contention was of course historical, chiefly the evidence for the claim that Jesus was the Messiah. But it was at the same time hermeneutical because the discussion to which Whiston's essay gave rise focused largely on whether the New Testament interpretations of the Old Testament prophecies ought to be understood literally or in some other way. What are the right principles for interpretation?

Whiston's essay provided the occasion for Collins, a controversialist of long standing, to take a delicious romp among the embattled enfilades of orthodox biblical interpretation. He argues tongue-in-cheek all the way, first in *Grounds and Reasons* and then, after it had been attacked in no fewer than thirty-five responses, three years later in *The Scheme of Literal Prophecy Considered*. The force of his argument is that the notion of the fulfillment of Old Testament prophecy held in the New, which is the basis for the claims of Jesus as Messiah, is either false or absurd.

It occurs to him—and most of his opponents agreed—that the Christian faith is invincibly established if it is properly based on the sacred books of the Old Testament. In that way the identity and authenticity of Jesus as the Messiah are reliably attested. To the contrary, it seems to him, without this "proof" of an ancient and inspired historical lineage, all of it heading up in the climax of Jesus and offered in evidence by Jesus and the New Testament writers themselves, Christianity would not only be uncertain but also false. Indeed, the whole messianic scheme makes no sense, it loses all its meaning, without the context of the Old Testament. If Jesus is he who was promised of old, one had best show that someone was indeed promised of old and that he had enough of the features of Jesus to make the latter fit the promise; the later revelation must harmonize with the earlier truth. The performance of miracles in connection with Jesus could not establish the basic messianic claims. In fact it could not even count in their favor, though its absence might be evidence against the claims, which are established only by demonstrating that, no matter what the appearance of things, the New Testament events really did possess the prophesied characteristics and so fulfilled the prophetic predictions.

At this point Collins strikes his blow. In fact, he says, Whiston is right that, as the text stands, the Old Testament passages cited in the New Testament simply cannot be applied literally to the situation described in the latter:

> these proofs, taken out of the Old, and urged in the New Testament, being, sometimes, either not found in the Old, or not urged in the New, according to the literal and obvious sense, which they seem to bear in their supposed places in the Old, and therefore not proofs according to scholastic rules; almost all Christian commentators on the Bible, and advocates for the Christian religion, both ancient and modern,

have judged them to be applied in a secondary, or typical, or
mystical, or allegorical, or enigmatical sense; that is, in a
sense different from the obvious and literal sense, which they
bear in the Old Testament.[1]

Several classic cases illustrate the point, and Collins cites and
argues them all. One is enough here: Matt. 1:22–23 claims that
the conception and birth of Jesus fulfilled the prophecy in Isaiah
7:14. But taken literally and in its own context that prophecy, far
from referring to Jesus, applies to a young woman in the days of
Ahaz, King of Judah.

Later in *Grounds and Reasons*, Collins easily disposes of Whiston's
thesis of a post-Christian and willful Jewish corruption of the Old
Testament text. But it is more to his purpose to observe that
orthodox defenders of the faith claim that the rules for nonliteral,
typical, mystical interpretation (it is obviously all one to him)
have long since been lost, so that in effect we do not know on what
principles the New Testament writers interpreted the Old Testament. In rebuttal he claims the similarity of the New Testament's
procedure to that of the rabbinical interpretation of texts, quoting
at length and with a great show of seriousness from "the learned
SURENHUSIUS, Professor of the Hebrew Tongue in the illustrious
School of Amsterdam," who has, lately and happily, after meeting
with a rabbi skilled in allegorical interpretation, not only
reconstructed the method but tested it successfully as well on the
pertinent New Testament explanations of Old Testament passages. The gist of the most learned Surenhusius's method may be
conveyed by the last of its ten rules, all of them dutifully set down
by Collins, and all of them very much of a kind: "changing the
order of words, adding words, and retrenching words; which is a
method often used by Paul." Collins cannot but dilate on the fact
that "by a most lucky accident of Mr. Surenhusius's meeting and
conference with a learned allegorical Rabbin, are the rules, by
which the Apostles cited and applied the Old Testament,
discovered to the world." It reminds him of the strikingly similar
upshot of a conference which Luther reports he had with the

Devil, whence he claimed to have received his arguments for the abolition of the sacrifice of the Mass. From all of which our author concludes that "the Rabbin establishes Christianity; and the Devil Protestantism." [2]

In short, the hitherto "lost" rules governing nonliteral interpretation are completely arbitrary nonsense and the interpretation itself therefore nonsensical, playing hob as it does with the literal sense of a passage. Collins has placed his opponents in a most unenviable quandary by putting before them two, and only two, alternatives. One either admits the applicability of rules for literal interpretation in this instance, in which case the New Testament claims concerning the meaning of the Old Testament passages which they have quoted are demonstrably false; or one says that the rules governing the interpretation of the Old Testament prophecies in the New Testament are those for nonliteral interpretation, which is equivalent to saying that the interpretation is meaningless because it has nothing to do with the words of the text of the prophecies. Literal and false, or typological and meaningless; those were his alternatives for the way the New Testament and the Christian tradition interpreted the Old Testament prophetic texts.

Collins received some very silly answers but he did not wholly lack for cogent rejoinders. Thomas Sherlock, longtime Master of the Temple who was later elevated to the episcopate, for instance argued that precise, literal, and intentional prediction come true is not the meaning of the claim that Old Testament prophecies are fulfilled in the New. Rather, the claim to fulfillment represents a retrospective view from the vantage point of what had happened in the New Testament, discerning a connected, providential scheme in the general bearing of the Old Testament texts, so that what was said and recounted there is now seen to have foreshadowed and led to the climax or fulfillment claimed by the New Testament writers.[3] It was a perfectly reasonable defense of typology or figuration, though it was in its own right well on its way toward more modernistic conceptions, both in the inclination to see typology as at least partially retrospective and in the view, reminiscent of Cocceius, of covenantal history as an unbroken sequence of events.

Sherlock in effect protested that Collins's disjunctive, supposedly all-inclusive alternative is apparent rather than real and does not render an account of all the possibilities. There is, he claims, an interpretation which is neither literal nor meaningless. It is not literal for it does not say that the prophetic utterances rendered a precise description of the later events to which they are applied, or that they did so because the prophets making the descriptions intended to predict these specific events. Yet its not being in this sense literal does not make such an interpretation purely arbitrary or nonsensical, as it would be if there were no real resemblance, similarity, or genuine connection between the texts from the Old Testament and the situation to which they are applied.

Collins's own concise description of a "type," while more old-fashioned than Sherlock's reasoning, fits the latter reasonably well and gives the lie to Collins's own insistence on either equating prophecy with prediction or making the typological application of the original texts wholly arbitrary and meaningless:

> A type is a mould or pattern of a thing, and has relation to that thing, whereof it is a mould or pattern; which thing is called the antitype: and in a theological sense, type is thus defined, a sign or symbol of some more excellent future thing originally designed by God to signify that future thing. And therefore when a prophecy is said to be typical, the meaning is, that one thing is designed to presignify or represent another thing, as a mould or pattern represents the thing, whereof it is a mould or pattern.[4]

This definition has nothing of that crazy quilt of the learned Surenhusius's rules for establishing artificially a similarity that does not exist intrinsically between two things. Nor on the other hand does the definition demand that the intentional description of a later event by the earlier text, with a one-to-one correspondence between their features, is the only meaningful basis for recognizing similarity and possibly some form or providential connection between the two. But Collins never made use of nor did he argue against the view of New Testament interpretation of Old Testament prophecy he himself has here set forth. It came admittedly very late in the second of his two essays in the controversy, but whether early or late, there is no indication that this kind of consideration ever modified his identification of typical interpretation with completely arbitrary "wire-drawing" manipulation. Though he referred to Sherlock's essay frequently and respectfully, he did not come to grips with the thrust of his thought.

But no matter who was right, Collins's view was the earnest of the future. If anyone wished to link in a connected series passages so far apart in time and evidently so different in their respective reference, the only way he could do so was by demonstrating the identity between the predictive description and the features of the later event to which it was (later) claimed the description referred. This in effect would amount to saying that in at least some of the pertinent prophetic utterances made hundreds of years earlier the speaker or writer had Jesus in mind, a position into which Collins would have been happy to cast his opponents; and some of them indeed seemed quite content to accept the inference.

Later in the century another kind of endeavor was made to exhibit a unity of meaning between Old and New Testaments. They are linked together in a common and developing history of religious ideas and outlook. But in England in 1725 our controversialists had no basis yet for this notion. It was of course to be based on the assumption of gradual, natural, and self-developing transitions in the history of human thought. The orthodox defenders against the Deists would have rejected this scheme. It lacked the overtone of a providential plan, at once intentional and therefore rationally discernible, but also partially inscrutable and therefore irreducible to full explanation. It was precisely this combination of apparent rationality and mystery that made the argument from prophecy so appealing to its proponents. Sher-

lock's *Use and Intent of Prophecy* is typical of the biblical interpretation of the time, for which the indispensable setting is God's
providential action in history, working through new and renewed
covenants unto the last still-hidden future day of total consummation.

Later advocates of the typological procedure like Sherlock did
not readily acknowledge a crisis in their interpretive ways. They
all appealed quite frankly to a pattern of providential design,
manifested if not yet fully exhibited in the history of the sacred
covenants. This constitutes the link between the two Testaments,
and between them and the rest of history. It was never clear
whether this doctrine of providential design was to be established
through the evidence furnished by the success of typological
interpretation or whether, on the other hand, the doctrine was the
indispensable assumption for making typological interpretation
operative and cogent. Whichever it was, and it was probably a
circular argument, the doctrine furnished a substitute for the
Deists' assumption, so natural as to be almost unconscious, that
the origin and sense of every rational statement is the intention in
the mind of the human author to give it that meaning which it
then has for others, especially its immediate audience. This
assumption was quite secondary, indeed superfluous for the
defenders of typological interpretation and of the typical fulfillment of prophecy. They had their own divine author who could
easily supplement if not supplant with a second, greater, and
more inclusive meaning the sense intended by a limited human
author and appropriate to his finite understanding. Yet the divine
author worked this more inclusive sense through the text's literal
words. To apprehend the divine meaning one did not have to
supplant literal with allegorical interpretation. Figural or typological interpretation, because it was thought to be historical, was
closer to literal than allegorical or other kinds of spiritual
interpretation.

The Deists' more orthodox opponents were still, even though
quite residually, operating on the Protestant Reformers' grounds
and those of the Western Christian tradition at large. The identity

of literal and historical sense of scripture involves a cognate unity on the part of God: the divine author of the book is the same as the governor of the history narrated in it. Being both author of the text's meaning and governor of actuality he unites meaning and fact, so that it does not occur to the orthodox interpreter that there is a distance between words and their reference of such a sort that each has a status logically independent of the other.

A statement God makes and intends literally, naturally refers to the state of affairs described in it. A description he furnishes is itself the reference or does duty for the latter. Moreover, in view of God's providential governance there is no reason why a statement he makes should not describe two events at the same time, the one literally and the other by prefiguration.

This extension is of two kinds. First, there is a temporal extension—a description God intends to refer to a future event, quite possibly beyond what its human author intends but linked providentially to the latter's description if not to his specific referential intention. Second, an expansion of the original pattern of meaning in its later application is obviously likely to accompany the temporal extension.

In a vague and attenuated way the orthodox defenders against the Deists were operating out of the complex and massive accumulation of interpretive tradition. However, some of them were more nearly akin to the mind-set of their opponents, and all the more easily the latters' prey, in insisting that the authors of some of the prophetic utterances personally foreknew the coming of Jesus and in that sense meant their statements to apply to him literally.

Sir Leslie Stephen rightly spoke of the "utter oblivion" in the argument for and against the claim to prophecy fulfilled, "of the principle that an effective argument must rest on some principles common to both parties," although with characteristic historical one-sidedness he assigned the blame for this state of affairs wholly to the obtuseness of the orthodox defenders, who simply could not get through their heads the full implications of the fact that their adversaries "held the Jewish writers to be ordinary human beings." [5] Against this assumption it was indeed impossible to argue by appeal to typical or figural fulfillment which, in the nature of the case, would work only when it was linked with belief in a providential design partially manifest in the pages of Holy Scripture.

There was of course no compelling reason whatever why the Deists should have adopted that belief from their inspection of the logical conditions under which the original prophetic statements make sense, conditions which seem to work in these instances as they do in all others of the rational use of language. To answer the question, whether and how the prophetic utterances make sense, and therefore better sense than that attributed to them in the New Testament and subsequent Christian tradition, the Deists had no need of historical-critical method. That procedure came later, largely in the wake of their own reflections. They needed only the basic analysis of what kinds of statements make sense because they can be reduced to regular and intelligible rules of the natural use of language and thought. Men like Collins did indeed go on the assumption that the Jewish writers were ordinary human beings and that the orthodox claim that this fact was irrelevant to the meaning of the texts was pure mystification. Let the defenders of orthodoxy demonstrate how any meaning of the prophetic texts other than the literal can make rational sense, or else let them show that the texts' literal, rational sense jibes with that bestowed upon them in the New Testament as backing for its claim about Jesus.

LITERAL MEANING, OSTENSIVE Reference, and LINGUISTIC RULES

Collins was a disciple of John Locke, and the conceptual tools provided by Locke did heavy duty in the present controversy, even though self-conscious reference to them was very sparse. By way of the "new philosophy," Collins expressed his conviction that the sense of the Jewish writers was that of ordinary human beings, and that it ought to be so interpreted. The lessons Locke had taught him he applied to the notion of prophecy, turning it into deliberate and literal prediction on the part of the only source whose words and meaning are accessible to the critic—the human writer. As a result he identified literal sense with historical reference in a new way.

Among Protestants hitherto (with the exception of the Socinians) a statement in the Bible was seen to be literal, or by extension, figural or typical if it was not clearly allegorical; and if it was literal about persons and events it was actually historical. Literal explicative meaning and historical reference were logically identical. But now Collins made that same identification in a wholly different way, doing so on the basis of the epistemological lessons he had learned from Locke, well before the rise of self-conscious historical method. And the consequence of this new way of relating literal sense with historical reference was the complete separation of literal and figurative (or typical) senses. Figurative meaning, hitherto naturally congruent with literal meaning, now became its opposite. We have already noted that Collins assigned the typical sense to the same class of reading as "mystical, or allegorical, or enigmatical sense; that is, . . . a sense different from the obvious and literal sense." The Reformers and the general tradition that came in their wake would have flatly denied this association of figuration with allegory and insisted that the very opposite is true.

The new view is difficult to state. In effect Collins's identification of literal and historical statements involved that he first break up their previous identity and then reintegrate them by subsuming literal meaning under the dominance of an independent criterion for deciding whether or not a statement is historical. A proposition is literal if it describes and refers to a state of affairs known or assumed on independent probable grounds to agree or disagree with the stated proposition. Whether Collins would have proceeded the same way in regard to other than historical statements is a moot point. One suspects that the answer is yes, since meaning for Locke and his followers generally had reference to the representation of independent reality, questions of meaning in the seventeenth and eighteenth centuries by and large being simply refinements of affirmations concerning the conditions of our knowledge of reality.

By placing before his opponents the seemingly disjunctive alternative that the New Testament claims about Old Testament prophecy are either literal, i.e. meaningful and in that case false, or typical, which is to say absurd, Collins in effect equated the meaning of literal or history-like statements with their actual historical reference. His (implicit) criterion for interpretation in this controversy about how biblical statements make sense was the same as that explicitly formulated by the early logical positivists some two hundred years later to cover all statements that are neither tautological nor emotive: the meaning of a statement is the method of its verification. If one can state the conditions under which a statement could be seen to be true (or false) it is meaningful or, the same thing, literally descriptive. Embodied in the argument over the fulfillment of prophecy was the breakup of the old identity of literal explicative meaning with historical reference or estimation, and their reintegration under an independent criterion which identifies meaning with reference to independently establishable fact claims. An exegetical or hermeneutical argument about determining the meaning of certain narrative texts has become an argument about the status of the fact claims apparently made in them.

It is clear that for Collins this step was a fait accompli and so self-evident that it could provide an ideal basis for polemical purposes in religious controversy. Moreover, the general identification of questions of meaning with those of knowledge of reality was such that many of his opponents, Edward Chandler in particular,[6] followed suit, arguing the meaningfulness of New Testament and traditional Christian interpretation of the Old Testament texts on the grounds of the actual, historically verifiable truth of the fulfillment of prophecy. Needless to say, they had a hard time against Collins.

A workable scheme of figural or typological interpretation assumed partial but significant access to the providential design through which God's truth and history cohere. This was a far cry from Locke and Collins. In this respect they simply lived in a different world, no matter what their actual belief about the providential implications of empirical and moral affairs. For Collins, following Locke, historical statements were simply and solely empirical, demanding a strength of assent which is suited to the persuasiveness of the evidence.[7] Where this assumption was operative one simply could not appeal to providential design as a theory for holding meaningful statements and reality together. That coherence had to be accounted for by an analysis of the relation of the immanent conditions of thought to sense perception and external reality.

Collins proceeded in two ways, both of them effectively grounding the meaning of statements outside themselves. First, he assigned the origin of specific meaning to the intention of the individual author. Second, he relied on a logical as well as epistemological analysis in which only literal interpretation makes sense, because unlike typological interpretation it involves a ruled use of language. At the same time the meaning of words, particularly in statements of descriptive prediction, is so completely derived from sense experience of the external world that meaning turns out to be identical with verifiability or with likelihood based on past observation. The upshot of analyzing the ruled use of language is that meaning becomes identical with ostensive reference. The meaning of a statement is the spatiotemporal occurrence or state of affairs to which it refers.

First, by taking account of the human author's intention *as an independent factor,* no matter whether his statement finally turns out to make sense in agreement or disagreement with that intention, Collins introduced a new element into the hermeneutical situation of biblical study. He was not alone; it was a typical move in that era in adducing the principles of textual interpretation, quite different from previous affirmations of the unity of intention with linguistic use. It is an important step in preparing the way for the practitioners of historical-critical method. Why scan the heavens speculatively when from the written word, from knowledge of historical conditions and the way human beings think, one can ascertain with great probability what the immediate and human rather than remote divine author had in mind? A few generations later, historical critics were to go on from there and suggest that while the author is indeed important, his intention is but one clue to the meaning of his words. The influence of an author's culture over his mind and outlook came to play a larger role than his conscious intention in the historian's determination of the meaning of his words.

The words become a clue, though not necessarily the only one, to the mind of the author where, rather than in the words alone, meaning resides. To this situation it makes little difference that in some philosophical views the mind is passive and sensation-controlled while in others it is not. The location of meaning outside the statement and inside the author's intention is complemented by a similar condition at the other end of the reach of the notion of meaning. There it is located, once again, not merely in the words but in the external reality to which the words refer. When this view is applied to the interpretation of scripture the implication is obvious. At both ends of the spectrum the use of language is governed by a sense of the setting for meaningfulness quite different from what had hitherto been prevalent in exegetical practice and accompanying theory. The immediacy of the world depicted and rendered accessible by the biblical words, and the rich but orderly and interconnected variety of levels of meaning they presented, faded away. Instead, the connection between language and its context is the reality of the author on the one hand and of the single, external reference of the words on the other.

The new assignment of an aspect of meaning to the author, his intention and (soon to come) his setting, caused painful confusion to orthodox (and pietist) interpreters, both in England and Germany. Incompletely weaned from the tradition that identified explicative (particularly literal) sense with historical judgment or reference, and yet moving toward the new reintegration of the two under the dominance of ostensive reference over literal sense, they or their supernaturalist successors now took up a new line of argument. They tended to regard obviously literal kinds of statements in the Bible as evidence of the truthfulness and integrity of the human authors, and thus as proper evidence in favor of the historical factuality of their accounts. Orthodox interpreters prior to the days of the "new philosophy" had not used this argument. (Since then it has never ceased completely among theological apologists.)

For the older interpreters neither the human author (alone or together with his setting) nor the empirical-historical fact described by the statement had the logical distinctness or independence from the words of the statement that was necessary to make this kind of argument as well as the skeptical counterargument cogent. But in the eighteenth century, once the kind of view represented by Collins had been set forth, the situation had changed. Thus Bishop Butler came to argue not simply the fulfillment of prophecy but the likely reliability of biblical reports from the simple, literalistic quality of the writing (which additionally implied their authors' trustworthiness).[8] We shall encounter the same argument again and again, for example in the writing of Johann Jakob Hess in the later part of the century. It is obviously quite different from the seemingly similar argument of an earlier day, represented by Calvin's suggestion that once we have accepted the authority of scripture our belief may be confirmed by discerning the excellence of God's Word through its simplicity, testifying to a truth greater and more excellent than human art and knowledge can attain.[9]

For men like Collins, the integrity of the prophets was neither here nor there. He had no particular stake in questioning it, although like many a Deist the level of morality he saw advocated in much of the Old Testament made him shudder. He construed the intention of the authors, in the meaning of whose statements he was interested, along much more narrow and specific lines. He argued vigorously that the prophets had indeed intended to predict—though not, of course, the things that Jesus and the New Testament writers would eventually have them predict. Indeed, the only way the prophetic statements can make sense is by checking them, under the assumption that the intention corresponded to the words, against such events as they appear to describe in the forecast, whether or not they later took place, and then against the shape of the events to which the New Testament authors apply them. It turns out of course that unless the prophets offended against the natural and rational use of language, either through some odd state of mind or because they were obfuscators or deliberate deceivers, their intention is quite different from what the New Testament authors make of their words. But of course linguistic oddity on the part of the prophets is much less likely than that the New Testament writers used the Old Testament words in a less than straightforward way, i.e. nonliterally, which is really to say nonsensically. That is what the learned Surenhusius's rules, which are really those of the New Testament's allegorical or spiritual interpretation of the Old Testament, come to. Typological interpretation falls under the same condemnation since it is not a literal and therefore precise description of a single referent.

From the consideration of the author's intention we turn to Collins's views on the rules governing the proper use of language. Most important of all, to Collins as to Locke there are finally only two kinds of ideas, those of sensation representing external substances and their qualities, and those of reflection by which we apprehend the operation of our own minds. Statements about empirical-historical events are obviously propositions derived from complex ideas of sensation. Indeed, all meaningful propositions that are not about ideas of reflection must refer to empirical states of affairs. In other words, the rational use of language is not only a matter of logical coherence but of externally received impressions or ideas to which words correspond. This fact underlies all else that Collins assumes. "Meanings" are in effect propositions about the external world for him. Literal language is their only proper expression and, unlike the earlier orthodox literalism about the Bible, Collins's literalism describes things that have no intrinsic connection with the words except to dominate them as signs representing things we know. The identity of meaning with reference involves the identification of understanding with knowledge. The meaningfulness of the biblical author's language must thus be governed by the same criteria that govern the meaning of any proposition.

First is the agreement or disagreement of ideas, without which there can be no knowledge at all because there can be no connection between any two ideas. Precisely this rule appears to Collins to be inapplicable to typological or allegorical or any other than literal interpretation. Thus any endeavor to reduce such talk to rules and therefore to sense is hopeless. It simply results in rules that are completely arbitrary because they violate the natural use of language. If one goes by them, one can never show, directly or by any intermediate idea, in what the claimed agreement between two ideas consists. After citing a particularly painful instance of typological or allegorical interpretation (from Hebrews, but Collins attributes it to Paul), Collins says: "It is not right to adjust Paul's discourses to our ways of reasoning, and of proving by such intermediate ideas, as either certainly or probably show the agreement or disagreement of the ideas contained in a proposition." [10]

Second, a mere elaboration of the first criterion, the specific form of agreement between two statements expressing what is claimed to be the same idea must be that of identity. Where a description fitting one event is said to be identical with the description of another which simply does not fit the first, we have nonsense; and, once again, nonliteral interpretation of the fulfillment of prophecy qualifies for that dubious distinction.

Third, any given idea or complex of ideas is what it is at the time, identical with itself and not with another idea at the same time. In regard to spatial and temporal events this means that in any description—retrospective, contemporaneous, or predictive— a person can have but one event or one kind of event in mind. A specific description has but one reference or one kind of reference, or, to put it another way, any proposition has but one meaning. To learn and apply this lesson there is no need to learn the rules of formal logic and bear them in mind. Rather, when we think and speak clearly, we naturally obey this principle. It is simply part of the contours of human understanding. Furthermore, a name or an idea refers to a real and specific thing when words are used properly. This and not an abstract and fixed essence of a species gives distinct meaning to the name. There are as many appropriate names as there are distinct things properly referred to, each name naming a distinct thing and the species to which it belongs, and not a preconceived, abstractly or mentally "real" essence beyond the ideas received by the senses.

Fourth, since words are signs of ideas, verbal propositions are significant to the extent that they express clear and determinate ideas. Where the ideas are those of sensation, the only way to test them for meaning and truth is to find out if they and the propositions expressing them conform properly to the things to which they refer.[11]

Collins undoubtedly agreed with the conclusions Locke himself drew from his theory of ideas and language for the interpretation of scripture, whatever his actual practice. The meaning of scripture (Locke called it "traditional revelation") cannot be conveyed, even if its original could have been received, except by ideas derived from those we already have. Whatever original revelation may have been, its communication has to be by way of propositions that make sense in the same way any others do. In other words, the interpretation of scripture must conform to the rules for the meaningful use of language. "For our simple ideas . . . which are the foundation, and sole matter of all our notions and knowledge, we must depend wholly on our reason, I mean our natural faculties; and can by no means receive them, or any of them, from traditional revelation." And thus no new simple idea can be conveyed by traditional revelation.[12]

Locke was no Deist. He set forth his latitudinarian position clearly if not at all succinctly in *On the Reasonableness of Christianity* and some shorter writings. But on the issue in question he would have been wholeheartedly on Collins's side: if language is to be used in a ruled, rational way, propositions cannot mean several things at the same time, nor do statements refer to states of affairs that do not correspond to the features described by the statements, except in the purely arbitrary application of someone claiming divine sanction for his perversion of thought and language. Typological or any other nonliteral interpretation cannot sit in judgment over the ordinary referential way statements using ideas of sensation make sense. The reverse is the true situation.

Collins summed up their common position in one of his few appeals to the fruits of philosophical analysis in *Grounds and Reasons*. He distinguished between meaningful statements or propositions (those of the prophets taken literally) and arbitrary or absurd ones (the same statements applied to Jesus allegorically or typically):

> To suppose that an author has but one meaning at a time to a proposition (which is to be found out by a critical examination of his words) and to cite that proposition from him, and argue from it in that one meaning, is to proceed by the common rules of grammar and logic; which, being human rules, are not difficult to be set forth and explained. But to suppose passages cited, explained and argued from in any other method, seems very extraordinary and difficult to understand, and to reduce to rules.[13]

Under Collins's guiding hand an argument over the meaning and interpretation of biblical narratives has turned into one over the reference of those narratives. Not only has explicative meaning been severed from and then reintegrated with historical reference by subordination to it, reversing the older understanding of the concomitance between explicative sense and historical reference, where historical judgment had been a function of literary or linguistic analysis; in addition, the ground rules for meaning-as-reference have now been drawn up. First is the logically independent factor of the interpreter's discernment of the human author and his intention. The author is wholly and ordinarily human because his intention is bound to be wholly congruent with the natural ruled use of thought and language which even a revelation cannot contravene, no matter what new information or doctrine it might impart. Second, then, are the logical and grammatical rules or principles that always inhere in the natural use of language, in accordance with which one must explain all statements. And finally is the fact that ideas of sensation and the words expressing them, including statements about history, always represent states of affairs in the external world. That is to say, theory of meaning is equivalent to theory of knowledge, and to understand is identical with being able to distinguish between what is true and what is false.

A historical criterion had now come to adjudicate the meaning of the history-like narrative biblical texts. The new way of uniting explication with historical reference and analysis served, at least in the interpretation of this kind of text, to make hermeneutics an auxiliary of a procedure which had all the structural ingredients needed to expand it into historical-critical method. There may have been other philosophical bases for the historical-critical interpretation of the Bible, but certainly this one was admirably fit for the purpose, granted only that consideration of the author would expand beyond the notion of his intention to that of the specific cultural and historically limited setting that serves to explain his thought and writing. Given that expansion, the dominance of meaning-as-reference over the explicative sense of the text and the reintegration of the two by critical examination of the referent was all that was additionally needed as philosophical support for the triumph of historical-critical interpretation of biblical narratives. The argument over the fulfillment of prophecy was indeed not an isolated grand cause bringing about a new situation by itself; but it exhibited more clearly than anything else the drastic change in the reading of biblical narratives, in the principles that go into their interpretation, and in the underlying new sensibility of a language-neutral external world which has taken the place of the narratively rendered temporal sequence satisfying the sensibility of an earlier day.

5 Hermeneutics and Meaning-as-Reference

The impact of the deistic controversies in England was soon felt in German theological discussion. Biblical commentators there in any case were beginning to meet similar problems though, it should be recalled, in a rather different context from that of the English debate. The Germans continued to be interested in the nature of the Bible as a series of written documents and not merely in its employment as evidence for or against the truth of the factual claims of revelation. But the shift in interpretation of narratives was much the same in Germany as in England. It was particularly important for theologically conservative commentators in Germany. They now had to meet an argument about the Bible and a way of interpreting it for which neither orthodox literalism nor pietist spiritual interpretation had prepared them.

These two theories therefore gave way quickly to a different defense of biblical and theological conservatism. For the sake of convenience, and falling in with one of the overly neat categories abounding in the history of ideas, I shall call it Supernaturalism. Its rise was marked not only by the impact of the deistic controversies but also by the increasing influence of Christian Wolff's rationalistic philosophy within German theological faculties, especially in his own university at Halle, earlier the great stronghold of pietist teaching.

Meaning as Historical or Ostensive Reference

Commentators of the supernaturalist persuasion argued the literal truth of scripture, demonstrating what they thought to be the specific nature of its inspiration and also setting forth reasons for the factual reliability of its reports. However, unlike the earlier orthodox and pietist theologians they no longer used scriptural inspiration as a kind of automatic warrant for claims on behalf of the texts. The two earlier views had obviously not involved testing

86

such claims by placing the texts in the broader setting of general, rational canons of meaning and general criteria for factual probability. This confrontation could now no longer be avoided.

In contrast to the orthodox and the Pietists, the Supernaturalists had to meet rationalistic and historical-critical interpretations of the Bible on the latter's home ground. They argued the historical factuality of the biblical reports of miracles and the fulfillment of prophecy, basing these claims on such arguments in favor of the Bible's reliable documentation of divine revelation as the apostolic origin of the New Testament writings, the integrity of the evangelists, the congruence of miracle with rational religion, the simplicity and life-likeness of the reports, and the historical fulfillment of Old Testament anticipations in the shape of New Testament events. It is a far cry from the earlier identification of explicative meaning with historical judgment, for which the fulfillment of prophecy was a function of the providentially ordered literal or figural harmony of earlier with later biblical narratives, a scheme that was at once literary and historical.

Supernaturalistic arguments may seem anachronistic and reactionary to a twentieth-century historian, but in their day they were actually part of a program of self-modernization in the theological camp, undertaken in response to such challenges as Deism and a new situation in biblical hermeneutics. They constituted an acknowledgment that, in the interpretation of the theologically significant biblical narratives, historical explanation governs explication of the text—not to say that it *is* explication of the text. Conservative commentators increasingly treated the narrative portions of the Bible as a factually reliable repository of divine revelation rather than the immediately inspired text that it had been to orthodox and pietist commentators. Liberal commentators doubted not only the inspiration—or at least equal inspiration throughout the Bible—but more especially the factual reliability of the narratives. The focus from both ends of the spectrum was increasingly on the identity of explicative meaning with the historical or ostensive reference of the texts.

S. J. Baumgarten

The Supernaturalists in Germany—theologians like Christoph Matthäus Pfaff (1686–1760), Lorenz von Mosheim (1694–1755), and the most influential and liberal of them all, Sigmund Jakob Baumgarten (1706–1757), professor at Halle—are the transitional figures between Protestant orthodoxy and Pietism, and the Neologians of the German Enlightenment who dominated biblical and theological study in the last half of the century.[1] They also found some direct successors to uphold their position, but the academic and pastoral ranks of these latter-day conservatives were greatly thinned by the turn of the century.

Baumgarten believed that even the words of scripture or the forms in which the books were written were inspired (*eingegeben*) by God; but he clearly did not drive the matter home with the insistence of some of his predecessors. It simply was not for him the strategic truth on which the place of the Bible as the direct authority and source of Christian belief depended. It could occupy so central a place only for those who saw it as the Word of God logically inseparable from the saving history described in it and from the efficacious appropriation of that narration. Instead, the Bible tended for Baumgarten to provide the indispensable *modus cognoscendi* for the revealed truth which it contains as a logically separable matter.

He was polemically engaged on a number of fronts, fighting the usual orthodox Protestant battles in behalf of the Bible's perspicuity and direct interpretability against Roman Catholic insistence on the need for the Church's teaching authority in interpretation, and the sufficiency of biblical revelation against the new inner revelations of the "fanatics." But he also thought it necessary to argue against "scorners of religion, atheists and Deists, or the cruder kind of naturalists"; and here the issue was whether the Bible really contains a more direct and immediate (*nähere und unmittelbare*) revelation of God. By now, in the middle of the eighteenth century he, a relatively conservative Lutheran, could nonetheless openly profess that God has manifested himself in a natural revelation in addition to that given in the sacred book. The biblical revelation, though disclosing mysteries above nature and reason, contains nothing contrary to them. And therefore the exegesis of the Bible has to proceed by ordinary rational analytical means.

Like many another commentator from now on, Baumgarten tended to distinguish sharply between the words and the subject matter of the Bible and to equate the latter much more than the former with revelation. To that extent his argument for the uniqueness and truth of the Bible was really a plea in behalf of a special, positive revelation. Scriptural revelation, he argued among other things, is not unworthy of God or for that matter insufficient for a universal purpose, and it does not contain false, contradictory, or unproven matters. The last accusation he countered by saying that not only is the falsity of biblical history undemonstrable, but also that its correctness "can be brought to the highest degree of probability or the greatest possible moral certainty in accordance with all the logical rules of a historical proof." He added that "so many agreed-upon, undeniable testimonies of antiquity serve to confirm the biblical history that one will have to reject all history if one will not accept that of the Bible." [2]

Such arguments, if they are not historical in the modern sense, are well on their way—at least in their acknowledgment of responsibility to a court of general credibility for anything, sacred or secular, that claims to be a fact. Baumgarten defended the credibility of the referent or subject matter of the Bible, the biblical history, against those who questioned it on philosophical or religious as well as on factual grounds. Whatever his beliefs about verbal inspiration, to this extent he moved on the same ground as Collins had done in the controversy over the fulfillment of prophecy. The historical referent—the factual history which claims to be revelation—governs and is the test for the explicative sense of the texts. They make sense to the extent that they can be shown to refer, and refer faithfully, to these events.

Assertions of this sort do not obtrude in Baumgarten's work, but they are noticeable and they have something of the casual ring of a position so obvious that it is taken for granted. And yet it is really the harbinger of a new day which had dawned with the application of newer criteria of meaning to the interpretation of biblical narratives during the deist controversy.

Similarly new for a conservative Lutheran was another emphasis which Baumgarten now cautiously put forth, while Collins had assumed it boldly a quarter of a century earlier. Collins had in effect argued the intention of the author as a logically independent factor in garnering the meaning of texts. Conservative Protestants, with their stress on the divine authorship and the verbal (or typological) structure and interconnectedness of texts as criteria for their meaning, had had no need for this assumption. We miss the point if we think they considered the view mischievous. In a sense they did not, but it never occurred to them to substitute it for the divine authorship. More important is the difference in their imagination. The Bible was for the older Protestants a coherent world of discourse in its own right, whose depictions and teachings had a reality of their own, though to be sure, it was the reality into which all men had to fit, and in one way or another did fit.

The transition from Luther and Calvin to Collins's *Grounds and Reasons* is a voyage from one world to another. The logical, hermeneutical difference bespeaks a chasm between worlds of thought and imagination. As Leslie Stephen noted, the two parties in the controversy over prophecy proceeded, without being aware of it, from two such completely different sets of assumptions and outlooks that any significant dispute between them, even meaningful disagreement, was unlikely. Collins's assumption that any biblical author is to be understood as an ordinary human being underlies his logical or technical move for gathering the intention or meaning of the author from the obvious reference of his words. Protestant verbal or typological interpretation of the biblical narratives in pre-deist days had nothing in common with such an assumption, either on a technical or logical level, or on the underlying one of a basic world view. But now, in the middle of the eighteenth century, it makes its way gently and gradually into the thought of such a conservative man as Baumgarten. He stressed that inspiration (*Eingebung*) is not to be confused with either enthusiasm or divine dictation. The human authors reflect rationally as they write and on what they write, and they use, in general, their own inward powers. The Reformers and their successors would not necessarily have denied the fact, but it would have been trivial in their eyes.[3]

Hermeneutics is clearly on its way toward a notion of explicative interpretation in which a biblical narrative makes sense in accordance with its author's intention and (before long) the culture he exemplifies. And the meaning of the narrative is the subject matter to which the words refer. For Baumgarten, as for other conservatives or Supernaturalists, the subject matter of the words is the revelation that forms the content of the Bible; and the specifically narrative (rather than merely doctrinal or parabolic) portions of the Bible tell with absolute reliability the factual sacred history in which the revealed truth is embodied. Emanuel Hirsch rightly says that with Baumgarten, "German Protestant theology moved into the decisive stage of transition from a Bible faith to a revelation faith, for which the Bible is essentially nothing but the specific, given document of revelation." [4] The transitional period to which Baumgarten belongs, about the middle of the eighteenth century, saw the beginnings of German scholarly leadership in historical criticism, and in nontheological, general hermeneutics of the Bible.

The difference between the Supernaturalists and the older conservatives is especially clear in their respective views of the unity of the Bible. It was an important matter not only because it was a crucial element in their common doctrinal heritage but also because modern commentators were beginning to question it seriously. Supernaturalists came to argue the scriptural unity not on the basis of a single divine authorship and consequently single sense of the text which could be welded together by figural or typological interpretation if necessary, but (once again) from the fulfillment of prophecy as a historical fact. They added to it reinforcing arguments such as the similarity of the effect all the parts of the Bible have on the devoutly inquiring mind.

A generation or so later a new line of thought began to develop on the topic of biblical unity, spanning part of the difference between conservative and more liberal theological interpreters. A tradition of "biblical theology" arose which combined a notion of a developing history of religious ideas and outlook within the pages of the Bible with a conviction of God's special presence to the Bible precisely through this religious history and the interpretive tradition accumulated by it. Theologians applied the word *Theopneustie*, a term as time-honored as it was unwieldly, to this drastic modification, half historical and half theological, of the older theory of the Bible's divine inspiration.

For the older conservatives the unity and *Theopneustie* of the Bible had lain *in verbis;* for the newer ones it was *in re*, and the *res* in this instance was primarily and crucially historical in a dual sense: it was the sequence of outer biblical history as well as a supposed historical connectedness of its ideas and the outlooks they embodied. The conjunction of *Theopneustie* with the developing history of religion within the Bible simply added an element of uncertainty to this situation. For the historical *res* or reference the stricter Supernaturalists had in mind was the actual occurrence of the supernatural events which the writers reported, whereas less strict but still conservative commentators added to it the history of Hebrew religion and interpretive tradition under divine guidance.

The case for the logical distinction but factual convergence between historical judgment and explicative hermeneutics was obviously very strong when even conservative theological views moved away from theories of direct divine inspiration of the words, beginning instead to defend the factuality of the revealed reports and (slightly later) the religious worth of the ideas they contained. From right to left, commentators came to appeal to arguments about what in the Bible was historically credible. Coincidentally they pled the subsumption of biblical words and statements under canons of general, not theologically, privileged meaning.

Historical criticism and general hermeneutics, in their common fight against special, privileged theological rules to govern biblical meaning, attacked the same "tyranny." The protests against exempting biblical historical claims from ordinary verification by appealing to divine authority went hand in hand with the protest against verbal infallibility (extending to Hebrew vowel points), layers of meaning, a hidden spiritual sense of statements, and the like. Much of the Bible was narrative and seemed, roughly, to cover a continuous chronological sequence, so that it appeared to be one long story. And since much of the traditional belief of Christianity was rendered by this story or history, the convergence between historical judgment and explicative hermeneutics tended to result in the dominance of historical procedure in interpretation. Could it verify the beliefs tied to the reports, the two together having traditionally been what the stories were about? Or did the historian have alternative suggestions about what happened? For whatever happened must surely be the meaning of the narrative texts. This dominance of history made interpretation relatively easy for some. Others who noted the logical distinction between the two procedures, but could not integrate them because they doubted that historical reference was the only meaning of all the biblical stories, had greater trouble. What was one to do if one believed there can be appropriate historical examination of a writing and that it may well refer to some facts, and yet that this is not what the text's words and concepts are all about?

The relation between the two procedures, historical criticism and explication of meaning, was virtually guaranteed for the simple reason that at that time, somewhat unlike our own day, the two things were usually combined in the same person. Textbooks and scholars of the later eighteenth century, no matter how much they distinguished between interpretive procedures, obviously expected to come up with a unitary reading of a text in their actual exegetical results. However one combined them, a variety of autonomous exegetical methods was bound to yield one "real" explication. The possibility of conflict or sheer unrelated heterogeneity among the elements of the interpretation of one text occurred to few people. Some isolated voices were to sound the alarm at the very end of the era of eighteenth-century hermeneutics but, by and large, confidence in exegetical procedure and in finally unitary interpretive results accompanied the marvelous taste of freedom from the yoke of authoritarianism which echoed through the writings.

Hermeneutical theory, like all other theory in the latter part of the eighteenth century, obeyed the slogan: Dare to think.[5] The sense of liberation which the era had brought to hermeneutics is expressed clearly if clumsily in the prose of Gottlob Wilhelm Meyer, a liberal historian of biblical interpretation. Writing in 1808 he contrasted the first and second halves of the previous century:

> If in the previous period the endeavors of those theoreticians who sought to maintain the subjugation of Protestant hermeneutics to dogmatics were of too great a weight to allow one to attribute real note or significant influence to the few contrary and freer attempts to withdraw it from this subjugation and raise it to greater independence, the ever more lively spirit of investigation of this latest period by contrast manifests itself in this—that the attempts to liberate hermeneutics more and more from these burdensome fetters attained not only ever greater number but ever greater repute and more decisive effectiveness, regardless of frequent resistance from various sides.[6]

The reader who has managed to reach the end of this sentence won't be surprised that this sort of outlook, constantly glancing over its own shoulder at the parallel conflict between dogmatics and biblical-historical criticism, edged ever closer to the latter. Freedom in the republic of scholarship, it seems, was undivided. Theory of interpretation, subjecting the meaning of biblical narrative texts to general criteria of grammatical, logical, moral and religious meaning, seemed to go hand in hand with a historical analysis for which credible historical explanation was a function of uniform and natural rather than suddenly and miraculously disrupted historical experience. But this alliance of historical-critical scholarship with hermeneutics was too close for some, and at the end of the eighteenth and the beginning of the nineteenth century it finally evoked a small chorus of protests on the part of a relatively conservative rationalist thinkers.

Outstanding among these was Carl Friedrich Stäudlin of Göttingen, who was not at all inimical to historical-critical procedure but thought that many of its proponents falsely claimed that it provides an exhaustive explicative interpretation of the texts. In that case—and the issue was wrapped in much confusion on both sides—the residuum after the work of historical criticism would be no more than a kind of practical application, something of obviously secondary significance. Can one reduce the teachings of any great man, the ideas of any great book to so small a substance? Stäudlin[7] had in mind views like Semler's and some of his as well as Ernesti's followers, particularly Karl Keil, for whom the chief part of explicative exegesis had consisted of the appropriate technical linguistic work and of "distinguishing and representing to oneself the historical circumstances of biblical discourse." Surely great texts amount to more than grammatical-historical exegesis implies!

In short, exegesis of the biblical narratives was not altogether or for every liberated spirit synonymous with working out their true historical reference and the "circumstances" of their words, despite the convergence of a free hermeneutical theory and a free ("presuppositionless," Strauss was to call it) historical science. But in general, Locke's theories, refracted through such deist controversies as that on prophecy and through later supernaturalist and historical-critical exegesis, exemplified a massive scholarly movement for which there was a direct convergence of the meaning of biblical narratives with the shape of the events to which they refer.

MEANING AS IDEAL REFERENCE

However, one philosophical tradition in eighteenth-century Germany, increasingly scorned as the years of the second half of the century went by but no less influential and pervasive for the fact, moved in a different direction. The philosophy of Christian Wolff was as important for general hermeneutics as the empiricist theory of ideas was for the relation between hermeneutics and historical-critical method. Wolff's theory, like Locke's, was not single-handedly a grand explanatory cause, but it exemplified in a powerfully influential way a particular philosophical strand that lay in back of much hermeneutical theory. Wolff himself, though known as a follower of Leibniz, learned almost as much from other philosophers, including Locke. But he was a thinker of considerable independence and great rigor. For years, before his banishment and after his recall as Professor of Mathematics and Philosophy at Halle, he exemplified the spirit of rationalism in the very fortress of pietist religion. The inculcation of true virtue by means of precise and orderly thinking was his goal. He defended revealed religion but only because, while it exceeded, it did not contradict natural religion and the deliverances of reason. His enormous literary output is marked by an almost incredible systematic and conceptual orderliness, and he left no conceivably pertinent topic untouched in his quest to set forth the totality of what he proudly called worldly wisdom, the penetration of all physical and spiritual reality by thought. Kant's critical philosophy was to demolish Wolff's system, but Kant honored the accomplishment and spirit of the man he dethroned.

Wolff's influence, or the impact of the kind of thinking he exemplified on the interpretation of the Bible, was largely subterranean, but it is evident in men like Baumgarten, whose formal procedure was patterned largely on Wolff's own. For general hermeneutics Wolff's logic was the most important aspect of his work. He divided the theoretical part of his logic into three sections, corresponding to the three operations of the understanding—conception, judgment, and inference. In the present context, the first of these is of greatest interest. All our words are connected with concepts, so that words, properly used, always signify. A concept in turn is a "representation of a subject matter [*Sache*] in our thoughts." [8]

In the description of concepts Wolff makes the moves that have the most important hermeneutical consequences. He distinguishes two kinds of conceptual definition or explanation. (He translated the Latin term *definitio* by the German *Erklärung*, one of the few technical usages in which he was not to be followed by the general tradition of German philosophical vocabulary.) The nominal definition or verbal explanation (*definitio nominalis, Worterklärung*) of a concept involves the statement of its specifying differentia, distinguishing it from others and providing its own internal coherence within the general compass of similarly general notions. Wolff cites as example the definition of a clock by its function: it is a machine for indicating the hours. Another example is the definition of reason as insight into the connectedness of truth.

The reality definition or subject-matter explanation (*definitio realis, Sacherklärung*), on the other hand, is concerned with the ultimate explanatory ground of the thing signified by the concept, in effect with the possibility deducible from and in turn explanatory of its actuality. This possibility we apprehend either by demonstration or experience. With the Scholastics Wolff urges that the possibility of a thing is properly implied in its thereness. Its possibility in turn depends on—if indeed it is not another name for—the essence of the subject matter, i.e. what it necessarily is: "One understands the essence of a thing when one grasps clearly how it became that which it is, or in what fashion it is possible. From which it follows further that the explanations of things bring their essence to view." As instances of *Realdefinition* or *Sacherklärung* Wolff suggests the explanation of a clock by its component parts rather than its function, and the explanation of reason from the powers of the soul that make it possible rather than from its insight into the coherence of truth.[9]

Clearly, the definition of a concept as that of a name of a possible reality means that Wolff grounds his logic in ontology and the conditions of human knowledge of reality. *"Quodsi in Logica omnia demonstranda,"* he said, *"petenda sunt principia ex Ontologia atque Psychologia."* [10] A concept is possible or rational instead of being empty verbiage when it is the concept of an essence or a possible reality. We must be on guard against nonsense which is, strictly speaking, talk of nothing, i.e. of what is impossible or in fact inconceivable because it is in violation of the principle of contradiction. Not that we cannot combine words ("iron gold," "a plant's natural love or hatred") in a way that makes grammatical or syntactical sense without amounting to proper concepts. But our duty is to distinguish mere words from things so that we do not deceive ourselves, "and thus we must admit no concept except one whose possibility we have rightly recognized." [11]

Words properly used refer; they signify or name possible things which have an ideal status in which they are known by way of the mind's apprehension of their actuality through the senses. In effect one may say that words describe those same "real essences" (though Wolff does not call them that) which Locke had so completely rejected. Their ontological status and derivation involves the ontological grounding of concepts as possible realities through the combination of the principles of non-contradiction and sufficient reason. The capacity we have for knowing concepts, and with them reality and its rationality, is argued from the analysis of psychology, i.e. the powers of the soul.[12]

Despite their large differences, Locke and Wolff had some important common consequences for biblical hermeneutics. Locke's "new philosophy" is a philosophical explanation or justification for the ostensive view or ostensive-referential analysis of the meaning of biblical narratives—the view that came in effect to subordinate explicative interpretation to historical-critical explanation. Locke's deistic followers tended to find the meaning of those parts of the Bible of which they approved in their universalizable religious and moral truths; but in their polemical discussions with conservative churchmen on the factual evidence for revelation they took biblical meaning to be ostensive. To the extent that scriptural ideas derived from those of sensation, the interpretation of the so-called Old Testament prophecies in the New Testament and later Christian exegesis must be subject to test by the agreement or disagreement of ideas. The meaning of the stories is their ostensive reference or their failure to refer to certain events.

Wolff's formal procedure was not opposed to the shift from the precritical logical equation of literal meaning with historical reference to the domination of explication by historical estimate. He stood for something else, partially different, partially complementary. Among German philosophers he more than anyone else shaped the conceptual instruments required for liberating principles of general explicative meaning from the fetters of pietist reading. The rules for understanding and the use of language demand a reading of the Bible as well as any other book in the ordinary conceptual way and by classification of its content as well as procedure. No text can be read unless it makes conceptual sense. Just as Locke finds no sense or knowledge where there is no connection of agreement or disagreement of ideas, so Wolff finds none where the principles of non-contradiction and sufficient reason are violated.

In the process of detailing principles of intelligent reading, it helps to distinguish the chief procedural means in any text: explanations, experiences, propositions and their demonstrations, and finally scholia or elucidations. Wolff classifies texts into historical and instructional kinds,[13] and he applies the demand for conceptual sense to the Bible, just as Locke had done, although he expresses himself a little more cautiously. Whereas Locke had argued that scripture had to be read through ideas native to us prior to the reading, Wolff, though he tends strongly to agree, leaves the matter a little less determinate.

By the second half of the century, when general hermeneutics began to flourish in biblical study, Wolff's overt influence had started to wane. Above all, the mathematical-deductive organizational scheme which he had hoped to apply to every arena of human inquiry, making logical inference the most creative exercise of the mind, was almost universally deplored. Nonetheless his formal logical scheme permeated hermeneutics. For example, Ernesti rejected a distinction between logical and grammatical use of language, quite possibly in opposition to Wolff's advocacy of both *Sacherklärung* and *Worterklärung*. (G. W. Meyer praises Ernesti for the independence of his hermeneutics from Wolff's school but does not specify what he is talking about.)[14] And yet he made the very distinction Wolff had made, if only to reject the notion that conceptual and linguistic analysis reaches to both *Erklärungen,* as Wolff had claimed. He said that exegesis (and hermeneutics) reaches only to *Worterklärung* and not to *Sacherklärung.*

Indeed, the distinction between *Sacherklärung* and *Worterklärung* came to be primary in the hermeneutics of the later eighteenth century. While it had antedated Wolff, he analyzed and systematized its philosophical basis in a way that proved definitive for hermeneutical practice for the rest of the century. Moreover, his use of *Sacherklärung* implied a shift for biblical interpretation similar to (and as drastic as) the change in relation between literal explication and historical judgment involved in the controversy over prophecy. For the older interpreters the *Sache* had been more important than the words if one found a state of affairs in which there was a conflict. Where a person, for instance, thought that by affirming verbal propositions or the stories in the Bible as true he had done his religious duty by scripture, he was apt to be reminded that he had not yet come to the subject matter. But such ways involved misunderstanding scripture; they were not the normative situation. Subject matter and word belong together naturally and fittingly. For Wolff, on the other hand, whether or not verbal explanation and subject matter explanation are congruent, they are logically distinct, and the priority obviously belongs to subject-matter explanation.

The distinction remained as sharp as this from now on in general hermeneutics for the rest of the century, even if one affirmed the inspiration of the words of the Bible as well as the revelation of its subject matter—no matter whether one saw the subject matter conservatively as special revelation and true doctrine or rationalistically as general universal religious and moral truth. Wolff's formal scheme cut across theological differences in its application to general hermeneutics. (Here as elsewhere Baumgarten turned out to be a loyal and influential follower of Wolff's scheme.)[15]

Wolff had in effect equated meaning with the transconceptual essence or possible reality to which a concept and word refer. The ultimate ground for meaning is ontology. Understanding is therefore factually if not formally identical with knowledge. To understand anything is to know its possible reality or essence; the sense of a statement is its reference. Locke and his followers had similarly held a theory of meaning-as-reference. But to the extent that for Locke ideas were those of sensation (rather than reflection, the only other "idea" one can have), they refer to substances or space–time occurrences and not to "real essences" and whatever stood behind them. His theory was one of ostensive reference. Wolff's theory of meaning-as-reference, on the other hand, is ideal. The reality to which a concept or a word refers is the ideality or possibility underlying either an actual thing or a general truth.

As it turned out, hermeneutical theorists later in the century, distinguishing between *Wort* and *Sache*, regarded the *Sache* of a biblical narrative as either space–time event (meaning as ostensive reference) or as teaching, which could in turn be either dogma or general religious ideas (meaning as ideal reference). In either case, or in a mixture of the two, meaning is referential. Quite properly these commentators did not discuss the epistemological or ontological status of "meaning" for biblical exegesis, but they obviously took for granted that one way or another, or in a mixture of ways, concepts and words refer objectively, so that in effect meaning is a function of knowing reality. Unlike Locke, Wolff thought he was able to supply a philosophical basis for ideal reference in the objective truth of nontemporal possibility.

Wolff no more than Locke was a sort of single pathfinder for hermeneutical theory of the Bible. But the distinction between *Worterklärung* and *Sacherklärung*, uniting as it did logic and ontology in explaining the status of words and concepts, rendered a service which seemed badly needed. It helped subsume the explanation of biblical statements under canons of ordinary and general rather than privileged meaning.

Wolff himself spoke of the estimation (*Beurteilung*) of written texts in the practical or applied portion of his Logic,[16] which corresponds to the theoretical part devoted to the analysis of judgment (*Urteil*). He divided all texts into those that present history, either natural or human, and those that convey teachings. (*Dogmata, seu veritates universales,* he called the latter in his *Latin Logic.*)[17] Of these, historical writings are easier to read because they tell only what took place, although once one reflects on such matters as their completeness, coherence, credibility and (above all) their use, the task becomes more difficult. But in this kind of writing, and even more in the other sort of text, one has to pay heed to the author's intention (once again!) and to judge of the subject by clear analysis of the use of words and concepts and by logical judgment of the content.

The reduction of texts to these two classes did not deny all value to works of literature but obviously assigned them to the second sort: the prime intention of the poet, and therefore the appropriate character of every literary product, must be to instruct. The work must convey useful ideas, constituting its meaning, more effectively by dressing them in pleasant garb. Wolff's own embryonic literary theory and the extensive work of his disciple Johann Christoph Gottsched, *Versuch einer critischen Dichtkunst vor die Deutschen,*[18] were completely intellectualistic, subscribing to the ideal of rational fiction in which pleasure is but a means to attain the goal of rational moral instruction. It was a heavy-footed adaptation of some elements of French neoclassicism in poetics.[19] Literary works, too, deal with the ideal subject matter to which they refer and which is their true meaning.

Here also Wolff helped set the standard for the unwritten code of theory of biblical interpretation until a time close to the end of the century: the slightest hint of aesthetic appreciation of the Bible would have been adapted into the moral and religious didacticism for which Wolff's theory of interpretation had set the stage. There were some exceptions; Bishop Lowth's lectures, *De sacra poesi Hebraeorum*, annotated by the distinguished Orientalist (and Neologian) Johann David Michaelis,[20] made a strong impression in German scholarly circles. The work was the first major effort to analyze some of the Old Testament literature through carefully worked-out formal poetic categories. Usually counted among the important products of English pre-Romanticism, it was so carefully confined to formal analysis that despite the warm reception it was accorded it made little difference to any other type of interpretation. In general, aesthetics had little bearing on scriptural interpretation (except in the unique instance of J. G. Herder); but even if the situation had been different, the influence of Wolff and Gottsched would only have strengthened the didactic as well as referential tendencies that we have observed all along. (German writers were not alone in the general divorce of the Bible from literary art; in England, for example, Dr. Johnson actually advocated it. It seemed to him unfitting and inappropriate to the sacred volume to mix the two things. The Bible best spoke for itself; the poet and literary critic should keep his hands away from it.)[21]

Explicative meaning was reference. Words referred to stable objects which were either space–time occurrences or didactic ideas, whether dogmatic or those of natural religion. But since the biblical narratives were history-like and the putative events formed the basis for assertions of religious truth, the presumption was in favor of their making sense historically, whether in the way they stood or through more or less drastic reconstruction of the events. In any case, the historical sense was stirring among the learned in the later eighteenth century, and in addition a long tradition of reading the Bible, no matter from what religious or irreligious point of view, had taken for granted that there was something historical in its narratives. Everything conspired to confine explicative hermeneutics to meaning as reference—to equate meaning with knowledge of potential or actual reality— and to make the primary reference historical rather than ideal.

General (not theologically privileged) hermeneutics and biblical-historical criticism grew up together, and historical criticism by and large was the dominant partner.

6 Biblical Hermeneutics and Religious Apologetics

Nonetheless there were differences between hermeneutical theory and historical procedure, and consequently those who reflected on hermeneutical principles felt a pull in another direction than that of equating interpretation with historical explanation. The historian had no obligation other than the strictest possible investigation he could muster into what had transpired and how to explain it. A rationalist age had a large investment in the belief that knowledge of history is a most useful acquisition for the man of culture and virtue. This was followed a generation or two later by a common conviction that history in effect renders man to himself. He has, it was thought, no given and constant nature but only the mirror of the past in which to observe the traces of the destiny he still pursues—the destiny which, in fact he *is*. But even then, no matter what a professional historian might think of such grandiose ideas he also knew that he owed careful, disinterested work to his subject, and that in its pursuit he must pay no ideological debts except to the most credible reconstruction of past thoughts, conditions, and events.

But the Bible embodied the most important part of the Western religious heritage. Even if one wanted no more from some of its texts than to know what they really said—assuming, as so many people have always done, that the texts didn't really manage to say it—one was already asking a question of explication which might not coincide fully with what the historian was about; it might even go beyond strictly historical reconstruction. But the full weight of the religious heritage on theory of interpretation of the Bible was of course greater yet. Just as history tended to dominate explication, especially of the narrative parts, so explication in general hermeneutical theory always moved to govern the applicative meaning or use of the Bible. To govern, yes, but not to eliminate it. Biblical hermeneutics was pivoted between the two interests of historical criticism and religious interpretation. More often than not these diverse interests were trying to adjust to each other in the same person. In any case, however, the tension was there, and it meant that hermeneutics was closer to religious questions than historical-critical method could be, until the question of the relation of "faith" and "history" arose in the next century.

TEXTUAL SENSE AND ITS RELIGIOUS APPLICATION

Application remained a challenge to most people who took the trouble to work at all seriously on the Bible, in large part because constructive suggestions about its right religious use were set forth with frequency and confidence. Everyone who had a philosophy of religion had not only a procedure for analyzing religion philosophically but also a proposal for what the right kind of philosophy of religion would be—and it usually meant what the right kind of philosophical religion would be. This normative point of view in analysis of course prevailed even more among Christian theologians. Usually the Bible was the raw material they shaped into a finished religious product.

The religious lessons drawn from the Bible and the instruments of applicative exegesis by which they were obtained may at times seem exceedingly banal. The Enlightenment is known for many great accomplishments, but religious profundity is not usually among them. Nor did the great minds of the period conceive that to be their task, even if they had had the capacity for it. But the fact remains that those scholars who worked on the Bible intensely usually had vigorous opinions about its worth, and to most of them it seemed likely that one reads the Bible to one's profit, no matter how much some individual parts may have to be ignored, improved, or assigned to the oblivion of a hopefully forgettable past. In any case, however, one had to draw the lessons from it by applying to it those general religious and moral ideas that were not the privileged product of a single mysteriously infused or revealed religious truth.

Most of the scholars of the German Enlightenment believed that applicative or practical hermeneutics was fully as general as theoretical or explicative hermeneutics. Just as explication has to operate with concepts, ideas, and propositions according to general canons of logic and grammar, of understanding, language, meaning, and knowledge (after the fashion of Locke or Wolff), so application must work with general canons of religious significance rather than mysteriously revealed, special Christian truths totally inaccessible to all but the initiate. This does not necessarily mean a surrender of belief in positive historical revelation, nor a denial of its pertinence to reading the Bible. But even scholars who tried to relate explication and application from a relatively conservative theological viewpoint thought that revelation as a canon for the interpretation of scripture has to be a reasonable thing, even if it goes beyond the deliverances of an *unaided* reason.

Explication tended to dominate application, but whether or not this was the case, the two seemed to cohere harmoniously. The profit one derived from the Bible appeared rather to be due to the subject matter or sense of the texts themselves than to any subtle relation between a text and the activity of reading it.

Among eighteenth-century scholars it was, in good pre-Kantian fashion, taken for granted that understanding and interpreting a text, for all its great importance, is really not a monumental problem, no matter how subtle a technical execution it might demand. One had to distinguish between explicative sense on the one hand and applicative meaningfulness or significance on the other (even though the distinction turned out in practice to be tenuous and obscure), but each of these two aspects was considered constant and reliable, and uninfluenced by one's reading. This was true even though the historical context of the text was thought to be important for the estimate of its sense, and changed circumstances similarly played a part in gathering its meaningfulness.

The difficulties of garnering and explicating the sense of texts were all considered to be technical rather than intrinsic. They are not due to irremovable conditions or limits of human nature, historical insight and temporal distance, the structure of mental operations, and the like. They may therefore be surmounted by training, practice, and the exploitation of the interpreter's innate capabilities. The world of eighteenth-century exegesis was by and large precritical (in the Kantian sense) and prerelativistic.

The words and larger linguistic combinations of given texts were thought to have a discernible, usually unequivocal sense, at least when the writers had performed well. The meaning of words and statements is a matter of convention, the conventions being governed by the author's intention (as read by his original audience), the aim discernible in the text, the common usage given words had at the time of writing, and finally the logical rules governing the meaningful use of language. Between the specifications of intention and usage there is no problematical distance; no matter what an author wanted to say, the treasury of words was there, preformed, inexhaustible, and at his disposal. Intrinsically there was no problem of communication. Likewise, there was no final problem of distance between the words of texts and their reiterative rendering by the interpreter. The prime principles and rules for interpretation are at the same time demands or requirements that are fulfillable, as we noted, through a combination of training and practice with native capability. Indeed their status as principles is unquestioned precisely because they are demands that *can* be met. J. A. Ernesti, the foremost practitioner of hermeneutical analysis in eighteenth-century Germany can therefore say simply and confidently: *Interpretatio igitur omnis duabus rebus continetur, sententiarum (idearum) verbis subiectarum intellectu, earumque idonea explicatione.*[1] Given these requirements or principles, the good interpreter meets them by combining acuteness of understanding with explanatory skill (*subtilitas intelligendi et subtilitas explicandi*). That these two qualities might be something more than purely technical and mutually supplementary instruments would never have occurred to Ernesti.

In short, the rules for interpretation are clear because they are devised to fit a normative and directly accessible sense of the verbal construct, a sense distinct from its meaningfulness or applicative significance. The lessons we think may be drawn from a text are not merely a matter of explicating or explaining its sense but of applying it significantly to our own condition or circumstances. Application is a logically different exercise from explication. Johann Salomo Semler, generally thought to be the most learned biblical critic of the eighteenth century, said that "hermeneutical skill depends upon one's knowing the Bible's use of language properly and precisely, as well as distinguishing and representing to oneself the historical circumstances of a biblical discourse; and on one's being able to speak today of these matters in such a way as the changed times and circumstances of our fellow-men demand." [2] The interpreter's task in this view seems to be like that of a skilled carpenter carefully prying loose a prefabricated frame from one building and then, having cut it down properly, fitting it into another with equal care.

Even though application was different from explication, the two were congruent because verbal constructs are accessible to the exegete who can compare verbal usage, circumstances then and now, etc., and as a result render his applicative verdict. This is the clear implication of Semler's remarks. Words and larger combinations were thought to be accessible because they refer to, or represent, states of affairs which one perceives, or else ideas which one grasps regardless of their linguistic embodiment.

Attention to basically accessible sense or meaning seemed to imply a primarily univocal use of language. In addition, individual words appeared to be the basic units of meaning. Meaning itself was thought of as a kind of unvarying subsistent medium in which words flourish or, to change the figure, a kind of conveyor belt onto which words are dropped for transportation to their proper reference or destiny. Language is a fit instrument because words have stable, lexically determined meanings. Here and there one is able to notice some uncertainties creep into this set of unspoken assumptions, but at best they introduce a remote undertone into a dominant melody. The general situation fits a comment on a hypothetical exchange made by Ludwig Wittgenstein: "You say to me: 'You understand this expression, don't you? Well then—I am using it in the sense you are familiar with.'—As if the sense were an atmosphere accompanying the word, which it carried with it into every kind of application." [3] Hermeneutical theory in the late eighteenth century is governed by the assumption of the accessibility of the original meaning or sense (*Sinn*) of texts, a sense that transcends and therefore controls the difference and relation between the activities of explication and application.

After the eighteenth century, hermeneutics was to become a unitary theory of the structure and procedures of human under-standing—unitary because understanding itself came to be thought of as a kind of internal, self-sufficient, and coherent complex, problematically related to texts and the thought struc-tures embodied in them. But for eighteenth-century hermeneuti-cal commentators, just as texts by virtue of their accessibility rule the exegesis made of them, so they rule the theory implicit in the practice of exegesis, as well as the aid theory may supply to practice. It was in this sense that Gottlob Wilhelm Meyer, who in the first decade of the nineteenth century wrote a five-volume history of biblical interpretation, meant his short definition of biblical hermeneutics: "The development of the principles [*Grund-sätze*] . . . of the investigation and apprehension of the sacred books, or the theory of exegesis [*Auslegung*]." [4] Eighteenth-century biblical hermeneutics was theory of exegesis. Understanding as a materially distinct function of interpretation did not make a basic difference to hermeneutical theory. Hence the simple difference and yet congruence between explication and application for most eighteenth-century commentators.

Applicative reading was no less objective in the scholarly reader's eye than explication. The abiding religious truth of the Bible, whatever it is, was to be determined right from the texts themselves, even if it could also be discovered elsewhere. The text is accessible to explicative and its subject matter to applicative reading. Belief in the authority and unity of the Bible declined but confidence in its meaningfulness remained strong, especially if one did not have to believe that all of it is equally meaningful.

Johann Salomo Semler (1725–91), Baumgarten's successor at Halle and generally regarded as the foremost historical-critical scholar and theologian among the Neologians of the later eighteenth century, thought that the application of scriptural interpretation should (and of course could) take place in accordance with universal moral and religious principles. ("Moral" had a broader meaning in Semler's day than now. Among other things it meant "spiritual" in contrast to "physical" truth or reality.[5]) The result, he affirmed, is that one can no longer believe in the equal inspiredness of all the books of the Bible. Nonetheless, the Bible remains the religious source of Christian truth, so that even those books that now retain merely historical interest still show the traces of their good office in the divine work of an earlier day. His *Abhandlung von freier Untersuchung des Kanons* (1771) was something of a landmark in theological scholarship because it was the most candid admission up to that time of a need to distinguish relative religious worth among the books of the Bible. Luther had done so in the sixteenth century, but that was a different matter because he had appealed to the Bible itself, its central meaning being Christ, for the basis of the distinction. Those books that preached Christ were inspired; others were not. But Semler appealed to more general criteria, presumably found within and outside scripture, chiefly the spiritual edification of men in all ages. And with great assurance he suggested the manner of distinguishing religious wheat from dross in the texts.

Scholarly German has never been known for its elegance, but Semler has the distinction of being generally acknowledged as the most graceless writer among the scholars of his era. A sample will do to present both his style and the substance of his thought on applicative interpretation:

> The *constant distinction* in content or sense of these books which Jews, learned in *Greek* as well as *Hebrew*, undeniably used to make, thus distinguishing in their so-called Holy Scripture clearly between *spirit, soul, and body,* makes it sufficiently clear

that the more understanding readers knew well indeed that
the difference in abilities, which readers or hearers bring
with them on their own, demands acknowledging a difference in *content* and value in these books; one could not
obligate readers, already well versed in assumption and
insight into principles and concepts which belong to an ever
improved *moral* condition and disposition, to find in the
narrated history itself (viz. the Pentateuch, Joshua, Judges,
etc.) an inner divinity and general usefulness toward the best
in instruction, *without intervention of their own representation of
much better truths.* . . . I hope that this short presentation
contains with sufficient clarity what I actually mean when I
maintain a *free* investigation of the so-called canon of Jews
and Christians . . . I believe that all those are, and more and
more become, true Christians who apply this use of the
powers of their souls honestly and without reservation to
these books which altogether are called *Holy Scripture*, in order
ever better to know God and be useful to him. . . . I am
therefore far from hating all so-called Naturalists . . . for the
sake of the freedom they used to refuse assent to the formerly
commonly held assertions of the general and undifferentiated
divinity of the whole so-called Bible. Every rational man, if
he is fortunate enough to apply his soul's power seriously, is
free, indeed obligated, to judge for himself on this matter
without fear of man.[6]

The spiritual truths at once brought to and found in the Bible
allow us to distinguish between wheat and chaff, and all grades in
between, in the "so-called Bible," even though in the present
essay Semler is as obscure about the content of these truths as he is
candid about the distinguishing effect they have on the Bible. (In
a once-celebrated essay written two years after Semler's death, the
Göttingen biblical scholar J. G. Eichhorn noted Semler's furtive-
ness about such matters as the canon, inspiration, and revelation.[7]) The qualitative gradations in the Bible itself should
indicate to us that there is a constant and growing movement of

man's spirit toward God, beginning with the Bible itself. In that sense the Bible, more particularly the New Testament, is the indispensable beginning and guide of our religion.

APPLICATIVE HERMENEUTICS: THE CONSERVATISM OF THE GERMAN ENLIGHTENMENT

With or without such reservations, in rich or thin hues, from orthodox to rationalist opinions, commentators depicted the issues and ways of interpreting the Bible applicatively. When it came to the meaningfulness of the Bible there were few pure skeptics or scoffers in the German Enlightenment, no matter what these same men did in historical or other explicative exegesis. One of the great differences between the English Deists and the German scholars of the later eighteenth century was that the Germans almost to a man took the Bible, especially the New Testament, to be a rich embodiment of religious truth. It did not matter that they had grave reservations over large parts of it or even that some of them (Semler, for instance) thought that all of it was subject to explanation as a product of its time. The meaning of the biblical texts was accessible and clear, and it was easy enough in principle to know the parts of the Bible that were still meaningful or worthy of application from those that were not. And the results of the harmony between explication and application were customarily favorable to the Bible.

In their own way the iconoclastic rebels against a historically uncritical adoration of the Bible as dogmatic truth were fully as zealous in their defense of the Bible's meaningfulness as their supernaturalist and pietist opponents. Among German New Testament critics, D. F. Strauss, a typical product of the eighteenth century despite his temporary philosophical allegiance to Hegel, was one of the most radical, and many a solemn mind reproached him not only for the substance but the irreverent tone of his attacks upon the credibility of the gospel story and its scholarly defenders. Nonetheless, Strauss was genuinely surprised by the virulence of the reaction to his *Life of Jesus*. For it appeared to him, his detractors quite to the contrary, that his negative historical results about the reliability of the narrative reports concerning the messianic uniqueness of Jesus opened the way for a genuinely positive reestimation of the religious meaning of the gospels, even if this was not part of his own most urgent agenda. He had liberated the narratives from their primitive mythological dross and, in the concluding section of his book, had pointed the way toward a reinterpretation of the myth of an individually incarnate Savior. No Deist fighting the battle of "external evidence" had ended up on that note. Beyond appropriating the instruments Hegel had handed him for appreciation of a de-mythologized New Testament, Strauss was simply part of a tradition that combined liberation from biblical orthodoxy with a lively sense for the Bible as a valuable source of religious insight.

Indeed, only Hermann Samuel Reimarus, deeply influenced by Wolff's rationalist philosophy and the Deists' critique of traditional Christianity, denied it. In his writings on the Bible, large fragments of which Lessing published some time after the author's death, Reimarus did grant that Jesus taught some of the principles of sound (i.e. natural) religion, but this is peripheral to the *actual* meaning of the gospel story, a tissue of errors on Jesus' part and lies by his disciples.[8] Not only exegetically but also hermeneutically, this constituted a precise reversal of practically everyone else's views, from right to left. All others tended to see the real meaning of the New Testament (the Old Testament being a more checkered affair for many) in whatever they found meaningful and lastingly significant there, consigning the obnoxious elements to the periphery.

As a result Reimarus found no followers even among those who appreciated him most and sympathized with some of his historical conclusions. Strauss,[9] despite a lively sympathy for Reimarus, not only denied his thesis that the resurrection story was a fraud perpetrated by the disciples, but even found the kernel of a religious, nonhistorical truth in the story. Lessing, Reimarus's great first editor and defender, and friend of his family, denied the authority of the Bible for religious belief, many of its supposed historical facts, and its origination of the religion which, together with much else, it contains. But that is not the same as saying that the central meaning of the contents is nefarious rather than religiously significant. Lessing, on the contrary, pleaded that the *Fragments* of Reimarus need disturb no genuine Christian but only the theologian who insists that religious convictions must rest on learning, hypothesis, evidences, and demonstrations of truth through reliable facts. The ordinary Christian knows the benefits of his religion, no matter what hypothesis explains the status of the Bible.

> In short: The letter is not the spirit; and the Bible is not religion. Consequently objections against the letter and against the Bible are not objections against the spirit and the religion. For the Bible manifestly contains more than pertains to religion; and it is mere hypothesis that it must be equally infallible in this additional respect. Furthermore, the religion was there before there was a Bible. Christianity existed before the Evangelists and Apostles wrote. . . . No matter how much depends on these writings; the whole truth of the religion cannot possibly rest on them . . . The religion is not true because the Evangelists and Apostles taught it, but they taught it because it is true. The written traditions must be explained from its inner truth, and all the written traditions cannot provide it with inner truth if it has none.[10]

Not the Bible but its subject matter is to be honored, and that subject matter was there independently of the Bible. And yet, to the extent that the Bible contains it, all honor to the Bible: "I am shocked! I am supposed to have denied that the Bible contains religion? . . . Are 'to be' and 'to contain' one and the same? Are these two sentences completely identical: The Bible contains religion; the Bible is religion? Surely in Hamburg one wouldn't want to deny me the whole difference between gross and net?" (In the quarrels over the meaning and truth of the Christian religion which arose in the wake of Lessing's publication of the *Fragments*, his chief opponent was the rigidly orthodox *Hauptpastor* Johann Melchior Goeze of the great commercial seaport of Hamburg.[11])

Lessing was remarkably ironic in his treatment of religious themes as soon as controversy moved close to an inquiry into his own views of Christianity. He carefully covered his tracks and was much clearer about what he was against than what he was for. Moreover, there are indications that his attitude toward the contribution of the positive religious traditions to the true, universal religion of the future remained quite ambivalent. But with all of this, it is still clear that his attitude toward the Bible was not that of the Deists or Reimarus: to the extent that its applicative meaning is true religion (whatever it may be), Lessing held the Bible in honor. And on that score he, unlike Reimarus, had little doubt. For example, no matter how much of the New Testament may be unreliable or misleadingly cast into a form that makes religion dependent on historical fact, he never regarded factual falsity and consequent doctrinal obscurantism as its heart. The Bible may be discriminatingly interpreted and appreciated in the light of more general religious ideas and truths.

Reimarus's posthumous writings would have found more wholehearted followers had they been published a few decades earlier, and in England rather than Germany.[12] As historical exegetes, many of the commentators of the German Enlightenment, Lessing among the most prominent, said things about the Bible and its authority devastating to people of traditional religious convictions. But as men reflecting on religion, and in that context on the Bible's applicative meaning, they were much kinder to it, whether they belonged to the most orthodox or the most radical persuasion. They were all confident of their ability to be just to both tasks and of the coherence of their critical explicative exegesis with their positive applicative reading. Once again Strauss was typical, priding himself on the congruence between the negative fruits of his *historical* analysis of the story of Jesus and a positive *philosophical* (or dogmatic) reconstruction of that very narrative.

APPLICATIVE MEANING AND RELIGIOUS APOLOGETICS

And so biblical hermeneutical principles, even though in one respect close to historical criticism, were also steadily and intimately related to religious and theological issues. Now Christian theology, even in that theologically rather confined period, was a varied thing. The literature that bore on the relation between theology and hermeneutics, though rather narrow in range, proved quite influential. The writings in this discussion were chiefly apologetical, in a slightly extended sense of that term, not so much defending the truth of Christianity against rival religious claims as arguing the religious and moral meaningfulness of its chief beliefs. The discussion partners of conservative or liberal theologians were for the most part not outright skeptics but believers in "natural religion" without revelation. At times the debate was one of outright opposition, at other times it was carried on in a spirit of compromise. One has to remember that not even the Deists themselves were anti-Christian to a man. Some of them, John Toland for example, thought they had divested the Christian religion in its own interests of such meaningless notions as the "mystery" of revelation.

Revelation or no, the business of much Christian theology then and much of the time since, on the part of those who sought to defend the religion as it stood (or as they thought it stood), as well as those who wished to improve it, has been that of arguing the intelligibility of its way of discoursing, the importance of its concerns for the life of mankind at large, and the meaningfulness of its real truth claims. *Plus ça change, plus c'est la même chose.* The discussion opened with John Locke's enormously influential *On the Reasonableness of Christianity*; its last works before the century ended and the mood (though certainly not the topic) changed were Kant's *Religion within the Limits of Reason Alone* and Fichte's early Kantian essay *Versuch einer Kritik aller Offenbarung*. Each of these works, and most of those between the first and the last, had a proposal for a true and significant way of seeing religion, including (chiefly) Christianity.

In the course of this quest, either to vindicate the reasonableness of Christianity or else reduce it to the reasonable religion that is its real meaning, the place and applicative meaning of the Bible were very important.

If the religious truths the Bible communicated were completely dependent for their meaning on the historical events through which they had originally come into currency, the Bible was of course at once an indispensable source of factual information and of religious truth. Moreover, its being the latter depended entirely on its also being the former. But if the religious meaning of the Bible (including the history-like narratives) did not depend logically on its connection with these stories and events, it was certainly factually dispensable; history in that case made no difference to religion. Was the Bible then also religiously dispensable? In principle the answer was yes, except to the extent that all spiritual ideas have to have some tangible form of communication or other in the process of human development. However, as we have noted, the religious dispensability of the Bible did not mean it was meaningless but only that the criterion of its religious significance had to come from somewhere else. The meaningfulness of the Bible depended on a broader religious context than its own specific pronouncements or beliefs. Lessing's plea that the Bible be seen to *contain* religion rather than *define* it was typical of the position that the Bible, though not religiously indispensable, is nonetheless religiously meaningful.

One can distinguish the various positions on the relation between the meaningfulness of the Bible and religious or theological apologetics by their answers to this question: Is the *religious* content of the Bible dependent on the historical factuality of the occurrences narrated in it? Traditionalists said yes. The mediating theologians—the English Latitudinarians beginning with John Locke, and later the Neologians in Germany, Semler most prominent among them—also said yes, but in muffled or ambiguous tones. They tended to insist that belief in the factual occurrences reported in the Bible, especially those connected with Jesus, was indispensable. At the same time they either said or hinted broadly that the religious meaning or truth communicated through these events must be understood by reference to a context of religion and morality broader than the Bible. The Deists and

Rationalists answered the question with a firm no. But no one in the German Enlightenment after the deist debates had been laid to rest, no matter what he thought of the bearing of the fact-like reports on the meaning of the texts, said the Bible was spiritually meaningless—except Reimarus behind the closed doors of his study. Apart from him, nobody from right to left answered *both* that the texts mean what they say *and* that they are religiously meaningless, misleading, or anachronistic.

Explicative meaning, we recall, was generally taken to be either ostensive or ideal reference, so that these stories too make sense by referring. Thus those who believed that they mean literally what they say went on automatically to argue the factual reality of the referent and, from there, the permanent religious significance of making the reference. All the miracle stories are true, and they form an essential part of the normative doctrine that Jesus is the Messiah, the Son of God incarnate. Again, God shaped the earth, life, and man at a specific point beginning temporal history. And similarly, at a specific time soon thereafter the first individual man named Adam and his wife Eve fell from grace in the manner depicted in the story in Genesis, with dire consequences for all their descendants. Because these things happened in this fashion the general doctrine based on them is still true and describes our condition also, unless we are redeemed. This was the Supernaturalists' position.

Those who believed that the stories do not make sense literally could argue in one of two ways. They could claim an ideal rather than an ostensive referent as the true explicative meaning of the stories. They would then plead that this, rather than a historical fact claim, is also their applicative, still meaningful significance. This was the position of the Rationalists. Or they could plead that the stories indeed do not make literal sense but nonetheless refer ostensively. In that case their explicative meaning is the historian's reconstruction of the historical occurrence to which they refer, and that reconstructed fact either is or is closely related to their abiding meaningfulness. They retain their significance because they refer to an inherently plausible rather than (as in the literal-historical reading) to a most unlikely or even inconceivable event.

The latter position had a certain instability because the religious significance of a reconstructed and rather ordinary historical event is hardly very great unless it is combined with some abiding ideal reference, either in the form of a revised traditional doctrine or a universal spiritual truth. This kind of compromise was attractive to a lot of people, though it always raised more problems of interpretation than it settled. In effect it was an affirmation that the stories have a dual referent, ostensive and ideal, both explicatively and applicatively. To combine them was no simple task.

The Rev. Dr. Conyers Middleton (1683–1750), an English writer of whom Gibbon said that he "rose to the highest pitch of scepticism in any way consistent with religion," [13] made some suggestions for reading the first three chapters of Genesis illustrative of this sort of compromise or mediation. He denied the literal reading of the account and yet insisted that this made no difference whatever, as long as one did not deny the central meaning—it was at once a metaphysical truth and something like a general fact or historical situation—which the account was intended to convey. It makes no difference in explicating the sense or discerning the religious meaning whether one reads the story of the creation and fall allegorically or literally. Having compared "the two principal and rival kinds of interpretation, the one according to the letter, the other to allegory," he went on to conclude: "I have ever been inclined to consider the particular story of the fall of man, as a moral fable or allegory, such as we frequently meet with in other parts, both of the Old and New Testament, in which certain religious duties and doctrines, with the genuine nature and effects of them, are represented as it were to our senses, by a fiction of persons and facts, which had no real existence." But no matter, for the doctrinal substance of the story may be preserved whether one takes it allegorically or literally, and that, after all, is the important point. The sense of the story is a certain congruence between what is a factual state of affairs and at the same time a doctrine, even if the description of *both* is allegorical:[14]

> For whether we interpret the story literally or allegorically, I take it to be exactly the same, with regard to its effects and influence on Christianity; which requires nothing more from it, than what is taught by both the kinds of interpretation, that this world had a beginning and creation from God; and that its principal inhabitant man, was originally formed to a state of happiness and perfection, which he lost and forfeited, by following his lusts and passions, in opposition to the will of his Creator.

In Middleton's view the particular story of Genesis 1-3 obviously makes sense because its real reference is a more general story with no particular protagonists, a story which is at the same time a theory about the origin of the world and the relation between the nature and destiny of man. Broadly speaking, its reference or explicative meaning is ideal, but the ideal referent has a kind of factual bearing. In some unspecifiable way the ideal truth is not merely exemplified over and over again; it is instead an actually historical sequence, though not of the specific, literal shape involving the particular times and dramatis personae set down in the account. Despite his characterization of the story as allegorical, Middleton is clearly cautious about divesting it of all factual reference. At any rate, metaphysical and factual references have a certain perhaps rather confusing and confused affinity for him.

If Middleton's explicative procedure and opinion are obviously of a compromising kind, clearly and unambiguously hostile only to the supernaturalist position, his motive in adopting his particular interpretive option was of a sort that would have been the same right across the lines of theological division—the interpretation of the Bible was undertaken in close relation to an apologetic enterprise; the explicative sense was turned to the kind of applicative accounting that would serve to make the texts and thereby the religion they represented meaningful, removing the threat of absurdity or anachronism. Having declared his preference for the allegorical interpretation of the Genesis story, Middleton candidly confessed: "I am the more readily induced to espouse this sense of it, from a persuasion, that it is not only the most probable and rational, but the most useful also to the defence of our religion, by clearing it of those difficulties, which are apt to shock and make us stumble as it were, at the very threshold." [15]

In sum: whether for or against fact claims in the Bible, for or against literal interpretation, men on the theological left, right, and center (again a very few radicals excepted) took the Bible to contain religious truth or meaningfulness and would interpret it in a way designed to strengthen that conviction. *Hermeneutics was in principle closer than historical criticism to an apologetical enterprise in theology or religious philosophy.*

The time would come when biblical scholars would pay slight if any attention to hermeneutics. In the nineteenth century, theological-apologetical as well as antitheological endeavors were to be much more directly and exclusively connected with issues of historical criticism; and in large part for that reason accounts of the historical life of Jesus (or the life of the historical Jesus) came to abound in great number. His was the crucial instance of the mutual pertinence of "faith" and "historical" judgments. But in the eighteenth century this was not yet the case. Biblical hermeneutics was a significant enterprise, and it looked not only over one but over both its shoulders, equally beholden to the rapidly developing method of "the higher criticism" of the Bible and to a connection with some sort of religious apologetic, whether left, right, or mediating.

The cards were overwhelmingly stacked against those few in England as in Germany—men like Anthony Collins, Thomas Woolston, Peter Annet, Thomas Chubb, and Hermann Samuel Reimarus—who both denied the supposed fact claims of the biblical narratives and yet insisted that these constituted their meaning, so that understanding the stories was equivalent to knowing they are factually erroneous and religiously meaningless if not nefarious. Even when the German scholars of the later eighteenth century distinguished between explicative and applicative interpretation, very few if any of them were prepared to support an explication of these stories that did not lead to any application whatever, or else to negative applicative conclusions.

7 Apologetics, Criticism, and the Loss of Narrative Interpretation

Biblical hermeneutics was theory of exegesis, Gottlob Wilhelm Meyer said. In the second half of the eighteenth century when general (nontheological) biblical hermeneutics developed rapidly in Germany, its principles of exegesis were pivoted between historical criticism and religious apologetics. The explicative meaning of the narrative texts came to be their ostensive or ideal reference. Their applicative meaning or religious meaningfulness was either a truth of revelation embodied in an indispensable historical event or a universal spiritual truth known independently of the texts but exemplified by them, or, finally, a compromise between the two positions amounting to the claim that while the historical fact is indispensable to revelation, the meaningfulness of revelation depends on its being set in some broader religious or moral context. No nonreferential explication existed until the mythical thesis was hesitantly applied to the biblical literature, but even "myth" as a critical-analytical category was not a complete change from meaning as ostensive reference. Almost everyone, a few of the Deists and Reimarus excepted, affirmed that explication harmonized with application. From left to right everybody thought that the Bible was religiously meaningful.

THE GOSPEL STORY AND THE HERMENEUTICS OF MEDIATING THEOLOGY

The chief beneficiary of this conservatism in general biblical hermeneutics was the New Testament story. Everyone who believed that the sense of the gospel narratives is the history of Jesus the Messiah believed also that the notion of historical salvation or revelation is itself meaningful. On the other hand, people who believed that monotheism, immortality, and the

124

realization of man's happiness through altruism are the substance of man's religion, equally available to all men at all times without any special revelation, discerned this as the true sense of the gospel narratives, the messianic history being merely their outward trapping. Nobody said that the *real* sense of the narratives was religiously meaningless or anachronistic.

The first of these perspectives actually conceals two divergent views. The Calvinist and Puritan inheritors in England and the Supernaturalists in Germany simply took it that all the narratives refer to actual events and describe them just as they happened. The mediating theologians who also commanded much of the biblical scholarship of the eighteenth century, first the Latitudinarians in England and then the Neologians in Germany, agreed with them to some extent, specifically on the necessity of a factual interpretation of the story of Jesus and a revealed religion. Beyond that, however, they leaned in the other, more rationalist, direction. Jesus was indeed the Messiah, so that a historical faith is necessary for one's spiritual well-being. However, this faith has meaning only as an indispensable solution to a universally experienced moral lack or dilemma. Thus the explicative sense of the narrative of Jesus the Messiah is indeed that of ostensive reference, but its religious application or meaningfulness is derived in part from general moral experience and religious principles and not only from the Bible itself.

Thinkers like Locke suggested that historical and spiritual faith coincide. The story of man's creation and fall refers to mankind's general religious and moral experience directly and not only by way of the historical incorporation of the experience into the specific factual history of Adam. Sometimes this independent appeal to man's universal moral need, which one may understand at least in part without awareness of the biblical story, is quite direct, as in Conyers Middleton's allegorical treatment of Genesis 1–3. Sometimes the appeal takes a more ambiguous form as in Locke's *On the Reasonableness of Christianity*,[1] where the author takes the story literally but still argues the case for the need of redemption on a more general basis.

In other words, the mediating theologians rejected the Calvinists', Puritans', and Supernaturalists' version of the notion of sin in which its meaningfulness was strictly dependent on its making specific ostensive, referential sense as history, told by the particular story of Adam and his progeny. These conservatives believed that the historical event of Adam's fall involves the guilt of all his descendants. The divine economy which has been at work in this historical sequence from eternity compensates for the disaster by condemning Adam's race to eternal punishment and misery, except for the salvation offered some in Jesus Christ's redeeming passion which had also been prepared from eternity.

The Latitudinarians and Neologians rejected this harsh version of sin based on the strict ostensive construal of the story in Genesis, and the consequent applicative interpretation of the story by a doctrine of original and ubiquitously inherited guilt and condemnation to eternal torment. But they turned their backs equally on the Deists' denial of the notion of human sinfulness in any form and of the concomitant need of a redeeming historical revelation. Mankind, it seemed to the mediating thinkers, having been gravely affected in its moral capacity and thus shorn of its natural immortality, proper moral understanding, and strength, needs a redeemer, a fact to which our natural experience in the world testifies. Redemption in history becomes intelligible from its natural context in our moral and religious experience, so that the wise man readily appreciates that rational, natural religion and morality need to be perfected from beyond themselves by a revealed religion which is above rather than against them. The mediating version of the concepts sin and revelation may be sharper than that: the redeeming historical revelation may in large part contradict rather than perfect our natural religion and morality; but even then it remains certain that without our antecedent awareness, either positive or negative, of such morality and religion, the revelation has no applicative meaning. Without that antecedent context, the Bible's story of historical revelation would be religiously meaningless.

God's design of man's nature toward the realization of perfect happiness had been vitiated by man's action. One way or another the need and hiatus created by this situation are eventually met by the coming of Jesus. The historicity of Jesus, including his specific time and place, is obviously not deducible from the general human situation and experience. The fact that he lived and really was the Messiah would have to be demonstrated by external or factual evidence such as miracles, the probability of his resurrection from the dead, and the general reliability of the written witness to him. But the religious meaningfulness of historical redemption or revelation, in contrast to the factual reference or ostensive meaning of the gospel narratives, depends on there being an antecedent or concomitant religious context, independent of the narratives, within which to interpret them.

Among more conservative mediating thinkers it was customary to augment this argument from the religious appropriateness of the Redeemer for the human situation with an argument that historical conditions when he came were exactly ripe for his appearance. Mediating theology, firmly committed to the positivity of Christian religion, nonetheless succeeded in reversing the direction of the interpretation of the biblical stories from precritical days, so that they now made sense by their inclusion in a wider frame of meaning.

The religious sensibility and philosophical outlook to which mediating theologians appealed changed drastically after the eighteenth century, but the logic of the argument and its use of the Bible remained essentially the same. Instead of external evidence, there were appeals to a leap of faith in the miracle of historical redemption, with or without corroboration by scientific historical investigation of the actual life of the historical Jesus. Instead of man's moral imperfection, there were appeals to internal conditions such as despair and the longing for the paradox of grace, or external conditions such as mankind's unredeemed alienation from itself in the process of its history and the concomitant loss of man's true self-hood in alien social structures and institutions. But the mediating theological argument remained the same: the explicative meaning of the gospel narratives is their ostensive reference to Jesus the Messiah. The correlative applicative or religious meaningfulness of the narratives is at least in part provided by their answering a universal human condition or need of which we are all at least implicitly aware. Their explicative sense is quite distinct from, but in harmony with, their religious meaning. The principle of general hermeneutics applying to their *explication* is that meaning is logical coherence in the statement of a proposition, and also that meaning is reference. The principle of general hermeneutics for their *applicative* interpretation is the full or partial pertinence of mankind's general religious and moral experience to the biblical narratives at issue.

In these respects the theology and hermeneutics of the mediating theological thinkers remained constant down to the middle of the twentieth century. Whatever their differences, John Locke, Samuel Clarke, Joseph Butler, Johann Salomo Semler, Johann Joachim Spalding, Friedrich Schleiermacher, Albrecht Ritschl, Wilhelm Herrmann, Emil Brunner, Rudolf Bultmann, Karl Rahner, Gerhard Ebeling, Wolfhart Pannenberg, and Jürgen Moltmann all agreed on these principles. Most of them have disavowed that they were out to "prove" the truth of Christianity, chiefly the assertion that Jesus Christ is the Redeemer—the claim with which (as it seemed to them) all other Christian doctrines must harmonize. But they have all been agreed that one way or another the religious *meaningfulness* (as distinct from demonstration of the truth) of the claim could, indeed must, be perspicuous through its relation to other accounts of general human experience.

To the mediating theologians, the unique truth of Christianity is actually discoverable only by divine, self-communicating grace (or revelation). And this, in turn, has to be grasped through the venture of an act of faith which remains just as risky and uncertain as the grace or revelation, to which it refers, stays indemonstrable. But the possibility of such a miracle—for it is nothing less—and the meaningfulness of what is communicated by it, involve more than an appeal to divine authority. They involve an appeal to the appropriateness of this miracle to the human condition; and that condition is one that all right-thinking men can or should be able to recognize. In other words, there is an area of human experience on which the light of the Christian gospel and that of natural, independent insight shine at the same time, illumining it in the same way. The degree to and manner in which the one mode of insight has to be bolstered by the other is a matter of difference among various mediating theologians, and they have invented a wide variety of often very complex ways of stating their views on this subject. But on the substantive point that both modes must be present and correlated they are all agreed. There is no such thing as revelation without someone to receive it, and receive it, moreover, as a significant answer to or illumination of general life questions.

I have used the term apologetics to cover (among other things) this appeal to a common ground between analysis of human experience by direct natural and by some distinctively Christian thought. This has been the chief characteristic of the mediating theology of modernity. Usually, apologetic mediating theologians have accused their predecessors of wanting to "prove" or "secure" the Christian gospel (that saving truth for the human condition comes through Jesus Christ), while they themselves only wanted to indicate how it could be "meaningful" to "modern man." And when their successors came along, they in turn usually said the same two things. Modern mediating theology gives an impression of constantly building, tearing down, rebuilding, and tearing down again the same edifice. (Notable instances of this procedure are the revolt of nineteenth-century Christian liberals against the "evidence"-seeking theology of the eighteenth century, the revolt of the so-called dialectical or neo-orthodox theologians against nineteenth-century liberalism in the 1920s, and contemporary arguments in favor of the meaningfulness of a specific Christian "language game" among all the other language games people play.)

The mediating theologians have always said that given the

pride and perversity of men, the belief that Jesus was Messiah may be an offense to them. Moreover, it may be difficult in view of the increasingly "secular," nonreligious thought of "modern man." But they also had to insist that it does make sense and is not experientially nonsensical. Furthermore, in regard to this central affirmation, at once historically factual and religiously true, the Bible meant what it said and is our indispensable source for the information. Even if the Bible generally no longer authorized what one believed—by providing either the reliably informative contents or the warrants for believing them—it had to provide and does provide the indispensable, factually informative, and religiously meaningful content in this instance.

RELIGIOUS APOLOGETICS AND THE LOSS OF NARRATIVE READING

The left-wing opponents of mediating and supernaturalist theology had of course to deny that these texts had to be read in this particular way, grounding religions in factual historical assertions. But mediating and left-wing parties were agreed that the criteria for what makes sense, as well as what can be religiously or morally significant, were general: whether or not the Bible provides us with reliable factual information, and whether or not this information is what the texts providing it are really all about, the Bible does not provide us with special canons by which religious ideas or claims become meaningful that wouldn't make sense in a wider context of meaning. It is no exaggeration to say that all across the theological spectrum the great reversal had taken place; interpretation was a matter of fitting the biblical story into another world with another story rather than incorporating that world into the biblical story.

No one who pretended to any sort of theology or religious reflection at all wanted to go counter to the "real" applicative meaning of biblical texts, once it had been determined what it was, even if one did not believe them on their own authority. Hence the right-wing and mediating theologians agreed that the New Testament made the affirmation about Jesus being the

Savior literally, and that it was to be understood that way (though this agreement did not always cover either the miracles he was reported to have performed or those with which he was purportedly associated, especially the virgin birth; nor, as we have noted, did it cover literal acceptance of such Old Testament accounts as the six-day creation or the fall, in the Book of Genesis). And those on the left of course denied that one either has to or can take this affirmation literally. Hence they denied that this is the real meaning of the texts, or they said it is impossible to find out from the texts the real shape of the occurrences to which they refer, e.g. what Jesus was really like or what he thought of himself, so that there is no way of checking the claim against the facts. Hence (once again) the texts must have meaning in some way other than literal or factual.

But almost no one, left, right, or center, wanted to be in the position of affirming at the same time that Jesus as the unique, indispensable Savior is the explicative sense of the texts, *and* that this affirmation is irrelevant or of merely anachronistic interest. If one affirmed the Messiahship of Jesus as the explicative sense of the story, one also affirmed it applicatively. If one denied this application one usually also denied it as the explicative sense. In this respect left-wing thinkers like Lessing and Strauss were apologists for the gospel narratives just as much as mediating or supernaturalist theologians: the explicative sense of the gospel stories is finally not their reference to a literal Messiah; this is only the stage of historical consciousness they represent. Their outward form or their real explicative sense is more general and harmonizes with universal religion. To have claimed otherwise would have meant saying not only that the *authority* of the Bible for belief is gone, but also that this portion of the Bible makes no religious sense at all, or else that its explication may have no carry-over whatever to application. It would have suggested that the truth claim cannot be affirmed and, additionally, that what it means is clear, and it is something that cannot have a negatively or positively signficant religious meaning for anybody today. This position was universally rejected among theologians and non-theologians. One either claimed that the texts really do mean what they state, that salvation comes through Jesus Christ alone and that this is a significant and not an anachronistic statement; or else one said that this, taken literally, would be an insignificant statement and therefore cannot be what the texts mean. And so it has, by and large, remained to the present day among those who have thought about the matter.

The question is: Why should the possibility be ruled out that this is indeed the meaning of the texts, and that it may well be religiously anachronistic or at least without direct religious consequence for anyone today? At one level the answer is very simple: whereas historical criticism had had from its very beginning a religiously neutral basis—no matter whether in fact any historian did, or for that matter can, keep his religious and moral convictions from interfering with the course and outcome of his investigations—the situation was very different in hermeneutics which was, as we have seen, apologetically implicated.

Certainly this was true for Protestant thought before the beginning of the period of our investigation, even though the cutting edge of the apologetics was different then, namely, to maintain against Roman Catholics that the Bible made sense (usually literal sense and/or figurative sense) without interpretive assistance either from the Church's magisterial office or from its accumulated doctrinal heritage. But it was true in a different sense in the eighteenth century. The specter now barely visible on the horizon was that important, indeed hitherto central portions of the Bible, no matter if they made referential sense, did not make abiding religious or moral sense at all, so that they are in effect really obsolete. And the accounts concerning Jesus as Messiah might be among these. What appeared, but not even sufficiently distinctly to be noticed by anyone except a few Deists who were mostly regarded as disgruntled cranks, was the suspicion that the accounts mean what they say, but that what they say is not only an untrue or unverifiable but is an insignificant claim as well—except as an ancient superstition about miraculous and personal divine intervention. That is to say, for instance, that the texts concerning unique redemption exclusively through Jesus cannot (in the barbaric jargon of a twentieth-century school of theology) be demythologized, because they have no other meaning than what they say. And what they say may no longer mean anything religiously significant. To explicate them properly is to erect a formidable barrier to any possible applicative sense. That was the impossible option which no thinker across the religious spectrum would have countenanced then or, for that matter, today.

With regard to the gospel narratives, the apologetical impulse from left to right meant that they could finally be interpreted only in two ways. Either their explicative and applicative meaning (for Supernaturalist and mediating theologians) is that of reference to Jesus as the Messiah in historical fact, or (for Rationalists and their successors) this is only their mythological form, their substance being something else, e.g. the presentation in individual, paradigmatic form of a message about true human life as God intended it. This message is rendered by way of a shape of life and a teaching authentic in quality and so compelling in authority that to grasp this possibility, to understand anything about it, is identical with deciding for or against the message.

Now two options were automatically eliminated by this apologetically motivated disjunctive alternative. First, there was Reimarus's claim that the story means what it says and is a lie. But second, the disjunction eliminates the explication of these accounts as primarily "narrative"—that they tell a story of salvation, an inalienable ingredient of which is the rendering of Jesus as Messiah, and that whether or not he was so in historical fact, or thought of himself as Messiah (i.e. whether the story refers or not), or whether the notion of a Messiah is still a meaningful notion, are different questions altogether. To the "narrative" perspective, these latter questions would have to do not with meaning or hermeneutics but with an entirely separable historical and theological judgment. Hermeneutically, it may well be the most natural thing to say that what these accounts are about is the story of Jesus the Messiah, even if there was no such person; or, if there was, he was not in fact the Messiah; and quite regardless of whether or not he (if he did exist) thought of himself as such; and regardless finally of the possible applicative significance of such a story and of the messianic concept to a modern context. Many elements may enter into the way a story makes sense, but its sheer narrative shape is an important and distinctive one which should not be confused with others—especially that of estimating its abiding religious meaning and that of assessing the narrative's cultural context or the reliability of the "facts" told in the story.

The apologetic urge from left to right, for which explication and application had to walk in harmony, was only one reason for the strange eclipse of the realistic narrative option in a situation in which many observers actually paid heed to that feature. Hermeneutics stood between religious apologetics and historical criticism, and these two worked against the narrative option. The historical critics in particular were the beneficiaries of the definition of meaning as ostensive reference, an early triumph of which we observed in the conflict over the fulfillment of prophecy.

Unlike the religious apologist, the historian as such had no interest in applicative interpretation but only in explication. For the historian the meaning of historical or history-like statements is the spatiotemporal occurrences or conditions to which they refer. His business is to reconstruct the most likely course of these putative events or, if he finds evidence that there were none, to give credible historical explanations for the accounts having been written in their specific way. In the process he must appeal to the ordinary, i.e. nonmiraculous, experience of men, to the cultural conditions under which the accounts were written, to the most likely specific motives for writing them, to the process by which they came to be, and finally to any parallels he may discover to the specific writings he is analyzing. These are the explanatory procedures one applies in rendering what counts as a satisfactory historical explanation. The explication of the statements is either their ostensive reference or a historical situation accounting for, and in turn illumined by, the statements. The real history of the biblical narratives in which the historian is interested is not what is narrated or the fruit of its narrative shape; rather, it is that to which the story refers or the conditions that substitute for such a reference. In short, he is interested not in the text as such but in some reconstructive context to which the text "really" refers and which renders it intelligible.

It is well to recall the example of the debate over the fulfillment of prophecy. Its upshot was the sharp logical distinction of historical judgment from explicative (in particular, literal) sense, and the immediate reintegration of the two things under the dominance of an understanding of meaning as ostensive reference. This is the philosophical context of historical criticism. Clearly, historical-critical analysis can be no more sympathetic than religious apologetics to an interpretation of the narrative text for which the narrative shape, theme, and course are of the greatest interest because they constitute the story's meaning, an interpretation that is not governed, as historical procedure is bound to be, by a theory of meaning either as ostensive (or ideal) reference or as an extension of such reference. This is not to say of course that historical explication is "wrong." It *is* to say, however, that the philosophical or conceptual apparatus, including the theory of meaning, underlying historical criticism of the gospel narratives tends to move it away from every explication of texts not directly governed by a referential theory of meaning or by the cognate identification of meaning with knowledge.

The situation has remained the same since the eighteenth century. The historical critic does something other than narrative interpretation with a narrative because he looks for what the narrative refers to or what reconstructed historical context outside itself explains it. He is not wrong when he does this, but unfortunately he is also not apt to see the logical difference between what he does and what a narrative interpretation might be and what it might yield. He is likely to think instead that a procedure that is neither a practical religious use of the narratives (a use which he sometimes though not always countenances), nor yet his own method with its particular conceptual tools, simply cannot exist; and certainly he does not believe that it can have the serious implications for a religious use of the narratives that he expects from the fruits of his own procedure. Nor would he easily tolerate the notion that his own procedure and narrative interpretation might have to live side by side without yielding a single overall fruit for a given narrative, that the two procedures might in given cases have divergent outcomes impossible to bring into harmonious balance.

In any case, whether one attributes it to the historical situation of the eighteenth-century interpreters or to their unhappy inability to make some appropriate logical distinctions, neither religious apologists nor historical critics were finally able to take proper and serious account of the narrative feature of the biblical stories. And this is all the more striking because all of them noted it and one way or another thought it significant.

Narrative Reading between Reference and Emotionalism

Clearly, a serious literary realism developed first as an art form and soon, although more slowly, also in literary-critical analysis in the eighteenth century; the preconditions were there for understanding the biblical narratives on the same terms. And indeed there was no dearth of commentators to draw attention to the Bible's "history-like" features. To be sure, a different historical "reality" was being depicted in the two eras. In the ancient day it was the intersection between God and man, in the later era the impact of constant and changing historical movements and social infra- and superstructures on individuals. But both shared the description of random and ordinary human beings caught up in a "real" world which defines them, in which they are at home, but which can also pin them down by the sweep of majestic forces of a moral or a morally neutral sort. The affinities between the depictive realism of the two periods were plain, despite their differences.

Such a literary development is always unlikely to be culturally or sociologically isolated. Eighteenth-century realism was not simply a literary movement but a broad apprehension of the world and man's place in it. Especially in matters religious, cultured people were apt to take for granted as a vitally important fact the reality and orderly change of the natural, moral, and social order. For many, mundane reality was not only man's temporal but increasingly also his spiritual home.

The high point of realistic narrative as an art form was the French novel of the nineteenth century, but its beginnings were evident in eighteenth-century France and England. About the same time a general hermeneutics for the Bible was breaking the fetters of the older inspiration-and-special-meaning theories. It was also the era when historical criticism, with Semler its most vigorous pioneer, began its triumphant march toward dominance in biblical exegesis, and the intellectual movement that came to be called historism or historicism first emerged. In view of such large-scale and interrelated intellectual developments, the failure to exploit the narrative option in biblical interpretation becomes all the more fascinating.

Despite the development of literary realism; despite the parallel growth of a realistic historiography of intellect, manners, customs, and imagination (from Montesquieu's *Esprit des lois* and Hume's *Natural History of Religions*, the work of Voltaire, Edward Gibbon, William Robertson, and Justus Moeser to Herder's *Geist der ebräischen Poesie* and his reflections on the philosophy of history); despite biblical hermeneutics and critical history, no one pursued the possibility that the biblical stories, including miracle reports, might make sense most nearly as realistic narratives—no matter what this would do to their permanent religious import or factual status.

There are various levels of explanation for this phenomenon. Religious apologetics of all hues presented one obstacle, and historical criticism another. Both worked to good effect in preventing the exploration of a narrative interpretation of the biblical stories. Both were of course deeply enmeshed in the question of the factual status of the narrated events. In that era it would have been unthinkable to forego positive or negative concern over this issue. It has remained an obsessive preoccupation of theologians and many biblical scholars ever since. Is there any reliable information about the "historical Jesus"? How can one get at it? Is it indispensable for the Christian religion? In other words, does "the essence" of Christianity depend on maintaining that the veracity of a historical fact is indispensable for the salvation of mankind?

Whatever the consensus of previous Christian belief about the place of specific historical events in the divine scheme of things, the isolation of the "fact" issue as such and its elevation to prime importance in religious argument was itself a function of the realism of the eighteenth century. It was a development unprecedented in prior Christian theological history. But curiously enough, this new and growing realistic sensibility, far from furthering the application of literary realism to the biblical narratives, actually hindered it. Once the Deist had raised the question of external evidence for revelation, the status of factuality for the meaning of revelation became a permanent item on the agenda of religious argument.

For the historians, or the biblical scholars on their historical side, the question of what took place, and how the reports about it finally took their present written shape, rightly became a consuming passion. This was a large part of their proper business. We have noted that in this process constriction of meaning to reference came very much into its own. Meaning-as-reference, ostensive or ideal, clearly involves a kind of realistic assumption: the idea in the minds of the writer and later interpreter alike stands for something "real," whether it is historical or spiritual. Assumptions about the way statements and texts are to be understood are very much of a piece with general epistemology. Meaning is reference; statements if they are logically coherent refer to true or actual states of affairs which we know. Theory of meaning is virtually identical with theory of the knowledge of reality.

The situation in the study of the Bible was at one with a prevailing outlook in philosophy. It mirrored not only what was going on in technical philosophy itself but also in theoretical assumptions about the natural sciences, in some (though not all) moral philosophy and practical aesthetic considerations. "Meaning" involved the proper representation of reality in accurate description through clear and distinct ideas. Where this could not be done, the use of words threatened to become vaporous, unclear and indistinct, an ephemeral dream.

In aesthetic theory the classicist estimation of a work of art as beautiful by rules as precise and objective as those applied to the solution of geometric problems became increasingly problematical as the century wore on. Empiricists tended to consign literary art to the pleasurable emotions and to the fortuitous association of ideas and images ungoverned by any intrinsic order.

Almost a century later John Stuart Mill asked: "Whom then shall we call poets?" He answered: "Those who are so constituted that emotions are the links of association by which their ideas, both serious and spiritual, are connected together." W. K. Wimsatt comments that "with these words Mill succeeded in reformulating briefly . . . a supposition which for about a hundred years had been becoming more and more normal to critical thought."[2] Toward the end of the century, just before Romanticism began to engulf aesthetic theory, German thinkers obviously felt a similar pressure toward emotionalism in the explanation of art, the beautiful, and taste, even though they struggled not to give in all the way. Nonetheless, for them also the assumption had come to an end that aesthetic construction is a partially sensible, partially rational cognition of a discernible intrinsic character of the world. One commentator rightly says that "in aesthetics the Copernican revolution of the critical philosophy was an accomplished fact before *The Critique of Judgment*."[3] Men like Kant and Schiller were caught between a conviction of the great importance of the man of artistic genius for mankind and a sense of the uncertain status of his works in the compass of man's contact with reality. Kant in *The Critique of Judgment* and Schiller in *On Naive and Sentimental Poetry* and *Letters on the Aesthetic Education of Man* refused to limit the artist's activity and his work's significance to the emotional life.

For Kant the function of the power of judgment is to raise to the level of intelligibility the human capacity for feeling pleasure and displeasure. To this capacity and to the judgment that orders it he assigned art and its appreciation, rather than to our knowledge of external reality as ordered by theoretical reason or to desire as ordered by pure practical reason. The assignment of beauty and aesthetic appreciation to feeling rather than cognitivity or desire was by no means original with Kant. It had gained ground soon after the writings on aesthetics by A. G. Baumgarten (the younger brother of the theologian), in suggestions of J. G. Sulzer and Moses Mendelssohn. Kant ordered and reconciled these three "faculties" of the soul, assigning the sense of beauty exactly as Sulzer and Mendelssohn had done. But in addition he ordered toward each other the cognate, autonomous, intelligible or supersensible realms of nature (cognitivity) and freedom (will, practical reason) by means of the power of judgment and such instruments in its employ as symbolization and analogy.

But for all this architectonic structuring and reconciling, and the crucial place that aesthetic and teleological judgments occupy in it, Kant was quite clear that providing a bridge between moral experience and perceptual and scientific knowledge remains a tentative business. It simply remained true for him that we do not have the intellectual intuition requisite for a genuine grasp of the real and intelligible world either in its internal unity or in the manner it coheres with our sensible experience. And we have to remain singularly tentative about our formal capacity to unite the ways we structure transcendentally the soul's faculties. We abide in a world of both objective and subjective darkness where only God knows the reason for the coherence of things. Within this large compass of uncertainty aesthetic experience remained for Kant a matter of analyzing the determination of the subject's experience rather than a recognition of objective beauty.

Obviously Kant struggled against a purely emotional view in aesthetics, even as he consigned the origination of the sense of beauty to feeling rather than cognition. The point is simply that it was bound to be a struggle, once meaning had become firmly identified with reference, and therefore with knowledge of the referent. In principle, the situation threatening to engulf everything that was not empirical knowledge subject to scientific or experimental check was similar to certain twentieth-century developments. Aesthetics was but one area of reflection which was threatened by consignment to emotionalism or meaninglessness.

Nowhere was the effect of this general attitude greater than in hermeneutics. Epistemological theory dominated the way texts mean and automatically turned inquiry into the sense of a passage into inquiry into its ostensive or ideal reference. One either followed this governing procedure on any topic devotedly or risked its spiritual or analytical homelessness, the journey of aesthetics from a didactic kind of Classicism to Subjectivism being one example. In the interpretation of ancient texts historical-critical method reinforced the dominant outlook. Together with the apologetical tendency that ruled every religious view from the stiffest orthodoxy to religious rationalism and insisted on an applicative significance of the narrative texts of the Bible, the historical-critical method was a powerful antidote to a serious consideration of narrative interpretation in its own right.

The beginnings of aesthetic appreciation and analysis of the Old Testament followed the general trend. The first of such critical studies, Bishop's Lowth's *De sacra poesi Hebraeorum,* appeared in 1753 and gained considerable influence among scholarly as well as nontechnical readers. Lowth confined himself to a strictly formal analysis, studiously avoiding questions of theology and therefore the ubiquitous pestering issue of the factuality of what was narrated.

> Since [he said] . . . in the sacred writings the only specimens of the primeval and genuine poetry are to be found, and since they are no less venerable for their antiquity than for their divine original, I conceived it my duty in the first place to investigate the nature of these writings, as far as might be consistent with the design of this institution: In other words, it is not my intention to expound to the student of theology

the oracles of divine truth; but to recommend to the notice of the youth who is addicted to the politer sciences, and studious of the elegancies of composition, some of the first and choicest specimens of poetic taste.[4]

Lowth's work was a powerful counter to Dr. Johnson's plea to keep literary judgments away from sacred subjects. But by disregarding theological and (automatically) factual questions, he also lost the lever which at that time would have been most likely to lead to consideration of realistic biblical narrative as a literary-critical genre. By nature or design he stayed away from any text that looked realistic and did not discuss the matter one way or another. The closest he came to it was in his treatment of Job,[5] but he was largely interested in showing that the work is not classical drama. And he was of course right; it is neither classical tragedy nor realistic narrative. In any case, in his native land, Lowth's effort remained without significant parallel.

THE ENGLISH NOVEL, ITS CULTURAL CONTEXT AND THE BIBLE

Beyond the level of technical explanations for the lack of narrative interpretation, there are some interesting cultural considerations to explain this curious state of affairs. *England and Germany were the two countries in which discussion of the biblical narratives was most intense in the eighteenth century. In England, where a serious body of realistic narrative literature and a certain amount of criticism of that literature was building up, there arose no corresponding cumulative tradition of criticism of the biblical writings, and that included no narrative interpretation of them. In Germany, on the other hand, where a body of critical analysis as well as general hermeneutics of the biblical writings built up rapidly in the latter half of the eighteenth century, there was no simultaneous development of realistic prose narrative and its critical appraisal.*

In England, the novel was making an increasingly significant impact on a large section of the reading public. A critical literature began to develop about it in the latter part of the century, the critics noting the break of the genre with that of the romance from which it arose. *Don Quixote*, ridiculing the figure of the heroic knight of romantic tales, was usually held to signal the historical beginnings of the shift. Mrs. Clara Reeve, a minor but significant writer and critic of the day, distinguished between the novel and the whole variety of romances both in their character and their effect:

> The Romance is an heroic fable, which treats of fabulous persons and things.—The novel is a picture of real life and manners, and of the times in which it is written. The Romance in lofty and elevated language, describes what never happened nor is likely to happen.—The novel gives a familiar relation to such things, as pass every day before our eyes, such as may happen to our friend, or to ourselves; and the perfection of it, is to represent every scene, in so easy and natural a manner, and to make them appear so probable, as to deceive us into a persuasion (at least while we are reading) that all is real, until we are affected by the joys and distresses of the persons in the story, as if they were our own.[6]

The novel developed at the same time as a cognate change in the writing and estimate of historical narrative took place. Both were regarded as having great moral utility, instructing those who are capable of learning, among them specially the young and impressionable, in private virtue and public duty, and a due knowledge of human nature and character. Mrs. Reeve was rather defensive about the instructional value of the novel, knowing that the more toplofty among her gentle readers looked down on many a novel's Gothic weirdness and gossipy appeal to lust, greed, fashion, and vanity. All the same, she firmly maintained that this literary form is well suited to her obviously and uprightly moralistic view of life.[7]

David Hume, hardly given to pious moralizing, had no qualms in claiming that the study of history profited its perusers greatly because, in addition to amusing the fancy, "it improves the understanding, and . . . strengthens virtue,"[8] although there is good reason to believe that he became progressively disenchanted about the lessons to be drawn from the past as he progressed in his own *History of England*.[9] Even so, Hume's earlier confident spirit was typical of the contemporary outlook on history writing, deeply influenced by the widely disseminated reading of the classical Greek and Roman historians, whose aim had been the inculcation of practical lessons from a knowledge of the human past.[10] Bolingbroke's famous phrase that history was "philosophy teaching by example" embodied the common view. The determined search for historical analogy made the tale an ancient historian told, as well as his purpose in writing, as contemporary to the present as was the customary historical setting of a novel, which usually was "of the times in which it is written" (as Mrs. Reeve said), and for the same didactic reason.

The practical usefulness common to history and the novel was but one aspect of the increasingly acknowledged similarity between them, including common procedures in the writing of both. One modern commentator on eighteenth-century writing distinguishes between the romance and the novel by attributing to the latter an awareness "of the ill-defined frontier between history and story, between truth and lie, between reality and fiction".[11]

It appeared that the frontier we cannot define we nonetheless know full well, so that consistency in ill-definition became important in maintaining the fiction that fiction is fact, to a degree that amounted to common and open conspiracy between writer and reader rather than to a mere willing suspension of disbelief on the part of the latter. So novels announced themselves as histories, not really intending to fool anybody for very long; and Samuel Richardson wrote to Bishop Warburton that he wished to maintain the fiction that Clarissa's letters were real, not because he wanted them to be "*thought* genuine," but, among other reasons, in order "to avoid hurting that kind of Historical Faith which Fiction itself is generally read with, tho' we know it to be Fiction".[12]

Fielding gave up part of the convention of pretense, but he maintained another and more significant part, that of *verisimilitude* to historical fact. He doubted the historians' ability to describe the real character of men from their public role and hence the explanation of historical movement from the description of public stance. He felt all the more keenly the responsibility of the novelist, precisely in his role as historian of private character:

> we who deal in private characters, who search into the most retired recesses and draw forth examples of virtue and vice from holes and corners of the world, are in a more dangerous situation. As we have no public notoriety, no concurrent testimony, no records to support and corroborate what we deliver, it becomes us not only to keep within the limits of possibility but of probability too; and this more especially in painting what is greatly good and amiable. Knavery and folly, though never so exorbitant, will more easily meet with assent, for ill nature adds great support and strength to faith.[13]

A. D. McKillop summarizes the mid-century development in fictional writing: "The emphasis shifted from a claim to actuality to a claim to probability, particularly as regards the possibilities of human nature."[14] But the pretense in either guise, actuality or verisimilitude, bespeaks a preference for "fact" over "fiction," if one equates fact with likelihood not only of character and occurrence but of broad societal and natural context as well. All of the novelist's techniques were designed to press that preference. As far as possible he wrote not episodes but continuous "historical" narrative, as life indeed is lived, even if he felt at liberty, as Fielding did, to lengthen or compress time spans in accordance with the intrinsic interest and importance of specific incidents. After all he, like the contemporary historian, was no mere chronicler or newspaper editor. He depicted neither heroic figures nor abstract qualities inherent in persons. He described recognizable sequences, and vices and virtues proceeding from credible motives on the part of recognizably human personalities. And these people were set within a specific (usually close to contemporary) historical time and within a definite and recognizable economic and social structure, interplay with which served to focus their character, station, and identity.

The writer's techniques did not merely express his preference for history-like reality over the incredible. He also used them to cross the obscure frontier from history to history-like fiction, while maintaining the integrity and similarity of the territory on either side. Richardson told his stories in letter form; most of the early novelists adopted the fictitious pose of editor, biographer, or historiographer. Fielding regarded his work as prose epic, deliberately reminding the reader at regular intervals that he, the reader, is not confronting reality immediately but only under the controlled guidance of the author, who remains a distinct and significant presence external to the narrative he holds before the reader as the image of reality.[15]

Once inside the territory of fiction, everything was depicted realistically or in history-like fashion. This does not mean that startling things might not be interspersed with the ordinary. On the contrary, of course; but they did not violate the rule of "familiarity." The novelists would have agreed with Diderot's dictum that the writer's art rejects the miraculous but not the marvelous since the natural order brings together the most extraordinary accidents. (It was up to the writer to see to it that the extraordinary did not appear contrived.) Fielding said substantially the same thing as Diderot:

> if the historian will confine himself to what really happened and utterly reject any circumstance which, though never so well attested, he must be well assured is false, he will sometimes fall into the marvellous, but never into the incredible. . . . It is by falling into fiction, therefore, that we generally offend against this rule of deserting probability, which the historian seldom if ever quits till he forsakes his character and commences a writer of romance.[16]

Unlike other forms of literature in England, this burgeoning tradition of prose fiction, hewing close to worldly reality—its logic not simply that of illustrated theme or system but that of cumulative rendering of persons and reality through narrative continuity in time—suffered no interruption during the romantic era. "Scott and Jane Austen are doubtless just what they would have been had the Preface to *Lyrical Ballads* not been written, and neither one gives any apparent indication of belonging to the same century as Byron, Delacroix, and Berlioz." [17] (But even the contrast between romantic lyricism and realistic depiction, clear though it is, ought not to be exaggerated: Wordsworth in the *Preface* and Coleridge in *Biographia Literaria* both draw attention to the imitation of real life, rusticity in particular in Wordsworth's poetry, though in the controversy between them Coleridge clearly works against and draws back from Wordsworth's tendency to idealize or unversalize rustic speech and character, and from Wordsworth's belief that poetry can be a direct embodiment of such speech.[18])

In England the development toward the full scope of what Erich Auerbach called serious modern realism proceeded neither so dramatically nor completely as it did in France in the nineteenth century. But basically the development was similar.[19] The difference (as Auerbach saw the matter) was awareness of the agitated movement of the overall historical background, which furnished the French novel's ultimate frame. The sense of the massive fluidity of that background allowed the lower classes to emerge as genuine agents and bearers of reality in their own right within the novel, and not merely as isolated individual characters interesting in their contrapuntal effect. On the other hand, the awareness of powerful, shifting historical forces and their infrastructures (as we might say today) transformed the novel's moralistic and individualistic perspective. Reality was instead constituted by the fateful depth portrayed in the transaction between these forces and the "random" individuals whom they engulf "as it were accidentally" and force to react one way or another.[20]

No doubt the English novel, much more than the French, continued to present social structures as given and eternally fixed. But even if the development was not so complete as it was in

France, there was a steadily expanding tradition of English literature, seriously depicting the relation of society and the individual and of people within the conventions set by given social structures. Imaginative expression imposed order on the perception of reality as the close interaction between ordinary persons, held together by common temporal experience and by the conventions of a political, economic, and social structure significant enough to generate serious moral existence.

This form of writing was neither a slavish imitation of the perceived external world nor simple moral didacticism about it. Governing themes, particularly of a moral or characterological kind were indeed present; but they could not be at odds with or force the rest of the artist's world in its verisimilitude to the temporally connected world of mundane reality. Such themes therefore had to be rendered in the process of the narrated world's cumulative chronological presentation, and not by an external ready-made imposition. Novels were not moral tales but ren- derings of a temporally connected world in which interpersonal and social experience was related to moral existence in a way that was as intimate as it was ambiguous. The ambiguity was the fruit of locating temporally sequential personal life within a broader, inescapably social rather than merely ethical context. This location made all the difference because it made the field of action amenable as much to historical narration and social, not to say informal sociological, observation as to moral description of behavior.

Gradually the impact of a locally quite diverse but nonetheless nationally coherent society with significant unifying foci of a moral, political, economic, and social kind made itself felt in writing as in other aspects of the common life. The novel reflected that coherence as well as the drastic changes within it which, despite their massiveness, still left a single national life. The shift in social makeup in which personal life and awareness were caught up as a result of the Industrial Revolution permeated the awareness of the middle-class readership, which was not only the novel's initial clientele but remained its natural readership no matter what the changes within the middle class itself or in the upper and lower levels of Britain's social structure. It is fascinating that this art form remained essentially the same and retained its hold on a large reading public's imagination when it mirrored a world in which the landed squire and his family and retainers formed the center and scope of reality, and later when it reflected a world in which rural cottage industries had been supplanted by towns and factories, and when the Enclosure Acts had done the rest to create a new reality by driving the rural poor into the new, burgeoning cities and slums.

By the close of the first third of the nineteenth century England, unlike Germany, had undergone not only its religious and philosophical but also its political, scientific, and economic revolutions. Even if the dust had not settled completely on all these great upheavals, between them they had shaped the nation. They created a climate favorable to this literary form which remained the same when other forms experienced the break of the romantic era. Indeed, the multiplex revolution enhanced the novelist's sense of the appropriateness of mundane reality for imaginative representation and scrutiny, and his moral and aesthetic concern with the quality of human life which is so firmly set within this mundane social and natural matrix. The continuity of political and legal institutions through all the changes no doubt contributed heavily to that sense of an unchanging historical order in the English novel on which Auerbach and others have commented.

Much of the Bible consists of realistic narration, so much so that there is no surprise in its being subjected again and again, in this era of burgeoning realism, to inquiry as to whether it was *really* true to reality. How probable were the things that were told? Unlike other story traditions of the ancient world (the comparison with Homer becoming increasingly common among scholars as the century wore on), *this* story tradition appeared to be true and have the marks of verisimilitude and of probable factuality. This was the case most especially if one left out of account all miracle stories. But even they seemed to have the marks of realism about them. It was often asked what other explanation than the genuine resurrection of Jesus would account for the startling but seemingly genuine and believable change of outlook among the disciples who, on their own admission, had been so cowardly and discouraged at the time of Jesus' trial and death.

But the new tradition of a *literary* realism was never applied to the technical task of biblical interpretation, so that speculation about the possible fruits of such a procedure at the time are as useless as they are fascinating. For reasons already mentioned it was not to be: the debate over the factuality of the biblical reports was far too central and crucial. On apologetic as well as historical grounds the question of the factuality of biblical reports, and the cognate debate over whether its putative factuality or the recognition of some central ideational themes was really the important thing about the Bible, prevented any serious attention to narrative shape in its own right.

In both cases what the biblical narratives are all about is something other than their character as cumulatively or accretively articulated stories whose themes emerge into full shape only through the narrative rendering and deployment itself. The curious, unmarked frontier between history and realistic fiction allows easy transition if one's interest is the rendering and exploration of a temporal framework through their logically similar narrative structure, perhaps most of all in the case of the biblical stories where the question of fact or fiction is so problematical. But when prime interest is concentrated on the fact issue—and it could hardly be otherwise in eighteenth-century examination of the Bible—the unmarked frontier is no longer merely real. Now it becomes impenetrable; one is either on one side of it or the other, and the decision between them is the crucial issue. The peculiar and intricate logic of narration is pushed into the background, and the similarity between the two kinds of writing is no longer significant except in a purely decorative sense. Empirical historical investigation into what most probably happened, together with supporting hypotheses and arguments, is a different enterprise from the endeavor to set forth a temporal world, which is the peculiar way in which realistic narrative means or makes sense. Not that one is more legitimate than the other. It is simply the case that one cannot do both at once, nor will the one kind of analysis do duty for the other.

In England, the interest in the historical factuality and/or the general themes of the biblical narratives subverted more than the technical appreciation of these writings as realistic narratives. Also pushed out of the way was all concern with what kinds of writings these narratives might be. Their narrative structure and their literary-historical origin and development were largely ignored. Whatever else the fruits of the deist debates, interest was concentrated from that day forward largely on criticism of the facts and not of the writings of the Bible. It was a procedure similar to that which F. C. Baur was later to pinpoint so accurately in the assumptions and procedures of D. F. Strauss's *The Life of Jesus*.[21] Although Bishop Lowth's *De sacra poesi Hebraeorum* and his commentary on Isaiah exercised some influence, they did not succeed in establishing a historical or literary-critical tradition of the biblical writings in the author's native land. T. K. Cheyne and more recent commentators have observed that only Warburton and Lowth—bitter antagonists as they were—and Alexander Geddes showed any talent for Old Testament criticism. The situation was essentially the same in the study of the New Testament.[22] Neither narratively nor historically-critically did the Bible as writing become the object of a tradition of scholarly commentary.

The burgeoning realistic outlook, increasingly embodied in the middle class of which men like David Hume were so proud for its contribution to political freedom and to the republic of the sciences, arts, and letters, was indeed reflected in common perspectives on the Bible. But it never shaped in the study of the Bible the same kind of imaginative and analytical grasp applied to the writing and reading of the novel. Realism in regard to the Bible meant the discussion of the fact question or else its treatment in the spirit of Bolingbroke's dictum about history, "philosophy teaching by example." In the latter case, the Bible's perennial themes were taken to be descriptive of the solid, real, and mundane world and its God taught by eighteenth-century science, and of the solid, real, and mundane virtues inculcated by history and philosophy. (Those like Gibbon, who were persuaded of the grandeur both of the well-being and the decay of past epochs conveyed by properly written history, were always a trifle contemptuous of the Bible's level of teaching.)

Like history and the novel, much biblical narrative in explicative interpretation is not "system" or pure factual description but the cumulative rendering of a temporal framework through realistic depiction and chronological continuity. But this made small impact on either pious use or technical scholarly analysis of the Bible. The argument from prophecy and its fulfillment, the logic of which rested in large part on just such a cumulative connection, receded from view early in the century. Its disappearance, as noted earlier, was due to its forced transfer from a formal narrative world of figural and literal interconnection to the arena of debate about the evidence for and against its factual claims. Its logic was basically altered, indeed destroyed, as a result of this shift from one world to another.

Such sense of a narrative framework as continued to exist among religious (and not merely scholarly) readers was now no longer chiefly that of providentially governed biblical history. In that scheme, earlier and later depictions within the Bible had been connected as type and antitype; but in addition, every present moral and historical experience had been fitted into it by bestowing on the present experience a figural interpretation that adapted it into the governing biblical narrative. All this had now changed. Such narrative sense as remained in the reading of the Bible found the connective narrative tissue which served simultaneously as its own effective thread to present experience in the history of the soul's conversion and perfection. This theme and transfer of narrative continuity took place either directly, as in the Methodists' devout use of the Bible to aid in tracing and treading the path from sin to perfection, or indirectly as in the allegory of

Christian's journey to Mount Zion with the aid and admonition of Evangelist and Interpreter in *The Pilgrim's Progress*.

Wesley's and Whitefield's preaching testified with powerful eloquence to their belief in the redeeming death of Christ and its efficacy for the Christian. In other words, it is not a lack of appreciation for the importance of the occurrence character (the "objectivity") of certain crucial events which makes the piety of the evangelical awakening in England something other than realistic. They are objective and objectively transforming events, though the crucial evidence by which they become religiously certain is not external but internal to the soul. (Christ is not reduced, as people often claim about early Methodism, to a subjective experience.) It is not the lack of an objective savior but the location of the cumulative narrative bond which indicates how loose and tentative is the hold of this profound religious movement on a context or world, temporal, eternal, or both, in which one may feel at home. The crucial and indispensable continuity or linkage in the story is the journey of the Christian person from sin through justification to sanctification or perfection.[23]

In figural interpretation the figure itself is real in its own place, time, and right, and without any detraction from that reality it prefigures the reality that will fulfill it. This figural relation not only brings into coherent relation events in biblical narration, but allows also the fitting of each present occurrence and experience into a real, narrative framework or world. Each person, each occurrence is a figure of that providential narrative in which it is also an ingredient. In that fashion all experience belongs in a real world.

In evangelical piety that relation is reversed; the atoning death of Jesus is indeed real in its own right and both necessary and efficacious for the redemption of the sinner. Nonetheless, though real in his own right, the atoning Redeemer is at the same time a figure or type of the Christian's journey; for this is the narrative framework, the meaningful pattern within which alone the occurrence of the cross finds its applicative sense. What is real, and what therefore the Christian really lives, is his own pilgrimage; and to its pattern he looks for the assurance that he is really living it.

8 Hermeneutics and Biblical Authority
in German Thought

The situation in Germany in the later eighteenth century was quite different from that of Britain, but the upshot for our topic was the same. Though a hermeneutics treating the biblical narratives as realistic stories hovered in the German much more than in the English atmosphere, in Germany too it finally came to nought. In Germany also, biblical interpreters took for granted the identity of meaning with reference, historical or ideal, after the fashion of Locke's and Wolff's philosophies; and theory of meaning was equivalent to theory of knowledge. Again similar to England was the entanglement of explicative interpretation of the Bible with religious apologetics and the consequent moves toward religiously applicative meaning whether conservative or liberal.

But the religious and cultural context for these technical similarities was quite different in the two countries. In England, where a serious body of realistic narrative literature as well as criticism of it was building up, no tradition of criticism of the biblical writings arose at the same time, so that the Bible never received the scrutiny or interpretation to which this perspective might have subjected it.

In Germany, unlike England, a body of critical analysis as well as general hermeneutics of the Bible accumulated rapidly in the later eighteenth century. Questions of the narrative shape of individual biblical writings as well as of the Bible as a whole played a considerable part in this development. However, it built up against a broader cultural background in which realistic prose narrative in literature as well as criticism did not develop to any really powerful degree. The realistic novel did not grow on German soil, despite tendencies toward literary realism in Lessing's plays, the *Sturm und Drang* writers, and the early Schiller. The cultural and literary context was lacking in which critical questions as well as those concerning the meaning of the narrative biblical writings might have been turned decisively from debate about their factuality to an inquiry about the autonomous meaning of their admittedly and specifically fact-like or history-like shape. The issue was broached often enough, but it was deflected each time by a sensibility that simply did not register the possibility of fact-like meaning which might not be fact. The meaning of the biblical narratives, insofar as they were read realistically, was automatically historical; and yet such a reading could always be combined with a reading of a piously inward or an ethicist sort. The old realistic sensibility was gone, in which the narrative itself rendered a world at once real and meaningful, which was identical with the narrative, while serving also to orient men's dispositions.

Biblical Study in the Later Eighteenth Century

Scholarly engrossment in the Bible produced three interacting types of biblical study: critical, hermeneutical, and theological. Historical criticism had taken its first uncertain steps in the seventeenth century and slowly gathered strength ever since. In addition to Spinoza, Hugo Grotius and Spinoza's contemporary Richard Simon had been eminent early precursors. Spinoza himself had suggested a natural history of the development of the Pentateuch. There were other names; but if it was to become a concerted intellectual movement, historical criticism had to be the subject of an ongoing literary discussion in books as well as learned journals, and in the university lecture rooms of the professors who increasingly dominated the discussion. In short, to become a major intellectual movement, historical criticism had to become an oral and literary tradition of its own. This task was accomplished in the theological faculties of German universities in the latter part of the eighteenth century, preeminently Göttingen, Halle, and the now long-forgotten Altdorf. No matter that the fruits of the discussion trenched directly on the faith of ordinary churchgoers and, until the second half of the nineteenth century, the interests of cultured nonprofessionals like Lessing: it was and remained largely an academic movement.

Göttingen in particular, the Hanoverian university, was the largest though by no means the only clearing house for English and German learned works in the later eighteenth century. Several generations of German scholars had already shown lively interest in the deistic debate, and most of the pertinent texts had been translated.[1] Beginning in 1748, Baumgarten had reviewed literature about Deism in his ongoing series, *Nachrichten von einer Hallischen Bibliothek*. But despite sympathy for some deist stands and a frequently similar estimate of what the basic problems were, and despite the impact of empiricist views on the early developments of historical criticism in Germany, the German Enlightenment was more conservative about religious matters than the earlier English progressives. Most striking, however, and virtually lacking in England, was the engrossment of German scholars in the Bible as a written document. The written source, in the particular shape in which it has come down to us, was part of the evidence to be examined. Criticism of the writings went along with, indeed became part of the criticism of facts. What counted as evidence for or against the reports contained in the Bible was the degree of external corroboration or the general likelihood of the reported events, as well as the character, likely origin and development, and internal consistency of the writings containing the reports.

This interest, often devout and not merely historical, literary, or critical, was nourished by the fading tradition of Lutheran and reformed orthodoxy that the text itself and not merely the things told in it constitutes the literal Word of God; in other words, that revelation within and the inspiration of the Bible are coherent, necessarily supplementary aspects of the same belief. For this carefully worked out theological position there was no precise parallel in England. It foreshadowed the persistence of a profound interest in the writings as such even when a more secular critical day had arrived and biblical inspiration waned. The pietist movement, much more lively than orthodoxy in the eighteenth century, heightened this fierce loyalty to the text's words, regarding them as a repository of literally and spiritually true meaning and "emphatic" profundity or mystery. Especially at Halle, the confluence of Pietism and Rationalism made for sometimes unlikely fusions between a critical, not to say skeptical, and an almost mystically devout reading of the scriptural text. The Pietists stressed a divinely inspired, often mysterious and special sense of the very words of scripture, open to those who read them devoutly and through the Spirit, rather than with the eyes either of a preconceived orthodox system or of rational philosophy. The Bible is inspired in a double sense: its very words are divinely given, its meaning itself therefore divine truth; and reading it becomes a means of grace to awaken men's spirits.

Interest in the text and therefore in the words of the Bible remained high among critics and theologians, whether pietist or rationalist. The Bible was a fascinating document in its own right for those who believed it to be inspired as well as for those who argued about the "facts" and "revelation" it contained. Hermeneutical developed together with historical-critical literature. The former explored the relation of ordinary and general meaning, logical, referential, and religious, to that peculiar to the supposedly inspired text. The latter applied to the Bible the literary, philological, and historical tools used in the analysis of other ancient documents, in order to arrive at reasonable conclusions about the writings' literary type, origin, historical context, and factual veracity. Establishment of the original biblical texts and harmonies of parallel writings, especially the gospels, which had often been the work of pietist scholars such as Johann Albrecht Bengel, became the raw material from which the "higher critics" built and which they needed before they could place much reliance on their own historical hypotheses.

A huge body of technical literature about the Bible developed in the last third of the eighteenth century, ranging from lexical, philological, textual and other aids to historical-critical studies proper, including the first of the so-called general historical and literary introductions to the literature of the Old and New Testaments. Then there were general hermeneutical studies of the Bible as well as special Old and New Testament hermeneutics. Finally, one must not forget the many "biblical theologies" which tried to relate the fruits of technical scholarship to the religious character, importance, and (it was hoped) unity of the canon, doing so without relapse into that orthodox use of the canon as a unified doctrinal textbook which had consisted of proof-texting the accepted dogmas of the orthodox Protestant Confessions from specific biblical passages.

RELIABILITY, UNITY, AND AUTHORITY OF THE BIBLE

In all these areas—historical criticism, hermeneutics, and theology—the biblical narratives garnered the greatest attention, particularly those which had in the past furnished the material for the chief Christian doctrines. Johann Gottfried Eichhorn published in 1779 his historical introduction to the first three chapters of Genesis, entitled *Die Urgeschichte*,[2] and the whole work was republished with notes and huge new introductions by Johann Philipp Gabler in 1790–93. In addition to historical introductions to the whole of the New Testament, for which the fourth edition in 1788 of Johann David Michaelis' *Einleitung in die göttlichen Schriften des neuen Bundes* is usually taken to be foundational,[3] the gospels gradually received particular attention. The "synoptic problem" involved consideration of the written and oral origins and mutual literary dependence or independence of the first three gospels and, in that connection, their reliability as sources for the purported history which is (among other things) their content.

Critical concentration on these particular portions of the Bible was obviously due in large part to their crucial impact on inherited belief. Creation, the fall, and salvation formed the basic sequence of Christian doctrine. Here, if anywhere, the historical critics had to insist that dogma, in Gabler's words, "must depend on exegesis and not conversely exegesis on dogma."[4]

But on these same narratives, religious interpreters likewise had to take a stand. In this connection Supernaturalists tenaciously argued the textual but even more the historical correctness of specific biblical reports, and Pietists insisted on the harmony between apparently variant accounts of the same events in the gospels. To the Pietists, even slight descriptive differences between parallel accounts indicated separate reference, such was their stake in the absolute truth of the words and not only the ostensive references of scripture. If one gospel says that Jesus fed four thousand people in the miracle of the loaves and fishes but the other mentions five thousand, they must refer to different occasions. So-called naturalistic interpreters, in contrast to both Pietists and Supernaturalists, went to great lengths, some of them absurd and fanciful, to reconstruct the "real" nonmiraculous events behind the reported ones. Both Supernaturalism and Naturalism were positions at once reacting to and logically dependent on biblical criticism and the immediately preceding philosophical position separating explicative meaning from reference, particularly ostensive reference, and then reintegrating them under the dominance of the latter.

With the rise of historical criticism and the gradually developing sense that all, including miraculous and other distinctly archaic statements in the Bible are the products of genuine and specific historical conditioning, and not merely the author's or speaker's (or even God's) accommodation to the original readers' level, the author's intention came to be undergirded or superseded as an explanatory factor by the cultural condition out of which the text arose. In any event, the clue to meaning now is no longer the text itself but its reconstruction from its context, intentional or cultural, or else its aid in reconstructing that context, which in circular fashion then serves to explain the text itself.

If the meaning of a text is the intention of the author in stating the proposition, it has that specific meaning and none other, as Collins had insisted in contrast to figural interpretation. On the other hand, if the meaning of a text is not only the author's intention but also the cultural context out of which he wrote, its specific reference is of secondary importance in any case, in contrast to literal-historical as well as figural readings. Its prime subject matter is its ingredience in and illustration of the outlook of its day. Even if the text or its subject matter bears on what comes later in history, it does not do so specifically but by its outlook and by the way this is taken up, gradually and naturally, into later perspectives.

Deist writers first and historical critics after them had to reject not only figural interpretation but a spiritual or mystical in addition to the literal sense of a text for much the same reason—that it is at best false but more likely absurd. Beyond the agreements there were two differences between Deists and historical critics. Historical critics were aware, as Deists generally were not, of the influence of cultural conditions on the sense of biblical writings; and critics were obviously interested in the character of the Bible as writing and not merely as reliable or unreliable report. The latter interest was bound to raise the question of what kind of unity might be found to pervade this literature. Whatever it was would have to be a substitute for figural interpretation which had traditionally served that function.

The direct impact on theology of critical method and a general rather than theologically privileged hermeneutics was twofold. First, "the higher criticism" forced a direct reexamination of the reliability, and in that sense of the authority, of the canon. This was always a matter of specific texts. But in the second place, as we have noted, criticism and general hermeneutics put into grave question the assumption of the whole canon's unitary meaning. Semler's ongoing *Abhandlung von freier Untersuchung des Kanons*, published as the controversy over the initial essay widened,[5] was epoch-making in its insistence that the Bible as such is not identical with God's word; that the question of the unity of the canon is purely historical, to be determined by the consideration of each book in its own direct historical context; and that many of the books, judged by this criterion, are clearly of purely historical and not permanent religious interest, let alone of a uniform and pervasive level of divine inspiration. Semler's differentiation between kinds of religious meaning and levels of religious truth according to cultural context makes him one of the prime ancestors of historical theology, the younger relative of historical criticism, which was to develop in the nineteenth century.

The fragmentation of a unitary canon was at least as grave a threat to the traditional status of the Bible as authority for belief as was the direct assault on its historical reliability. If the Bible is a library of books from a variety of different contexts, consisting of sometimes conflicting meanings, some more and others less valuable, the choice between them and the criterion for normative religious meaning among all those that emerge out of the variety of these writings is in human rather than divine hands. The divine authority of the Bible in prescribing belief is possible only if its meaning is the same throughout, if it is esentially clear, and if it is the product of special divine communication rather than the fruit of human understanding gained naturally from other sources and then applied to the Bible. Where one has to appeal to an authoritative canon within a larger, nonauthoritative one, the basis for selection is not the divine authority of the book in question but an extrinsically derived scale of what constitutes religious meaningfulness and possible truth, which is then applied to the Bible. Whether or not the divine communication of a unitary meaning of the Bible's text is a sufficient condition, it is certainly a necessary condition of its authority in matters doctrinal.

Both questions, that of the Bible's reliability and that of its unity in meaning focused on the history-like narratives and the doctrines that had traditionally been associated with them: creation, the fall, the stages of Israelite history looking toward messianic fulfillment, the New Testament, and the second coming of Christ. While historical criticism and theological claims met most directly over the issue of the factual reliability of the several texts, the point of coordination between theology and hermeneutics was the unitary meaning of the canon, especially if its parts could be shown to be historically conditioned. But obviously, all three types of considerations—historical-critical judgment, normative theological or religious affirmations, and hermeneutics—

became a tangled web. J. P. Gabler was the first to state clearly that dogmatic theology must depend on the results of exegesis, which to him meant historical-critical analysis of the texts. While this sweeping claim, reiterated by Strauss in the nineteenth century, met with heavy resistance, there was nevertheless an increasingly strong determination on the part of all but the most conservative commentators that theology and historical criticism at least should not be in conflict, even if criticism could not furnish the foundation for theological interpretation. (The most notable puristic stand against all biblical criticism, that of the Berlin theologian, publicist, and ecclesiastical politician Ernst Wilhelm Hengstenberg, came in the nineteenth century.)

Pietists, biblical critics, and some others alike thought they were getting back to the Bible directly although, to be sure, the slogan meant rather different things to the various approaches and depended on what they thought hindered direct access. Freed from the chains of dogmatic or philosophical interpretation, or from its position as a confessional textbook, it was thought that the Bible would serve as the direct basis for theological assertions. Its unitary subject matter would stand out in its own right. Paradoxically, then, the later eighteenth century saw both a grave questioning of and a rising appeal to the Bible's direct authority. In short, a specifically and self-consciously biblical theology arose which claimed not only that the Bible itself (with or without historical criticism) is the direct basis of belief but also that it has a significantly unitary meaning—even if the adherents of "biblical theology" often had little more than the name in common.

The specter of figural interpretation, which had provided biblical unity in precritical days, haunted the search, at once general-hermeneutical and theological, for unitary meaning. The figural, direct juxtaposition of two texts widely separated in time smacked not only of the anathematized "layers of meaning" but also of an arbitrary intrusion of Supernaturalism into explanation of the Bible's unitary meaning. In addition to introducing layers of meaning, figural interpretation invited outrageous historical argumentation. What seemed needed instead was an explanation of the Bible's unity based on natural and general canons of meaning. If the unitary divine purpose and unitary *Theopneustie* or inspiredness of the Bible were to be made evident, it had to be done by means that were in harmony with such general and natural procedures. This was the joint task of hermeneutics and biblical theology.

9   The Quest for A Unitary Meaning

Three divergent directions laid claim to the valid use of the term biblical theology.[1] First, there were those who thought that biblical in contrast to systematic or dogmatic theology was based on a historically worked-out differentiation of the variety of the Bible's contents, followed by whatever inductive generalizations one could make about permanent and normative in contrast to merely time-conditioned concepts in the whole of the canon. These in turn could serve as the basis of normative, abiding theological claims. "Biblical theology" was therefore a completely historical investigation, and "dogmatic theology" had to await its results before it could undertake its own work. This was the position that Johann Philipp Gabler adopted in his Altdorf inaugural lecture of 1787, "De iusto discrimine theologiae biblicae et dogmaticae regundisque recte utriusque finibus." [2]

GABLER AND STÄUDLIN

Gabler contrasted the strictly scientific procedure of biblical theology to dogmatic theology which is always dependent on the contemporaneous situation in thought and culture. The results that biblical theology obtains have a permanent validity which dogmatic theology cannot and should not try to match. Biblical theology is a purely historical undertaking, gathering, comparing, and classifying the thought and words of the individual biblical authors, wholly ignoring the question of whether they were inspired. But beyond that, once one trenches on dogmatic theology one would have to say that since the Bible is obviously the product of many authors and many levels of religion and culture, one cannot claim for all of them an equal measure of *Theopneustie*.

Obviously, biblical theology in this sense came to converge toward historical-critical rather than theological analysis. It meant working out from a text's words, as used at the time they were written, and the single, and never more than single, meaning of the text and its author, quite regardless of one's estimate of the soundness of his position. On this grammatical-historical procedure and its estimate of the verbal sense Gabler agreed with Ernesti and with his own contemporary, Ernesti's student and follower, the Leipzig professor K. A. G. Keil. But to grammatical-historical interpretation, Gabler added consideration of the historical circumstances under which the text was written, as an element in estimating its explicative sense. On this matter he was in agreement with Semler rather than Ernesti, who had held back from expanding grammatical-historical into broader historical-critical investigation. Finally Gabler, in agreement with his teacher J. G. Eichhorn and his Altdorf colleague G. L. Bauer, went on to claim historical and philosophical criticism as the appropriate means for working out a text's true subject matter, which in turn was the root meaning reconstructed by these means. The subject matter (*die Sache*) in contrast to the merely verbal sense given to the text by its author, now became the genuine explicative sense of the text.[3] Biblical theology in Gabler's sense came to be a mixture of historical criticism and general hermeneutical procedure, both together laying down the conditions for an evaluation of what is permanently valuable in the Bible.

The upshot of the view that Semler, Gabler, and Keil (but not Ernesti) held in common was that historical-critical principles, and a hermeneutics subordinated to historical criticism, became not merely the indispensable basis but in effect the sum and substance of the interpretive structure for dogmatic theology. Grammatical-historical and historical-critical analysis together rendered the full explicative meaning of texts for Gabler. The rest was simply collation, generalization, and the application of common-sense philosophical judgments to distinguish pervasive biblical concepts that are still religiously normative today from those that are superannuated because they applied only to the writers' own primitve time.

Gabler and Keil were bitterly opposed by certain scholars

whose theological and philosophical views were just as rationalist as their own, but who were more conservative in their hermeneutics. C. F. Stäudlin of Göttingen no more believed in miracles than did Gabler, and for both of them religious and moral ideas were, if true, trans-historical and fixed metaphysical entities. But Stäudlin argued against Keil and Gabler, not indeed that historical criticism or for that matter grammatical-historical interpretation was misplaced but that the scope of both procedures, singly or together, in explicative hermeneutics was limited, and that normative or permanently valid ideas are part of the explicative and not merely applicative meaning of texts.[4] The argument between the two positions was perhaps a tempest in a teapot, since both sides held to the same religious outlook, but it did serve to indicate something of the thinness of the distinction between explicative and applicative interpretation. Clearly, there was resistance to the assumption that normative and religiously significant uses of the biblical texts were an automatic distillate of grammatical-historical and historical-critical reading. If, Stäudlin thought, one confines one's reading to this sort of perusal and analysis, the result was instead apt to be that one would never recognize any religious dimensions to the texts at all. They have to be read applicatively, with their *Theopneustie* in mind and with one's own religious, rational, and meditative disposition at work. Nonetheless, such applicative reading is not merely *Eisegesis* or simply a peculiar slant on the texts, but rather a genuine explicative reading in accordance with the nature of the texts themselves, discovering genuine dimensions in them which remained hidden from a merely historical reading.

G. T. Zachariä

The second group of men calling themselves biblical in contrast to systematic or dogmatic theologians, began with a much more nearly traditional view both of the character and content of the Bible and of the nature of theology. Their aim was in effect to demonstrate the correctness of traditional Protestant doctrines from a conceptual analysis of the Bible, ordering the doctrines into a coherent whole partially through a logical and partially through a historical scheme. However, in the process the doctrinal concepts became more and more filled with a rationalist content, reminiscent of the opinions of Conyers Middleton. Thus the meaning of the fall was equated more and more with a general loss of happiness after an originally happy state of all mankind, with only a tenuous connection being made between the story in Genesis and the general assertion thought to be its meaning. Furthermore, the continuity of the two testaments—one of the motivating forces of every biblical theology, since all of them sought ways of arguing unitary biblical meaning in the face of historically and hermeneutically provoked doubts—was seen to lie in the unity of their concepts or religious ideas. One could claim that these ideas underwent no essential development from the one Testament to the next; only their form changed from a basically sensuous to a more appropriate spiritual shape. Or one could claim, with nineteenth-century representatives of this way of thinking, that there was a genuine conceptual development not only of the shape or form but also of the content or essence of biblical-religious concepts. In either case it was easy to make an almost imperceptible shift from traditional to rationalist notions of what constitutes the heart of biblical-theological ideas. And in any event, the heart of the Bible is its religious concepts.

Gotthilf Traugott Zachariä (1729–77), a Göttingen professor influenced by S. J. Baumgarten under whom he had studied, and by Ernesti's grammatical-historical approach to hermeneutics, wrote a *Biblische Theologie oder Untersuchung des biblischen Grundes der vornehmsten theologischen Lehren* (four parts, 1771–75). He welcomed critical-historical procedure but considered it peripheral to, because logically different from, *Glaubenslehre*.[5] (It is, however, questionable that he distinguished properly between grammatical-historical and historical-critical procedure.) Like Ernesti, he affirmed both the *Theopneustie* of the divine books and writers[6] and the ordinary meaning of the books, vigorously defending a general and ordinary hermeneutics of the Bible against pietistic beliefs in a special spiritual or double sense of the texts. ("Understanding

[*Verstand*] of Holy Scripture is no different from that of other human writings, and the investigation of its particular character [*Beschaffenheit*] cannot rest on biblical grounds and demonstrations"; pp. 6f.) This combination of the inspiration and yet ordinary meaningfulness of the Bible persuaded him that exegesis is the better and well nigh the only part of dogma (p. LXXIX), cutting his ties to the highly structured and technical analytical procedures of Protestant scholasticism.

Zachariä affirmed the usual traditional dogmas, for example historical revelation, original sin, atonement and the Trinity. He argued the historical factuality of the literally meant biblical accounts, rejecting all allegorical interpretation, for instance that of the first three chapters of Genesis.[7] He claimed the literal historical credibility of the creation accounts, and gave as one of his reasons the fact that they depict the process at the level of simple, direct, sensible experience, without appeal to the physical or "invisible" historical causes which a scientist or historian would try to explain. It was a procedure, he thought, both reliable and quite appropriate to the rude level of the Hebrew people for whom Moses accommodatingly wrote (pt. 2, pp. 20f.). We have encountered this theme frequently: realistic depiction, especially simplicity, is taken to be evidence in favor of historical factuality. The argument is a residue of the precritical identity of grammatical or literal reading and historical reference.

Though the structure of Zachariä's book is partly that of the divine *oeconomia temporum* depicted in the Bible, the scripture functions for him chiefly, as he says over and over again, as a source of knowledge (*Erkenntnisgrund*). Thus the sensuous representations of the Old Testament were fit means for guiding earlier generations to the spiritual ideas which they contain and which are brought out with greater spiritual perspicuity in the New Testament.[8] And while our own spiritual wisdom and clarity certainly do not exceed those of apostles and evangelists, it is obvious that with them we also read the Old Testament at a level higher than that of its original readers (though not its writers). This insistence lands Zachariä in a handsome contradiction, not without parallel in his day. He has argued not only the literal in contrast to the allegorical meaning of biblical narratives, but on that basis their factuality as well. But now it turns out that he also regards them—the Bible being a source of knowledge and particularly of concepts or ideas—as sensuous rather than literal (or "spiritual") formulations of truth. In other words, he locates the meaning of biblical stories at once in their ostensive reference and in their ideal reference clothed in sensuous form—the narratives are simultaneously factual accounts and allegories. Not only is it exceedingly difficult to maintain both ideal and ostensive reference for the same statement, but the position obviously violates also the doctrine of single meaning to which Zachariä wants to adhere. In the poems and some of the prophecies and "even in the historical books God frequently had to be guided by the sensuous thought modes of the time, in order to meet the Israelites appropriately in accordance with their concepts" (pt. 1, p. 175). The doctrine of accommodation (on God's and Moses's part) forces Zachariä into the very allegorical interpretation of the stories which he had rejected on grammatical-historical grounds.

Concerning the relation of revelation to history Zachariä was obviously a Supernaturalist, claiming direct divine intervention in history through miraculous occurrences faithfully reported in the Bible. But hermeneutically he was clearly moving in a rationalist direction, and since he was writing a biblical theology, in which the interpretation of biblical concepts became the sum and substance of theology, this was the more important factor. This double focus is an excellent illustration of the often quite unconscious proximity in that era between two stances which it became increasingly unnatural to hold together as modern secular world views advanced. While realistic narrative interpretation functioned historically for Zachariä, it finally was hermeneutically insignificant. He tended to opt instead for meaning as ideal reference: even though the accounts are true, their meaning lies in the concepts sensuously and therefore allegorically represented in them. The doctrine of accommodation, to which he together with so many other commentators in the eighteenth century adhered, obviously forced the narrative into a didactic, non-narrative interpretive framework.

What were the true ideas, represented sensuously in the Old Testament and more explicitly in the New? Zachariä was a typical mediating theologian, for whom the meaning of the central, factual christological and soteriological doctrines depended on their being put into a context of meaning wider and more general than that of the story or storied world in which they were set. The truths whose truth is largely to be taken on faith (together with attention to factual evidence), but whose meaning must be more broadly understood, are that there is one God who had created the world and made man for the happiness which he lost through his own blindness, and which God restored in Jesus Christ. This was the bond of continuity, partly historical but partly that of a conceptual scheme, holding together the two Testaments. Time and again Zachariä first set forth his exegesis and then a section on the "theological truths" to be drawn from it, truths which turn out to be general concepts and propositions of a rationalist sort, even though he may have defended in the prior section the grammatical-historical or realistic reading of the same passages. Thus he says, after a brief introductory exegesis of Genesis 1:1 and 2: "The theological truths which we learn from this description after separating out everything sensuous amount to this: (1) God has created everything which now makes up the whole world, otherwise called heaven and earth . . . (2) The matter of the earth was also created by God before its full formation, just as much as its individual, formed parts" (pt. 2, p. 14).

Conyers Middleton had argued that whether or not Genesis was allegorical or historical, its meaning is the same. He did however opt for the allegorical alternative, a happy choice for the sake of consistency, in view of his assertion that the meaning of the stories is a general proposition. Zachariä was not quite so fortunate; he wanted to have things both ways. The story was to function specifically or within its own narrative context, and that meant to him that it was to function literally and historically. And yet its meaning was not set within this particular storied world but within a different universe of discourse, the connecting and explanatory links of which consisted at least in part of general propositions and concepts. Sin and redemption are universal conditions, the first of them only confusedly referable to the particular biblical narrative, the second at least in part gathering its meaning from its conceptual connection with the universal features of the first.

When the meaning of the biblical stories becomes their ideal reference, so that they are interpreted by more generally derived notions, it cannot be long before the suggestion will arise that the same ideal truths to be discovered in the Bible may be found in more appropriate forms and concepts elsewhere and in later times. One is invited to observe religious-ideational progress within the Bible itself and its continuation in later history. The customary term for designating this outlook and theory came to be progressive revelation, though at the turn from the eighteenth to the nineteenth century it was referred to as "the perfectibility of Christianity." Zachariä stopped well short of such a notion, which found its classic expression in Lessing's *The Education of the Human Race*. By contrast Zachariä had, as we have seen, insisted on the equal inspiredness of all the texts of the Bible and an at least partial dependence of the meaning on the narratives. And yet the progress in the forms that biblical ideas took, from sensuous to spiritual, and the fact that the meaning of the Bible lies in concepts, pointed "biblical theology" in a new direction: the unity of the canon lies in the development of the moral and religious ideas taught in it, the purest of them—and they are obviously the teaching of Jesus—being the norm for what is accepted and what is rejected from among the rest. It is a rationalist reduction of biblical meaning and biblical unity, in which ideas are self-contained entities undergoing self-explanatory progressive development. This version of biblical theology, of which Zachariä was the first representative, was carried on in the biblical theologies of Christoph Friedrich von Ammon (1766–1850) and Daniel Georg Conrad von Cölln (1788–1833).[9]

COCCEIUS, BENGEL, AND THE
HEILSGESCHICHTLICHE SCHULE

In the third place, there was a use of biblical theology, at once more complex and richer than the previous two. There were those who, influenced by the seventeenth-century theologian Johannes Cocceius as well as Pietism, saw the unity of the Bible in the one sacred history it depicts as well as in the pervasive *Theopneustie* which makes it a means of grace to the faithful. This movement interacted deeply with the development of Romanticism, philosophical Idealism, and Historicism at the end of the eighteenth century, for which all interpretation, including that of the Bible, was profoundly influenced by the stance of the interpreter and his quest for a cognate spirit within the text. In a variety of ways this complex intellectual movement was climaxed for biblical hermeneutics in the biblical theology and its notion of a special "salvation history" which characterized the thought of twentieth-century neo-orthodoxy in Christian thought. The roots and expressions of this view require more detailed examination than that I have devoted to the other two types of biblical theology.

The third group of biblical theologians, from the eighteenth to the twentieth century, claimed that the continuity of Old and New Testaments is historical, earlier outlooks and events anticipating by a kind of built-in incompleteness the events and meaning patterns that fulfilled them later. It was, moreover, a gradually increasing fulfillment in which there must be no large temporal gaps as there had been in figural interpretation. And the relation between earlier and later moments must, again unlike figuration, be more nearly general than specific in character. The several, separate accounts of the several segments of the one biblical history could be joined only tentatively by indicating, wherever possible, a generic similarity and parallel contents between them. For the rest, they remained separate accounts of separate episodes in the same broad temporal sequence, some of which are sufficiently open-textured to anticipate later episodes. And no temporal links can be left out. If, for example, late Jewish religious culture has an increasingly messianic outlook, this and not some specific and much earlier Old Testament reference is the indispensable anticipatory context for making sense of the story of the origin of Christianity in the New Testament. Moreover, the unity of the several accounts is external to the accounts themselves; it is the "real" and logically separable historical or temporal continuity among the segments of time, depicted separately by the separate accounts.

All this is a far cry from figuration's joining of separate accounts into a single narrative, coherent or identical with the temporal sequence rendered by it, through the direct and specific juxtaposition of earlier and later events. Instead, the relation of what is earlier and later is now seen to be historical rather than storied, even if the history's segments and their accumulation are accurately mirrored in the sum of the individual stories. The meaning of the whole Bible is the linkage in gradual development of the times mirrored in its parts. The unity of the Bible came for these "biblical theologians" to be the unity of a specific theme, particularly that of salvation, which is enacted gradually in the general shape of events, and the general shape of the cumulative interpretation of writings of a religious and cultural community. Biblical unity is not the enactment of a single pattern of meaning through a specific set of interactions constituting a single story consummated over a temporal span. It is the history of the tradition of the writings about the events depicted.

The sense of divine purpose given with figural interpretation, where it had been exhibited directly and without recourse to a theoretical explanation or the setting forth of temporal causal links, had to be altered accordingly. For figuration or typology, the cogent suggestion of a divine plan was always dependent on its being directly exhibited in the juxtaposition of widely separated and specific occurrences and their meaning. This view now seemed arbitrary and magical. God's purpose must be identified and enacted by the cumulative history presented in the Bible and the purposiveness demonstrably immanent to it. All in all, the criteria for meaning developed by these biblical theologians for the most part not only avoided conflict with historical criticism but also sought to be in harmony with those views which regarded religious meaning as accessible to people who knew how to discern general patterns of meaning in history and human experience.

In this third kind of biblical theology one finds the most strenuous endeavor to discover a modern substitute for figuration to show forth the unity of the canon. The beginnings of biblical theology in this sense, in which the unitary theme or meaning of the Bible is inseparable from its arrangement into the cumulative account of or witness to a history of salvation, are generally thought to be evident in the seventeenth century.

Cocceius's kinship with and his probable influence on Pietism in Germany has long been acknowledged. His chiliastic views found strong echoes there, as did his understanding of the unity of scripture as the *oeconomia temporum*, the temporally differentiated stages of the covenantal relation between God and man that heads up in the Kingdom of God. His periodization of Old Testament and church history also influenced later practice, especially among Pietists who saw this structure as God's implementation of his ways among men, even in their rebellion against him. Württemberg or Swabian Pietism even more strongly than the more subjectively oriented northern Pietism of Halle expanded Cocceius's scheme of a periodized sacred history, shaped toward the first and second comings of Christ.

Bengel on Letter, Spirit, and History

Johann Albrecht Bengel (1687–1752), a great Swabian New Testament philologist, commentator, and translator, agreed with Cocceius's realistic eschatology and his rejection of scholastic modes of biblical interpretation. The temporally sequential bond by which salvation is worked out in Bengel's view, and his close textual analysis of individual passages, both mean that Bengel did very little with typological or figural interpretation. One observes in his case a pattern increasingly typical in a theology based on the Bible as the account of salvation history. First, the letter of the Bible is taken very seriously; indeed the focus of the Bible's inspiration hovers ambiguously between the literal words and the inspired fidelity, the *Theopneustie,* of the sacred writers. Between them hovers, equally ambiguously, a point of transition where a literal and a spiritual sense are claimed to fit together, specifically in the reader's understanding. Second, the meaning of the inspired words is their reference to the sacred events they portray in historical sequence. Here, then, the inspired words operate meaningfully not only because they or their writers are directly inspired by God but also because they refer ostensively with descriptive accuracy. This is true to such an extent that hidden but real and accurate reference to events yet in the future may be worked out from some biblical statements: they are not *figures* of such future events; they actually refer to them predictively or prophetically. The verbal literalism of Pietists like Bengel apart, their salvation-history view of the unity of the Bible in effect claims that the unity lies in the temporal sequence of world history depicted by the stories, or arcanely hinted at by scriptural texts, and not in a logical identity between the depiction and the reality rendered by it.

Bengel liked to quote Luther that theology "is nothing but grammar, applied to the words of the Holy Spirit." [10] Literal grammatical meaning, literal understanding, was his craft. His critical work, in a great translation of the New Testament published in 1734, was confined to criticism of the text. His aim was to establish the true text in the face of all the variant readings. This true text is the true Word of God, of which theology is the statement of the grammatical rules. Literal reading was for him therefore the philological and lexical rather than the nonmetaphorical or nonallegorical meaning of statements. It was a philological rather than literary reading of the text, reinforcing the absence of figural interpretation from his commentary, the *Gnomon novi testamenti.* As a literal reader and a purely textual or "lower" critic he avoided questions of historical or "higher" criticism, particularly those of the genuineness of texts. He took the authenticity of a text for granted, once one had got beyond the verbal variations in its documentary tradition. In his own day even his lower criticism was controversial enough. But it obviously led, and led rapidly, to genuinely historical criticism of the Bible. And once propositional meaning and ostensive reference had become identified under the independent authority of the latter, "literal sense" would no longer signify the directly descriptive or depictive literary sense of a passage but only its philological and lexical meaning, exactly as Bengel had held. As a result the real meaning of the passage would then be a matter for the historical critic to explain, since he alone could show the space–time occurrence to which it referred or its context in real historical life. After Bengel's day the estimate of the verbal sense rapidly assumed the position of an important technical aid to interpretation, which nonetheless came to be of secondary significance in the order of explanation.

The loss of a literary reading of the biblical stories and the concomitant loss of figural interpretation did not mean that Bengel lacked completely for a broader framework of interpretation than the philological. Bengel was self-consciously orthodox, and proudly acknowledged the close connection between his literal and his theological reading of the Bible. He rejected the Protestant scholastic reduction of the Bible to the proof-texting interpretation of a series of dogmas. The doctrine of emphasis which endowed the words of the Bible with as much force, overtone, and hidden spiritual meaning as they could bear was for him a bridge from the isolated and purely grammatical or philological reading of single passages to an understanding of the Bible as a unitary whole. Yet unlike some other pietist commentators he always insisted on the close connection between literal and spiritual reading. "Most learned men," he wrote, "shun the spirit, and, consequently, do not treat even the letter rightly." [11]

It was a reciprocal relation. There is an inner word or meaning given with the outer word; and appropriate to this state of affairs there is a grammatical reading, open to all who have the training and native ability, and a spiritual reading restricted to those who are awakened to it by the Holy Spirit. There is a special stance, in other words, which allows religious access to the truth of scripture, i.e. to its applicative interpretation and to its explicative meaning. To understand properly is to be awakened and to grasp the kindred spirit, the *Theopneustie,* of sacred texts and/or writers. The most striking impact of this position was to come when historical criticism had loosened the tight connection that prevailed in Bengel's as in Spener's and Francke's day between grammatical and inner or mystical sense, and between literal and spiritual understanding. Once the common biblical world in its apparently common outward meaning started to break up, a kind of reading became all-important, which stressed the self's distinctive perspective upon the text. The view came to prevail that such a distinctive perspective alone allows a living connection with the Bible.

However, the doctrine of emphasis and of the mystical sense of scripture in conjunction with literal reading could have an additional impact, closer to the kind of reading Cocceius had given the Bible. Bengel's *Ordo temporum* (1741) is a projection from the Bible's report of the sequence of the history of salvation to its future consummation in Christ's thousand-year reign. No longer figural interpretation, the knowledge of this history is a mixture of mystical expansion upon the literal sense's "hidden" meaning and the assumption that prophecy is predictive ostensive reference by a kind of historical extrapolation of past signs into future events. The numerical schemes of the Bible, especially those of the Book of Revelation, now allow to the devout mind a kind of inexact but nonetheless basically correct plotting of the course and the periodization not only of past events but also of those that are still hidden in the future.

The doctrine of emphasis and the experimentation with the reference of numerical schemes to events in the overarching world of common history disappeared soon enough from responsible scholarship, although both have remained standard ploys in

Christian folk piety. But Bengel was an earnest of the future in a variety of ways. Combining responsible scholarship with single-minded devoutness, he sought to unite the Bible's inspiredness with its content as a reliable record not so much of dogma as of the sequence of historical facts in which the divine economy of salvation is at work, and both of these with a critical analysis of the text as a written source or document. If the philological side of his work previews the relation of Pietism to historical criticism, the other, "spiritual" side is an earnest of biblical theology of the *heilsgeschichtliche* type. The economy of salvation is the content of the Bible, its meaning as a unitary canon constituted by its reference to the immanently connected temporal sequence of saving facts including the Bible as well as all history, and by the inspiredness of the text or (increasingly) the writers. The Bible is thus a unity in meaning, on the one hand because it is the reliable record of a special and connected historical sequence, on the other because it is pervaded by one and the same spirit working through writers and text and calling upon the reader for the same stance of faith.

BIBLICAL THEOLOGY AS THE HISTORY OF SALVATION

As one moves beyond the eighteenth into the nineteenth century, the ultimate identity that Cocceius and Bengel could assume between the special history of salvation and universal history began to break up, and the *heilsgeschichtliche Schule*'s framework for the meaningfulness and unity of biblical reference becomes increasingly that special history alone, giving it an awkward logical status. Since this school of thought had subsumed the biblical narratives' meaning under the heading of real, ostensive reference just as much as some of the more rationalist commentators had done, that history as factual data in temporal sequence would presumably have to belong in the same temporal framework with any other temporal sequences. In principle it should, like all historical data, be equally accessible to the understanding of all men. But it is obviously not understood in the same way by pious and by secular commentators, nor do pious commentators know how to relate the sacred history to the rest of the historical world. The relation of this sequence to ordinary historical events was never cleared up in the scheme of salvation history. Moreover, the scheme was made more complex to avoid head-on collision with such matters. Increasingly, salvation history, while remaining the real reference and therefore the unitary meaning of the Bible, was taken to be an amalgam of the cumulative occurrences and the cumulative responses to them. The "saving facts" are real and historical but not in an ordinary way that would open them up to religiously neutral verification. The reference of the Bible and thus its meaning is the interaction of a sequence of temporal occurrences with a sequence of interpretations within the sacred writings. Interpretation is obviously a distinct item from the occurrence both in the object of analysis and in the stance of the interpreter. Unlike the relation between occurrence and meaning in Calvin and the great sweep of the Western tradition of figural interpretation, "meaning" or "interpretive sense" here is no longer constituted by the cumulative and specific occurrence pattern of the story. We are far from "realistic" interpretation. In the first place the unitary meaning of the biblical narratives is totally subordinated to the history of salvation as their logically separable historical reference. In addition, the historical reference in question now is as much a phenomenon in the history of mind or spirit as it is a realistic phenomenon. History of salvation and history of interpreted and reinterpreted tradition join together.

In addition to regarding biblical unity as constituted by realistic history as well as the response ingredient in it, members of the *heilsgeschichtliche Schule,* like some more liberal commentators, began to view the unity of factual and saving meaning in scripture as a matter of the distinctive positioning of the reader or interpreter. The Bible is not simply, if at all, a book of dogma for intellectual assent. While it is a book of facts, it is obviously far more than that. Its inspiration and its topics involve writer, text, and reader in a common mode of disposition or faith. To hold these and other aspects of meaning together is in effect to unite explicative and applicative meaning. To do so is to affirm that the Bible's unitary meaning is not accessible except by the special self-positioning of the reader as a person toward the text and what it "witnesses to." One's special stance comes to enter into, but it is first of all independent of, any "world," biblical or otherwise. From this stance the self then takes up a position toward its meaningful world. In effect, the reader's material contribution to the meaning of the text by his personal position toward it involves the further affirmation that the reader must enter a present context directly related to the same religiously meaningful reality he finds in the Bible, so that all three are involved in the same spiritual framework. And into it the Bible's special history is also drawn. The history of salvation is thus an overarching reality or world which encompasses a self's present relation to God or Christ, together with the history of such relations and the factual occurrences in which it was embodied, as witnessed by the Bible. The Bible becomes a "witness" to a history, rather than a narrative text. Its meaning is a unitary complex consisting of the history of saving events, the history of the witnesses' faithful response to them and finally the present faithful stance toward that complex history as a present and future reality.

Among nineteenth-century theologians Gottfried Menken (1768–1831), Johann Tobias Beck (1804–78), and, above all, J. C. K. von Hofmann (1810–77), and the so-called Erlangen confessional school represented different versions of this view. It came down, with all its ambiguities, into the biblical theology that formed part of twentieth-century neo-orthodoxy. With all its profession of the narrative unity of the biblical writing within the one history of salvation to which it witnesses, this outlook was obviously far from realistic narrative interpretation. In realistic narrative, the meaning of a story is a function of the specific storied representation. In the *heilsgeschichtliche* version of biblical theology its meaning is a function of the temporal sequence of events and interpretive tradition to which the story refers, together with the interpretive stance taken toward this complex sequence. Meaning is the upshot of the interaction of these factors. Event and interpretation are logically distinct but not separately available. The meaning of a realistic passage is the event and its interpretation. Precritical realistic narrative interpretation on the other hand never gave such an independent status to the positioning perspective upon the story, nor did it separate story sequence from actual sequence.

10 Herder on the Bible: The Realistic Spirit in History

Pietism leading to a salvation-historical interpretation of the narrative unity of the Bible was not alone in bringing together the history of events with the history of group perspective, and with the material contribution of a distinctively present self-positioning to their interpretation. A similar outlook characterized the important romantic reaction in theology against the fashions of the religious Enlightenment at the end of the eighteenth century. Its most distinguished representatives were Johann Gottfried Herder (1744–1803), and Friedrich Schleiermacher (1768–1834) a generation later. Schleiermacher, a far greater technical scholar and theologian than Herder, was concerned with the unity of the New Testament only, denying any material or more than "merely" historical continuity between Judaism and early Christianity. Herder on the other hand, a much more distinguished literary commentator than Schleiermacher, was an ardent admirer of the Old Testament; and though he was skeptical of any reduction of the variety of the biblical writings to an artificial unity, he clearly affirmed a continuity of spirit and content between the two Testaments in his *Letters Concerning the Study of Theology*[1] (hereafter cited by number).

Deeply influenced by the Pietism of his widely known mentor and friend, Johann Georg Hamann (1730–88), Herder also felt the impact of the writings of men like Jean-Jacques Rousseau in his quest for an expression of the "inwardness and individuality of the human soul" as the "ultimate depth of historical life." [2] From Hamann in particular came Herder's persuasion that poetry is "the mother tongue of the human race." [3] It was an important point, for in his hands it shaped the twin convictions that poetry is in its origins no mere deliberate artifact, and language no mere signpost representing sense data and the substances for which they stand, views at which Rousseau had already hinted in his *Second Discourse*. Among the earliest, most primitive peoples in particular, language is the immediate, natural and naive (two terms of highest encomium) expression of their way of life, their sensibility, their natural and communal spirit. As Goethe phrased Herder's views when he reflected much later in the tenth book of *Dichtung und Wahrheit* on their momentous first conversations in Strassbourg, "Poetry is a gift to the world and its peoples, not the private inheritance of a few elegant, educated men." [4]

A gift indeed it was, at once divine and human, to be read as humanly as possible. That precisely was Herder's injunction also in the instance of that noblest expression of the most ancient and natural poetic spirit, the Old Testament: "In human fashion must one read the Bible; for it is a book written by men for men: Human is the language, human the external means with which it was written and preserved; human finally is the sense with which it may be grasped, every aid that illumines it, as well as the aim and use to which it is to be applied." [5] The contrast with Bishop Lowth is instructive. Lowth too had looked for the origin of poetry in religion and in the popular imagination. Nonetheless his analysis of Hebrew poetry had been an endeavor to classify it in accordance with proper technical categories derived from Greek, Roman, and neoclassical usage. Herder's attitude toward Lowth's *de sacra poesi Hebraeorum* was quite ambivalent. He admired the work but criticized what we would call its formalism. By contrast, and quite characteristically, Herder called his own equivalent endeavor (published 1782–83) "Concerning the *Spirit* of Hebrew Poetry." [6] He was always concerned with entering the "spirit" of an age, a man, a people or a work. His endeavor was to his mind not only different from but often impeded in principle by technical, categorial investigation.

It seemed to Herder that understanding an ancient language in its poetic effulgence is a matter of entering imaginatively and empathetically the world of the imagination and culture that produced it. (He enriched the German language with the term *Einfühlung* to describe the process.[7]) This is what the interpreter must learn to do, rather than merely gain technical mastery over the special metaphorical and rhythmic structure, and the specific genre constituting the language-world of a particular kind of poetry. It has frequently been noted that in Herder's hands interpretation is not a technical or critical analysis of aesthetic products but an empathetic submission to the author, his depictions, and the atmosphere out of which they arise.[8]

> Become [he declaims in a famous passage about the Old Testament] with shepherds a shepherd, with a people of the sod a man of the land, with the ancients of the Orient an Easterner, if you wish to relish these writings in the atmosphere of their origin; and be on guard especially against abstractions of dull, new academic prisons, and even more against all so-called artistry which our social circles force and press on those sacred archetypes of the most ancient days.[9]

Paradoxically, this total surrender, which was the price of entry into the spirit of any specific past to which one was relating himself, was necessarily accompanied by an equally pervasive detachment from it at every other level. The *Einfühlung* into another specific, historical spirit or age, though aesthetically uncritical, was confined solely to the aesthetic mode. No particular past manifestation had any more normative claim on one's own religious, philosophical, moral, or even aesthetic positioning of oneself than any other. He did believe that the Bible contained normative religious truth, but the threat of inconsistency hung over this view. He saved himself from it by turning the Bible, and divine revelation with it, into the fullest expression of the one human spirit under the educative guidance of divine providence. To read the Bible, including its poetic spirit, in the fullest human manner—rather than merely with the eyes of technical criticism or traditional dogmatism—is also to read it as a divine gift.

If ancient poetry was a spontaneous and natural expression, rather than deliberately or self-consciously poetic in design, no technical depiction or genre-assignment can do justice to it. One's recapitulative experience of the spirit out of which it arose, sympathetically noting the authenticity and appropriateness of the particular written expression to the original spirit, is the sum total of understanding. Less romantic, more rationalistically inclined commentators—particularly in the burgeoning analysis of biblical stories as a species of "myth," which arose in the wake of the pioneering Göttingen classical scholar Christian Gottlob Heyne (1729–1812)—took Herder's step but refused to stop where he did. For them, the critical question of the factual verification or the historical origin of the biblical stories became all-important, or they consigned them to technical genres such as myth or allegory. The latter option, obviating the historical fact question where it seemed useless, was supplied as an alternative designation for understanding the stories. Herder refused to take this further more technical step beyond empathy, not so much because it was wrong but because it was peripheral and because it would elide what he thought to be genuine understanding. He was not by any means uninterested in the question of the historical factuality of the stories of the Bible, and he certainly stressed the realistic character of some of them vigorously. But the context in which he raised the issues of factuality or fact-likeness allowed them no ultimate explanatory status in their own right. Neither the one nor the other serves as an ultimate interpretive device. The essential thing was to understand the spirit that led to this kind of realistic writing. Anything less than that was neither explanation of the writings nor explanation of our understanding of them. Presumably as a result of this attitude, he failed to distinguish between factuality and fact-likeness, even though as an aesthetic rather than historical commentator he came closer than any other major figure at the end of the eighteenth-century to taking realistic narrative seriously as a literary explanatory category, and not merely as a clue to the historical or nonhistorical status of the stories. (Johann Jakob Hess, a Swiss pastor and theologian of far narrower compass of interests than Herder, came closest to his views on the realism of the biblical stories.)

In the last analysis, Herder not only could not distinguish

clearly between factuality and fact-likeness, but both—as realistic story pattern—were dependent variables of the one true explanatory constant they represented in common: the experience or the spirit of the culture from which they had been written. In the case of the Old and New Testament writings, this was largely a historical experience or spirit, as Herder never tired of stressing.[10] But he left the meaning of history in this context ambiguous in a virtually systematic way. Characteristically he used it to refer to the past, *res gestae,* but at the same time to narrative accounts of the past, especially to documentary accounts we now have before us of happenings still earlier than the accounts themselves. Finally, and most typically, history could also mean the kind of consciousness represented by a specific kind of account, namely, a specifically historical consciousness. To be "historical," then, an account need not be of any specific occurrence that had actually taken place.

Hartlich and Sachs[11] claim that Herder did not care about the question of the biblical stories' factuality, but this is an oversimplification. Anyone who reads Herder with care is bound to note his deep concern about this matter, together with (and often despite) the ambiguity of his use of "history" which we have noted and which led him to an aesthetic rather than factual view of what it is to understand the history-like or historical writings of the Bible. To his imaginary correspondent in *Letters Concerning the Study of Theology* he wrote: "I would fault you greatly, my friend, for staying with the study of theology if you are not convinced of the historical truth of the first Christian history" (vol. 10, no. 14). Again, "Christianity has an infinite stake in the simplicity and truth of this story. Whoever turns a gospel of Christ into a novel has wounded my heart, even though he had done so with the most beautiful novel in the world" (vol. 10, no. 19). "The basis of all Christianity is historical occurrence and the pure grasp of it—simple, plain faith actively expressed" (vol. 10, no. 14).

Since Hartlich and Sachs themselves can see no explanatory categories beyond the disjunctive, exhaustive, and ultimate categories of "history" or "myth" in the face of the "fact" question concerning history-like biblical accounts, they can subject Herder, with his ambiguity about history as a category of explanation, to a brisk verdict of inadequate analytical discernment, especially of the historical variety. This is the source of their drastic oversimplification of his view. Herder was indeed uninterested in the factuality or nonfactuality of the accounts in Genesis, dwelling instead on their peculiar aesthetic character. But he had considerable interest in the factual content of subsequent stories, and he was passionately committed to a belief in a factual core of the accounts in the synoptic gospels. His arguments for the historicity of the latter were indeed not critical in a sophisticated sense; he appealed largely to their immediate convincingness or appropriateness, for example to their artless simplicity, an argument one encounters again and again in the eighteenth century. But in any case, his interest in the historical veracity and integrity of the accounts is obvious. In this vein he criticizes not only Reimarus's imputation of dishonesty to the Evangelists' explanation of Jesus's purpose, but also the thesis of Lessing, whom he greatly admired, that miracles are improbable (vol. 10, no. 13). On the other hand, Herder was anything but a biblical literalist. This is shown by the fruits of his considerable effort to analyze the literary origin of the gospels. He found it in a common oral preaching source which transmitted the words of Jesus more faithfully than their narrative framework. (Critical though he was of Lessing on the notion of miracle, he was heavily dependent on him in this literary source-critical work.[12])

However, while he insisted that the central fact claims of the gospels and certain other biblical stories were absolutely indispensable to a *Christian* reading of the Bible, he did so in the broader interpretive context of their place in the history of the human spirit in its various unique and distinctive written self-expressions. And therefore the fact claim, no matter how important for the theological candidate and the Christian in general, is taken up exegetically or hermeneutically into a wider framework. Neither technical literary classification nor status as factual report is for Herder the explanation of a writing's meaning. Hermeneutically

a biblical writing, even if it reported facts, was something more
and logically different from a report. (Nor, for that matter, was it
a myth even if it contained nothing but fiction.) Even when
Herder makes an ardent plea for the factual veracity of early
Christianity or the simple, realistic quality of a particular biblical
writing, his own exegetical point of view has a way of remaining
at the aesthetic level, in the sense that the reader's most important
task remains neither the reference nor the realism of the account
but the direct *Einfühlung* into the spirit whose written expression
the account is.

Herder was strongly persuaded that the written expression is
perfectly congruent with its subject matter; but it is not itself the
subject matter of the Bible—a simple but crucial difference
between Herder and any kind of realistic narrative interpretation.
Given that distinction in essence between depiction and meaning,
it finally does not matter whether there is harmony between
subject matter and depiction (as Herder constantly maintained),
or hiatus; the important thing is that the narrative itself does not
directly render what it depicts. The narrative is neither logically
(or essentially) identical with the subject matter depicted, nor
does it render directly accessible the temporal sequence talked
about. The cohesion of depiction with subject matter on the one
hand, and of subject matter with its accessibility to present
understanding on the other, requires something more than the
narrative account itself.

There is, for Herder, a convergence in harmony of these
logically distinct elements in interpretation. Fact claim as well as
realistic rendering converge toward the original cultural spirit
appropriate to both, of which they are fit expressions. But for that
spirit to be rendered effectively, there has to be a convergence
between fact claim, depiction, and ancient spirit, and also
between this amalgam and the appropriate stance of present spirit
or present self-positioning. This ambivalence in the location of
meaning undercuts any sharp distinction between explicative and
applicative sense, a fact of which the very notion of *Einfühlung* is
almost a guarantee. In addition, the convergence of all these

factors forbids the clear-cut identification of exegetical meaning
with factual affirmation or fact-like narrative depiction. He
believes in the latter, and yet he believes even more in the spirit
that gives rise to it.

In a way, therefore, Emanuel Hirsch is absolutely right in
attributing a well-nigh systematic ambiguity to Herder's position
on the historical factuality of biblical miracles:[13]

> Herder objects profoundly to destroying the distinctiveness of
> biblical history by mixing with it modern notions that are
> foreign to it. This history is full of miracle at least in the sense
> that the people taking part in it and the narrators reporting
> it constantly experience miracle and incomprehensible di-
> vine activity. If one explains away their experience in a
> consistently natural way one destroys everything: Divine
> revelation and nurture become dissimulation. Best off is he
> who takes the miracle in it simply as the historical experience
> of those concerned and of the witnesses, and exceeds the
> limits of our knowledge neither by assertion of the supernatu-
> ral intervention of God nor by reductionist explanation. Such
> a man holds to the truth and cares little about the rest.
> Accordingly, Herder moves out of the way—with a consist-
> ency that can irritate to the point of fury the critic who wants
> to nail him down precisely—of every ultimate, determinate
> opinion, and remains at the level of relativity in understand-
> ing the opinion of experiencers and witnesses in their
> humanly significant traits, in accordance with the truth of
> the heart expressed in it, and in justifying it as right for them.

But Hirsch's point (and to some extent that of Hartlich and Sachs
also) is more nearly correct at a different level from that at which
it is expressed. For despite Herder's view that natural instead of
miraculous explanation should prevail wherever possible, he
clearly does affirm his belief in the factual truth of many biblical
miracles, especially those of the New Testament, and centrally
that of the resurrection. Rather than at the level of the
affirmation or denial of fact claims, the systematic ambiguity

apparently so irritating to critics comes at the corresponding
hermeneutical level: whether or not the factuality or the fact-likeness—the realistic nature of an admittedly realistic narrative
account, including a miraculous one—is a significant element in
its meaning. It is in this respect that Herder can be thoroughly
ambiguous. He can affirm the factual truth of an account or its
realistic character as writing, or both, and he can even stress the
importance of both; and yet he can remain quite ambiguous as to
whether the meaning of the account is the spatiotemporal
occurrences to which it refers or the depiction it renders, or
whether the meaning is the spirit or outlook that generated such a
writing. And in the long run it is the latter that is more important
and, if anything, becomes the clue to the former.

That is to say, then, that in Herder's view it is the spirit of the
biblical writings that is to be taken as strongly realistic and as
explaining the realism of the writings. The biblical stories are
historical or history-like; they are neither myths or allegories nor
heroic or epic inventions but natural, simple, and straightforward
accounts of actions from credible dispositions. They are to be read
as humanly as possible not only because they are not the
mechanical products of direct divine dictation, but also because
they are not deliberate, elevated, poetic contrivances on the part
of their human authors. They present credible motives, inter-
changes, and activities, appropriate in each case to the level of the
human and historical development in which the text in question
originated, and to the setting whence it arose. Herder's ambiguity
lies at this rather than the level suggested by Hirsch, or in his
supposed inability, attributed to him by Hartlich and Sachs, to
resolve a dichotomy between history and myth in the explanation
of these stories. He is either unable or he refuses to see that he has
to make up his mind between the location of meaning in realistic
depiction on the one hand or, on the other, in the natural,
realistic, historical spirit fitly expressed in the writings.

If the outlook, spirit, or consciousness represented (no matter
how fitly) by a narrative text, rather than the text itself, is the
text's meaning, or even if this is one alternative in an ambiguous

position, then meaning is no longer the product of the cumulative narrative but has instead become a function of a universal and distinctively human phenomenon—that of cultural spirit, differentiated into a variety of irreducibly unique historical expressions of itself. The basic and indispensable condition for understanding this phenomenon, which rapidly became a technical explanatory category as well, is that the interpreter knows himself to be partaking of a specific historical location, that of the present. Once the interpretive perspective has in this fashion become a condition for understanding explicative meaning, the realistic narrative stance has been destroyed, no matter how strongly the realistic quality or spirit of the writing is affirmed.

Calvin had already put his finger on the difference between realistic narrative interpretation and the kind of perspective Herder would adopt much later, when he argued that figural meaning is part of the specific historical context in which the figure arises, and not a pattern retrospectively applied to the earlier context from the vantage point of a later situation. It is precisely this affirmation that Herder could no longer make clearly. To be sure, the historical and interpretive continuity expressed in figural interpretation (which he affirmed) lay for him in the continuity of outlook or spirit expressed in it. But this continuity, given indeed in historical development, was not itself or conceivable without the stance of retrospective interpretive empathy.

Moreover, in Herder's view typology or figuration requires more than this interpretive, retrospective stance. He no longer sees it as the reference, at once literary and historical, which a specific earlier event has to a later, without detraction from its own reality or meaning. While Herder detested the spirit of Rationalism and Deism in religion, he could not return to a pattern of thought antedating these developments. He could not—indeed, he would have been the last to try to—undo the intellectual history of his own century. The literal fulfillment of specific prophecies in exact detail hundreds of years later was no more credible to him than it had been to Anthony Collins early in the century. For Herder, history develops slowly and without missing stages between earlier and later times. Figuration changes for him from the connectedness of two temporally widely separated specific occurrences to a slowly accumulating and general sense of anticipation reaching a climactic fulfillment.

His antirationalist or at least nonrationalistic historical relativism dictated to Herder a kind of aesthetic submissiveness to each ancient depiction in turn, which a man like Voltaire would have scorned completely, but it also allowed—indeed it forced—his normative independence from every one of them and therefore moved him toward cultural explanations not so much of biblical events as of their meaning, and of the connections of meaning among events and their depictions. This attitude gave a cast at once traditional and yet modernistic to his view of the Bible, much to the confusion of contemporary and later commentators. Not quite consistently with this relativism Herder found the simplicity and naturalness of spirit pervading the Bible, "the book of books," a convincing expression of its unique truth. It is a persuasive expression of the fact that a mysterious providence is cumulatively at work in its pervasive outlook, but in such a way that the natural, historical meaningfulness of the book is utilized and not subverted.

Not one to reduce historical and literary variety to uniformity, Herder nevertheless found in the Bible a unity which was largely that of history—in his ambiguous sense, i.e. the amalgam of cumulative events and changing, developing outlooks—together with the spiritual perspective which is at once the present interpretive view and the applicative meaning of the Bible. "You are right, my friend," he writes to his imaginary correspondent (vol. 11, no. 39),

> that if the sum of what the Bible teaches us is theology, and in its application practical theology, the chief perspective of pupil and teacher must be directed upon this. As a consequence it does not matter alone what every splint and nail signified individually in its own place, but what it means to

us now, beyond times and cultures, in the totality of the
building in which providence has placed it. The purpose of
the first is simply its own isolated knowledge; the second is
necessary for its use for our time. The first makes the biblical
antiquarian, the second the biblical theologian.

He goes on to say that it is our part, not that of those within the
pages of the as yet uncompleted Bible, to see the whole of the
building, a point to be remembered particularly in connection
with typology. The question is not

> whether this or that person in the Old Testament recognized
> himself clearly as a type, or whether his time recognized him
> as such, but whether in the sequence of times he was pointed
> to as an archetype. . . . Only later illumination, the clear
> succession of the developing sense in the sequence of time,
> together with the analogy of the whole, shows us the building
> in its light and shadow.

In this sense of a view of the Bible as a whole which we can
exercise, Herder urges a *Symbolik* of the Bible, i.e. recourse to
analogies and figures providing a sense of its unity. This unity is
real enough, but for its realization our later perspective is
indispensable. The result of such a view, it seems to him, is that
"the sum of the Old and New Testaments is Christ with his
invisible, eternal kingdom. What else would there be for human
nature to hope and strive for than just this kingdom which
prophets promised, which Christ brought to the world, toward
which all those of every age worked who were good and true?"
(ibid.).

It is a retrospective interpretation in which the self-positioning
of the interpreter is indispensable. If that stance is the condition
for knowing the bond of the Bible, the bond itself is the Bible's
history—a history that is at once the outworking of God's
providence and the continuous quest of the human race. Com-
menting on the use of texts in preaching, Herder says that most of
them are history or narrative (*Geschichte*), parables, and the

teaching interwoven with them (vol. 11, no. 40). Again: "Why is the largest part of the Bible history? And why is all poetry, doctrine, prophetic language [in it] based on simple history? Why otherwise than because God wanted to speak to us in scripture as he speaks to us in nature, in his intimate word as in his open works—naturally and actively" (vol. 10, no. 12). But once more we must remember to interpret history, even "fact," in his ambiguous sense. There is no fact without spirit, without consciousness, spirit, or interpretation—then as now. And there is no spirit of the past that is not understood in relation to the present interpreting spirit. There is therefore, in this historicizing and aestheticizing context, no explication that is not on its own terms also application.

In this complex sense as well as context, "history" is at once the revelation of God and the cultural development of natural human consciousness. "The more human, the more internal to human beings, the more intimate and natural one conceives God's work and word to be, the more certain one can be that one conceives of it as it was originally, nobly and divinely. Everything unnatural is ungodly; that which is most supernaturally-divine becomes most natural" (ibid.). History, rather than dogma or verbal inspiration *ex machina*, is the instrument of divine revelation. But revelation-as-history has both for its aim and its procedure the education of the human race to its full human and humane stature. Herder expressed these notions not in the same way as Lessing in *The Education of the Human Race*, but express them he did. For Lessing the religious development of mankind was itself the revelation of God and not merely the instrument of that revelation. That development was finally not only the aim of but the substitute for revealed religion. Independently of Lessing, though with full awareness of his views, Herder expressed a similar opinion,[14] though in a more conservative and synergistic vein, divine and human actions merging, rather than being (as for Lessing) identical in essence.

If history is education, then no matter what the impact of events, the focus and connective bond and thus the narrative tissue of history lies in the development of mankind's spirit in the process of education, and not in the interaction of specific persons and specific events. As it turns out, the pattern of biblical figuration and thus of the unity of "the whole building" fits into this scheme for Herder. The connective web between earlier and later biblical accounts is indeed in one sense figural, earlier views and pronouncements being images, figures, or archetypes of what comes later, especially of the Messiah. Herder notes that figural fulfillment is neither a forced retrospective accommodation, artificially or even dishonestly adapting an earlier and different meaning to a later situation for purposes of popular teaching, nor on the other hand is it the miraculous proof of scriptural truth by the demonstration that an event was predicted and described in accurate detail hundreds of years earlier.

Rather than being either a rationalistic or a mechanical-orthodox device, figuration is the broad anticipation of a later and richer spiritual condition by an earlier, questing, spiritual outlook. No specific Old Testament prophetic passage is to be torn out of its context and applied necessarily to Christ (vol. 10, no. 18). But from within its general historical and the speaker's personal thought-context, a passage may well be a broad anticipation of the future. Prophecy (*Weissagung*) becomes a broad "vista into the future [*Aussicht in die Zukunft*]. . . . "If it was Christ who founded the actually eternal kingdom which David, Solomon and their successors could not found, then he belongs not indirectly but most directly into their prophecies; only that they at the time could not yet or could only darkly see the mode and shape of his kingdom, but kept to God's word and in confidence gave themselves over to the future." Clear and specific reference of a prophecy to a specific later event "destroys completely the prophetic spirit, the only gradually increasing clarity and generally the primitive impression of each prophecy." The words of the men of the Old Testament arose, like those of others, from the urgings of their hearts, and hence from within their temporal conditions. The shape which these words were to assume in the passage of time they could not see; only the future could see it.

The meaning of a single text is not one specific conceptual construct but a historically changing phenomenon (ibid.).

The chain of prophecies and images gradually clarifies God's purpose and its increasingly specific contours. In this gradual and nonmechanistic sense one may indeed speak of a genuine fulfillment of the Old Testament in the New, not only completing the Old Testament but also saving it from an abrupt and purely adventitious ending. Though the process is gradual, general, and anticipatory, it is more than mere natural anticipation: God's providence is at work through the historical direction. The historical facts, including miracle but especially the fulfillment of prophecy, are the foundation of Christianity. Though the fulfillment can be seen only retrospectively as the synergistic effect of providential revelation and immanent, natural historical education, its substance is a *genuine* fulfillment of earlier vistas by later events and the fuller perspectives that go with them (ibid.).

In its very ambiguity Herder's was an extraordinarily rich, subtle, and delicately balanced performance. Revelation or divine providence and immanent historical development flow harmoniously and synergistically into each other, without detriment to either. The balance and mutual supplementation of historical occurrences—including such miracles as the resurrection of Jesus—with religious apprehension is equally delicate and complete. the thread of the biblical narratives' continuity, and thus of the unity of the Bible, does indeed lie in the increasing clarification of God's purpose in the consciousness or spirit of his people, but not without the lesson coming to their spirit by the external historical circumstances, the sheer or positive events told in the Bible. Finally, Herder balances the forward motion of this historical unfolding perfectly with the condition indispensable for understanding it in its unity as divine and human process—the spiritual kinship that a present interpretive positioning must have with the historically distinctive religious positioning toward which it is directed. Explicative sense merges perfectly and fully into applicative meaning in the quest for the unitary meaning of the Bible in the midst of its many and distinct historical expressions.

Hirsch rightly says that Herder dissolved the notions of an unvarying dogma, and that what remains is on the one hand the history of dogma and on the other a biblical theology, that is, a Christian perspective constantly renewed by its contact with the Bible, "which gives to the preacher clarity and perspective for guiding his hearers to the living understanding of God's word." He is right, further, in distinguishing between Herder and the Pietists because Herder, no matter how conservative he sounded, was not interested in returning from an ecclesiastically dogmatic to a simpler, more directly biblicist doctrine and piety. Instead, Herder was concerned with "the making contemporary [*Vergegenwärtigung*] of biblical history as the most profound human and religious means of education." [15] The mergence of explication with application, the well-nigh programmatic indispensability of *Einfühlung*, the centrality of spirit with its unity-in-differentiation between past outlooks and present self-positioning all testify to this transportation of the past into the present which is the fruit of the reverse movement—the self-distancing of the interpreter from his nonetheless ineluctably present location in time through empathetic, imaginative entry into the past. *Vergegenwärtigung* of the Bible was indeed what Herder sought for. In the process of this quest the historical "facts" and realistic depictions merged with the presentation of the past consciousness or spirit in which they were written, to form together the meaning of the Bible for present spirit or consciousness. Perhaps this mergence was in part indeed a function of Herder's admitted—and regretted—inability to achieve conceptual and depictive power and clarity.[16] But it was also the warp and woof of his thinking. In the words of a recent commentator on Herder's understanding of the Old Testament, "within the hermeneutical circle his point of departure is quite clearly the present time, he himself who steps from here into the past." [17] And understanding the spirit of the past in its own right he sought to bring it into the present from which he himself began.

Herder was the one major commentator in Germany at the end of the eighteenth century who came close to a realistic interpretation of the explicative meaning of biblical narrative, without reducing that realism either to evidence in favor of historical veracity or to part of an accommodationist theory of the biblical stories. He did not simply identify realistic depiction with ostensive or ideal reference.

But on the other hand he also did not finally come to grips with realistic reading as an interpretive procedure in its own right. His explanation of the unitary and significant meaning of the Bible finally hovers between the spatiotemporal reference of realistic accounts—and whenever he takes this path their peculiar narrative mode does, after all, become evidence for their essential factual correctness and in that sense their historicity—and the unique, realistic, or historical spirit or consciousness of the Jewish people, which was fitly expressed in a realistic rather than heroic or artificially poetic mode, down to the very language and poetic idiom of the Bible.[18] More pervasively than the reduction of meaning to ostensive reference, one may observe in his procedure the inevitable religious-apologetic motif which kept realistic narrative interpretation at bay. This was done by casting the Bible directly into the larger framework of applicative meaningfulness. In Herder's case this meant incorporating the Bible's meaning into a developing "spirit" which speaks aesthetically-religiously to our own spirit. Realistic and figural reading, which had allowed the reader to be incorporated and thus located in the world made accessible by the narration, here gives way to an independent spiritual self-positioning which then locates itself as well as specific past epochs by relating itself to earlier spiritual positionings, locating them in turn by their presently accessible, or spiritually present recapitulation.

The result is a modern substitute for the unitary meaning of the Bible that had been provided in earlier days by figural interpretation as a fit extension of literal reading. Now that this cohesion has been ruptured and the older kind of figuration consigned to superstition, Herder has offered a highly ambiguous alternative suggestion for the unitary meaning of the Bible, a suggestion which has substituted a spiritual-historical bond for the earlier realism and in turn wedded this bond both dubiously and inconstantly to claims of the unitary meaning of the Bible as at least partially factual and true history.

Taken one way, Herder's reflections on the Bible and its unity—the prime problem, we recall, that hermeneutics in contrast to historical criticism posed for the Bible's theological authority—resemble those of the biblical theology which built up from Cocceius through Pietism to the *heilsgeschichtliche Schule.* Unlike the Pietists, Herder wrote at a level naturally combining an aesthetic stance with that of a historical relativist; but he shared the Pietists' conviction that the unitary content of the Bible is the history of saving events, self-differentiated into a sequence of temporal stages. This sequence is at once aimed providentially toward Christ and yet an immanently connected historical development toward the climax of biblical history in him. It is at the same time also the history of inspired, faithful interpretation, tradition, or outlook, that spirit extending to the very language of the Bible in its distinctiveness. Furthermore, this sequence constituting the Bible's unity is accessible in all its fullness only to a present, self-conscious, self-positioning in kinship to the spirit that permeates the Bible itself.

The difference between Herder and the Pietists involves more than his aesthetic view of the Bible's meaning and authority, his generally far more sophisticated, acculturated views of God, man, and history. In addition, the emphasis on self-positioning that he shares with them is not so much, as it was for them, a direct and religious relation to the religious "objects" of the Bible (Jesus, his blood atonement, and his love, the divine Spirit directly speaking to our hearts from the pages of the Bible, etc.) but a direct relation to the spiritual history in which these objects are ingredient. Yet in their own much more provincial way Pietism and the later *heilsgeschichtliche Schule* were themselves related to the romantic and idealistic modes of sensibility and reflection rapidly rising to dominance in the haute culture of German classical thought and literature at the end of the eighteenth century. It is simply impossible to exaggerate the self-conscious novelty and power of the full-orbed conviction at the end of that century, no matter how far one may see its roots extending into previous history, that a free and self-conscious self-positioning toward the world is an independent and indispensable factor in shaping the depiction of that world with its bearing on the self. It matters little whether this self was the Pietist's self dispositioning itself religiously, that of the Romantic dispositioning itself aesthetically in acute awareness of its own sensibility, that of the philosophical Idealist dispositioning itself in conceptual self-reflexiveness, or that of the budding Existentialist, dispositioning itself in self-committing agency.

With Herder's thought we are well on the road that led many a sensitive commentator, either by way of Pietism or directly to Romanticism and Idealism as modes of interpretation, with their eventual claim to the complete uniqueness of the *Geisteswissenschaften* within the spectrum of human knowledge, their tendency toward historical relativism or "historicism," and, above all, toward the idealist conviction that the knowledge of every spiritual, cultural object (if not all data) has to be analyzed under the scheme of a subject–object, self–other or spirit–world correlation. Even if, for the post-Kantians, this bifurcation must be overcome or even seen as issuing from a precognitive subject–object unity, it is the starting point for knowledge and self-definition. Herder's thought bears a family resemblance to Kant's, their later acrimonious arguments notwithstanding. Though he did not consciously rise to the development of the technical subject–object schema, his view of history bears all the marks of the preschematic sensibility underlying it.

11 The Lack of Realism in German Letters

Herder was by no means isolated in the outlook which is finally so utterly inimical to a realistic perspective of historical and history-like narrative. In the fourteenth book of *Dichtung und Wahrheit*, the book in which he described his first contact with the brothers Jacobi and with that most charming, idiosyncratic, and importunate of meddlers with other people's religious privacy, Johann Kaspar Lavater, Goethe reminisced briefly about a peculiar awareness he first noticed in himself in full strength during his stay in Cologne in 1774. It was decidedly ambivalent in character.[1]

> A feeling that became powerful and expressed itself in various strange ways was the sensibility of the past and the present in one—an intuition which brought something special into the present. Expressed in many of my larger and smaller works, it is beneficent in poetry even if the moment of its immediate expression in life itself must appear strange, inexplicable, and perhaps unpleasant.

The Cologne Cathedral, frozen in unfinished state hundreds of years earlier, was like a ruin to his eyes. A half-executed, monumental conception, it died, incomplete in the midst of its own growth, and that moment of death was preserved to the present viewer. He found it depressing. On the other hand, upon being taken to the impeccably preserved home of a patrician family long since gone, he was aware of the predominantly beneficent side of the same feeling, stimulated in particular by the cheerful and lively family portrait over the fireplace, which gave a vivid semblance of contemporaneity to the whole setting.

Friedrich Meinecke, who cites the experience, speculates that this feeling may well have been a significant point of coordination for Goethe's poetic art and his feeling about history, including his well-known ambivalence and unease, not to say distaste, in the presence of history and historiography.[2] Goethe's fear of history was unusual, but his sensibility of "the past and present in one" was typical and became a cornerstone in the conditions underlying historicism. It was more than insight that past forms of life develop and endure into the present, that we and our institutions —language, culture, state, family—would not be what we are without the preceding history. Rather, it referred to a distinctive mode of consciousness on which our apprehension of the human past depends.

This mode involved an element of imagination and sensibility rather than conceptualization, though philosophers who became deeply engrossed in history, Hegel preeminently, would make strenuous efforts to raise both the mode of cognition and the resulting depictions to the "scientific" or ideational level. Not so Goethe nor, one may suspect, Herder. Goethe, who always called himself a realist, was in any case suspicious of the "German" habit of preferring ideational to sensible grasp, and "abstract" thought to impressions. As he expressed it in an oft-quoted rhetorical exclamation about his German compatriots in the *Conversations with Eckermann:* "Why don't you have the courage for once to give yourselves over to impressions, to enjoy yourselves, to be moved and edified, yes, to be instructed and kindled to greatness? Don't always think that everything is vain if it isn't some abstract notion or idea!"[3] Nonetheless, the non- or pre-ideational sense of the past and present in one was a link between him and those for whom that same sense was lifted to the ideational level, and history was a preoccupation with the endurance of the past in present time. For Goethe this sense was occasioned by outward impressions, to which he in any case always responded with exquisite delicacy and almost painful vividness. Herder's sensibility and imagination were doubtless awakened somewhat differently and were in some respects more nearly inward and linguistic than sensuous. But the similarity in the upshot is striking: past occurrences and forms of life, cut off from their specific and unsubstitutable temporal moorings, are transported with spectral or wraith-like vividness into present experience, brought into it in their very difference from our own forms of life by our inner or outer sensibility. The transport heightens not only the awareness of the past but also of the present, and one's awareness of oneself as present and aware of both present and past.

Meinecke, agreeing with earlier scholars, cites a parallel though not identical instance to that of Goethe from Herder's early manhood. It was an awareness of "strong impressions of a present which is at the same time still living past" (Meinecke does not draw attention to the similarity).[4] In particular, Herder very likely witnessed a wild and primitive Latvian peasant celebration of midsummer night in 1765, an experience that Meinecke associates with his impassioned Rousseauesque search in history, lore, and ballad for an idealized primitive mankind, which in its poetic innocence was the original and unspoiled work of God. (Herder was one of many German enthusiasts for James Mac-Pherson's famous balladic forgery *Ossian.*) In his own way, and with a far less ambivalent and more affirmative attitude toward history than Goethe, Herder too saw the unity of past and present in apprehension.

There turned out to be no more deeply ingrained antirealistic element than this in later eighteenth-century German *haute culture* and its attitude toward history and the task of its depiction. There was nothing quite comparable to it among British history writers or novelists, no matter how seriously they took their own roles as narrators, as Fielding and Gibbon for instance certainly did. Hume, praising the beneficent results gained from the study of history, wrote:[5]

> if we consider the shortness of human life, and our limited knowledge, even of what passes in our own time, we must be sensible that we should be for ever children in understanding, were it not for this invention, which extends our experience

to all past ages, and to the most distant nations; making them contribute as much to our improvement in wisdom, as if they had actually lain under our observation. A man acquainted with history may, in some respect, be said to have lived from the beginning of the world, and to have been making continual additions to his stock of knowledge in every century.

There is no appeal to the privileged position of the experienced present in this statement, and no exhortation to enter into specific past experiences from such a privileged and inalienable position of awareness and self-awareness. Quite apart from all those differences of outlook separating Hume from historicism—for example, the remainder of a notion of perfection and other rationalist tendencies which impeded his discernment of the genuine development of unique and "inner-historical" necessities (so Meinecke)[6]—Hume's felicitous simile indicates that the connection of historical depiction lies in the depiction itself that renders the unitary and sequential world of which the reader discovers himself to be a part. The narrative continuity itself makes accessible the world one needs to understand it. One's own understanding of his world is just as cumulative as the world that is made accessible to him in accretive depiction: he becomes a cultural human being through the historical narrative for which he has a natural affinity because he is part of the world effectively rendered by it; in the mode of knowledge he *is* as old as the history he knows.

Despite superficial resemblances, the spirit of Hume's statement is a world away from Herder's exhortation to become with ancient shepherds a shepherd and, in general, to establish that bond between past and present within one's own self-consciousness which then, and only then, allows the world to unfold in the continuity of its collective historical-spiritual individualities or essences.

Herder's advocacy of empathy as the condition for the connection between past and present, so unlike Hume's metaphor of the history reader's ancient lineage, is but one expression of the burgeoning sense, expressed most articulately in Kant's practical philosophy, that the human self is free, even if the source of its freedom and the manner of its fitting into the natural, casually connected world remains a mystery. The uniqueness and otherness of the self (the subject) from the world (the object) is the condition of human freedom. Its *realization* is the creation of a world, moral for some, religious for others, aesthetic for yet others, in which the self finds an affinity, a home for its sense of being free. For some, the historical world—ambivalently situated as it is between natural casual connectedness and human-spiritual relatedness—became the embodiment of this human freedom, so intimately related to the sense of presence and self-awareness. But even then it is obviously as a distinctive human reality, not to say creation, and not as an overarching "real" world that history is the story of human freedom.

In some writers this preoccupation with human freedom turned into a profound search for and study of the classically balanced individual as the sole motive force of the common life. Schiller, for instance, after his passionate early drama of social and political protest against a morally decadent and politically tyrannical princely absolutism, *Kabale und Liebe* (1784; first called *Luise Millerin*), turned increasingly in an individualistic and classical direction. It came to a climax in his *Briefe über die ästhetische Erziehung des Menschen*, in which the only revolutionary possibility for the common life lies in the harmonious equilibrium of the individual's moral and sensual drives. This alone is the means to the realization of genuine freedom, not only for the individual but for society. To be sure, Schiller's turn in this direction was in part a product of his revulsion against the wilder manifestations of the French Revolution, but the signs of the turn antedated the Revolution, just as Goethe also moved to a classicist stance before the great French upheaval had made its impact, in *Iphigenie auf Tauris* (1787) and *Torquato Tasso* (1789).

In the long run the revival of a classicist ideal of human

balance and harmony was as antagonistic toward a realistic depiction of history as the romantic vision of man's spontaneity in inward sensibility and the advocacy of its untrammeled and immediate outward expression. In Germany, both generally led to a reinforcement of conservative political views, despite early contrary signs among the forerunners of the Romantics, the *Sturm und Drang* writers. The revival of the classical ideal in German letters simply strengthened the tendency. In both, the sense of the reality of inwardness and its tension with external reality prevented, on stylistic and substantive grounds, a development of realistic narrative. Narrative realism, which had begun to develop vigorously in the English novel, did not make the same kind of headway in Germany.

THE LEVEL OF REALISTIC DEPICTION

This situation was the more intriguing for the fact that in some of Lessing's plays, particularly in the "serious comedy" *Minna von Barnhelm* (1767) and the bourgeois tragedy *Emilia Galotti* (1772), a real advance toward realistic literature had been made, in part under the influence of Diderot whom Lessing had translated in 1760. "No more philosophical spirit," he had stated in his preface to *The Theater of Diderot* (1760) "has been occupied with the theater since Aristotle," contrasting Diderot's severe criticism of French classicism favorably with the praise accorded it by "the insipid minds among us, at whose head stands Professor Gottsched." He reacted favorably to Diderot's distinction between farcical and moving comedy (an outgrowth of the *comédie larmoyante*, which had made its appearance in France slightly before Diderot's day).[7] When the time came he aimed to make his own *Nathan der Weise* "as affecting a piece as I have ever written." [8] Diderot also helped move him toward the form of the domestic drama, a mixture of previously fixed genres, portraying a private world in which believable everyday virtues and vices come together as they do in life. Indeed, characters are shaped by the life situation (the "conditions," as Diderot had phrased it) in which they are set, rather than by purely self-subsistent, self-explanatory human qualities which appear in a social and natural vacuum.[9]

As early as 1754 Lessing had said: "I daresay that only those are true comedies which depict virtues as well as vices, the decorous as well as the unfitting, because it is precisely through this mixture that they come closest to their original—human life." [10] He sought to fulfill the ideal of such a true, lifelike comedy in his *Minna von Barnhelm*. Not only that, but the play fits Diderot's notion of "conditions" in a broader sense, at once social and political, than Diderot himself had probably had in mind. As Goethe, who had seen *Minna* in his student days in Leipzig, was to note:[11] "It is the first theater production taken from significant life, of specific temporal content, which for that reason had an effect that can never be calculated."

The work was not only specific, it was also realistic in being contemporary. It was concluded only four years after the end of the Seven Years' War, which had left a particularly painful residue of bitterness between Prussians and Saxons. The play is about a lovers' quarrel and reconciliation, in which the contemporary situation contributes directly to the theme, setting, and plot, if not to the development of the characters. A recently impoverished Prussian major, a man of great kindness and a rigid code of honor, is wrongly under the king's suspicion of having violated the code. His fiancée is a gay, charming, and wealthy Saxon girl who intrigues almost too skillfully against the officer's insistence that even though he loves her, honor forbids his marrying her. Though the chief protagonists are aristocrats, their relation to each other and to the subordinate characters is nonetheless typical of the private and sentimentally realistic quality which is the mark of the bourgeois novel.

Even though he is vindicated, Major von Tellheim is portrayed as a man of clumsy stubbornness, easily the prey of a particularly winsome species of feminine guile. Both his honor and her guile are a mixture of what is good and what is misguided. His pride in particular, however, is capable of inflicting great hurt on the feelings of a subordinate, Paul Werner, Tellheim's former sergeant major, who displays a self-sacrificial devotion fully as pure as the officer's motives. Distinctions of rank and class are carefully preserved in some particular virtues and excellences assigned to the characters, but not in their qualities of passion and motive power for good. Indeed, the strength of loyal affection between Tellheim and Werner clearly cuts across class lines, establishing a bond that moves toward the equality of farmer and aristocrat.

In this connection, the symbolism of money—which Lessing used frequently, not least in *Nathan der Weise*[12]—enters directly into the relation, an expression of the contextual "conditions" under which human beings act out what they are. A debt freely forgiven by Tellheim becomes a direct expression of his aristocratic honorableness; a debt he himself cannot pay is a direct threat to his honor. But on the other hand Werner's self-sacrificing offer of money to him is a gesture that is as startling as it is appropriate to their relation and transforms it at least temporarily. It first appears that it is unseemly for Tellheim to be Werner's debtor; but the occasion reminds them that in battle Tellheim twice owed his life to Werner. The symbolism marks the watershed: once this greater debt is remembered the major modifies his stand increasingly, to the point that he can finally say to his sergeant major: "If I promise on my honor that I'll tell you when I haven't any more money, that you'll be the first and only person from whom I'll borrow—will you be satisfied?" [13] There is a significant proportion between money and life: one can owe both to another person, so that each can become the expression of the other and thus the setting or even medium of relation between people. Money, like battle, can become the condition equalizing class differences, shaping two human beings toward each other in unexpected equality. For good or ill—and here for good, in contrast to Balzac's later and always ominous use of money as symbol as well as social reality—it is the wedding of bourgeois social values with bourgeois personal, private realism.

Lessing's acceptance of money and (especially in *Nathan*) commercial life as a significant condition enhancing or even

expressing personal qualities and relationships, is reminiscent of
Wesley's frequently repeated Sermon on the Use of Money with
its three "plain rules": "Gain all you can, save all you can, give
all you can." Here too money is regarded as a fit medium for the
enhancement of personal intercourse. But it is precisely the
realistic quality of Lessing's treatment in *Minna von Barnhelm* that
distinguishes it from Wesley's. For the latter the acquisition,
saving, and spending of money was an external means to express
and test the internal self-discipline of the Christian person:
"Calmly and seriously inquire, 'In expending this, am I acting
according to my character? Am I acting herein, not as a
proprietor, but as a steward of my Lord's goods?' " [14] Money to
Lessing was much more than an external means for individual
self-shaping. It was one significant social element entering into
individual character, molding personal relations in a social
context.

Yet when all is said and done, the element of realism remains
comparatively incomplete even in this play. The depiction of
character is finally a strictly moral, characterological business.
The characters are stereotyped. Each, in all his plausible mixture
of ordinary good and evil, still acts out of a set pattern of
disposition and behavior into which social dynamics enter only
weakly and externally. Their interaction therefore is strictly
private and personal, and transformation in their life attitudes
takes place only at that level. The Prussian state is a kind of deus
ex machina personified in the figure of Frederick the Great, and
the background of social conflict or problematic remains undevel-
oped. Despite the fact that war and military service are not
glorified, neither of these realities nor those larger forces that
stand behind them enter deeply into the play's development.

Political consciousness and fierce protest against political
absolutism developed only with *Sturm und Drang,* reaching its
epitome in Schiller's *Kabale und Liebe,* a tragedy of love thwarted
by ruthless court intrigue, tyrannical cruelty, and rigid social
stratification. But, as Erich Auerbach has shown, this play is no
more fully realistic than Lessing's *Minna von Barnhelm* and *Emilia*

Galotti. Its exaltation of love in conflict with narrow convention and an unnatural social structure rested on a sense of erotic love as part of ordinary reality and a fit subject for tragedy. "It became clearly erotic and at the same time touching and sentimental. It was in this form that the revolutionaries of *Sturm und Drang* seized upon it and, following Rousseau's footsteps, again gave it the highest tragic dignity, without abandoning any of its bourgeois, realistic, and sentimental element." But the "sentimentally touching" style, the narrowness of the circumstances portrayed, the exaggerated, gruesomely rhetorical details, the failure to explain either the functioning and wider setting of the oppressive institutions or the reasons for their decline and, above all, the "inner lack of freedom of the subjects of the principality" who are portrayed as having no glimmer that this situation is anything but eternally fixed and right, prevent *Kabale und Liebe* from attaining a fully realistic level.[15]

To turn from drama to the novel: practice as well as theory of the novel were by no means unknown in Germany in the later eighteenth century, and English fiction—Richardson, Fielding, Sterne, Smollet—was widely read and discussed. One of the earliest comprehensive critical essays devoted exclusively to the novel was Friedrich von Blanckenburg's *Versuch über den Roman* (1774), a wide-ranging, well-informed layman's effort to guide upcoming young novelists in the writing of this relatively new and still often despised genre. Blanckenburg's chief and most admired model was C. M. Wieland's *Die Geschichte des Agathon* (1766–67, revised edition 1773), illustrating not only the critic's own predilection but also the turn which the art of the novel was generally taking in Germany. Agathon is a *Bildungsroman*, the type of novel which was to reach its apex in Goethe's *Wilhelm Meister.* "The improvement and shaping which a character can receive through various occurrences or, more precisely still, his inner history, is the essential and peculiar element of a novel," Blanckenburg wrote; external events recede to the periphery and receive their signifiance from being causes of the "internal actions," in effect shaping the sensibility of the protagonist. "And in fact," says the twentieth-century editor of Blanckenburg's book, "the German developmental novel found its high artistic form above all through the consistent focus of narration on the inner improvement of an individual character." He adds that "to the concentration on the internal development of a single person corresponds the lack of a disposition favoring an ambitious and at the same time fascinating social novel, such as developed rapidly in the nineteenth century beyond the frontiers of Germany." [16] Despite the popularity of Scott, Dickens and Balzac in Germany, the balance of internal character development with portrayal of the external social world in German fiction had to await the later works of Theodor Fontane and the novels of Thomas Mann.

A much more explicit depreciation of the realistic social novel may be found a generation after Blanckenburg in the critical writings of Friedrich Schlegel.[17] An admirer of the novel form as he understood it, he took it to be at its best a highly romantic, subjective, fantastic form of literature. He rejected realistic works like those of Fielding with condescending impatience: they give us lifelike depictions of the way people curse, squires deport themselves, etc.[18] He remained firmly fixed in this early opinion. He admired "arabesques" and other plays of fantasy that take pure depiction only in order to distort or dissolve it. Hence he always praised the work of Sterne. But not so the novel as "a distinctive genre of poesy, and a regularly narrating prose depiction of occurrences in contemporary social life." He said in his 1812 Vienna lectures on ancient and modern literature that in this whole endeavor "to connect poesy so directly with reality and try to present it in prose, there is something not completely soluble, something downright mistaken." [19]

HISTORICISM AND REALISM

Realistic writing and its appreciation in late eighteenth-century Germany did not develop beyond the level attained by Lessing and the early Schiller. Romantic writing and criticism obviously tended in the very opposite direction. In Schlegel's estimation even the depiction of the connected development of a credible character through the impetus of external events, a typical Enlightenment motif, is no longer an object of praise. Historiographical stance paralleled that of fiction. It is a curious fact, noted by Auerbach, that the rise of historicism in Germany in the same era, which might have been expected to aid the development of both realistic fiction and history writing, did not in fact do so. We have already seen the peculiar disposition of this thought movement, as represented by Herder, to spiritualize history by turning it into the development of the stages of collective-spiritual individualities, in large part as a result of the fact that the knowing subject occupies a distinctive, self-positioning location toward the historical world. Historicism is the rendering of mankind's unfinished story in which man, in his encounter with determinate historical situations and developments, actually encounters himself writ large. But the universal self or man he meets is never met—as a Rationalist might claim—in direct, universal trans-historical form. The universal historical being of man is met only as the specific spirit of a specific age and group. In the great historian Leopold von Ranke's typically broad terms, "Everything is general and individual spiritual life," where general means nothing more than the most broadly encompassing historical collectivity, and individual means much the same—the collectively individual spirit of an age or group.[20] Historical spirit, the condition or subject of historiography, meets itself, historical spirit, in history.

Linking the historically specific with universal history by means of the notion of historical-spiritual development was one expression of a puzzling situation which Auerbach in particular noted. On the one hand, historicism was an apprehension of the specificity and irreducibly historical particularity of cultural change. But on the other hand, as a movement in German thought it led to the very opposite of this apprehension, to a vast universalization in defining the content of historical change. One reason why historicism failed to move toward realistic depiction was the enormous universalizing tendency we have observed in Herder and which reached its philosophical epitome in Hegel's descriptive explanation of spirit or reason as the unitary moving force of history. In more moderate form this spiritualizing, universalizing tendency, for which life, spirit, self-consciousness, or some other mode of man's self-grasp as generically unique is the subject of culture and history, has remained the same ever since. The tendency toward universalization and spiritualization was due to the fact that finally the subject matter and bond of historical development was a universal subject, whose character-izing quality was taken to be that of culturally embodied or diffused consciousness. The historical subject matter in historicist perspective is finally the one universal human spirit, even though always in specific cultural form.

The cultural setting for this intellectual development was a thoroughly fragmented political situation and a backward econ-omy, each tending to paralyze the other. The imposing figure of Frederick the Great of Prussia, bestriding the German scene of the latter eighteenth century, only accentuated the small ambience of his own and every other German realm. Even Prussia, to say nothing of the other German principalities except Austria (which was a multinational conglomerate in any case), was no major European political or cultural force, except as Frederick's own genius raised it temporarily to that level. Moreover, his enlight-ened indulgence of intellectual and religious freedom stood in broad contrast to his political despotism, typical of the period and much more characteristic of the conditions prevailing in the rest of Germany. It was a period of highly personal government. Apart from Austria, the situation in the smaller German states was obviously bound to be even more provincial.

In all of this, German nationalism both flourished and was the object of grave suspicion. In concept and fact political nation-hood, a firm cultural setting for the development of the realistic novel in England, lagged far behind in Germany. The French Revolution and Napoleon's conquest of Germany were to change the situation drastically, especially in Prussia, but in the latter part of the eighteenth century, when German intellectual and literary thought began to rise to its greatest height, the general cultural context for this movement was extraordinarily provincial. By the end of the eighteenth century England had had its political, economic, and religious revolutions and had emerged as a national entity. In Germany, as Heinrich Heine was to observe astutely and fearfully as much as two generations later, revolution had so far been confined to religion and philosophy. It is to be remembered that the first stage of that revolution, the German Reformation of the sixteenth century, had been accompanied by a terrible repression of the peasants. At the end of the eighteenth century, when Germany was still overwhelmingly agrarian, the legal and economic situation of that large mass was still virtually the same, with the partial exception of the agrarian reforms that had recently occurred in Austria under Joseph II. The important social changes that did take place were confined to the growing burgher class, but even among them social mobility was still very limited.[21]

In short, seldom has a major intellectual and literary movement, such as that which took place in Germany in the late eighteenth century, begun from so fragmented, narrow, and provincial a political base, and in so stagnant a social and political climate. Given that background, it is not surprising that even younger intellectuals like Goethe and Schiller, some of whom had at first sympathized with the French Revolution, rapidly came to find it a spiritually alien, profoundly threatening and incomprehensible force of frightening power. For them, too, sociopolitical conditions were either eternally fixed or deeply and unintelligibly disturbing. They drew back from depicting human nature and destiny through the interaction of human beings with the upheaval of the large-scale social and historical forces generally characteristic of their own era. It is not surprising that both German literature and German historical writing and reflection eschewed realism in favor of more ethicizing or spiritualistic depictions and foci for continuity. Rather, it is surprising that the historicist view, with its strong emphasis on ceaseless cultural change due more to specifically historical than natural factors, developed at all.

Erich Auerbach has commented with great perspicacity on the results of the entanglement of a sweeping intellectual movement such as early historicism in such narrow political, economic, and cultural circumstances. Historicism oscillated between the depiction of richly concrete but completely localized historical phenomena on the one hand, and vast, universalizing, and spiritualizing commentary on the other. The serious treatment of a human arena of manageable scope in a broad but still specific historical context such as that of a national life was precisely what was missing.[22]

> Contemporary conditions in Germany did not easily lend themselves to broad realistic treatment. The social picture was heterogeneous; the general life was conducted in the confused setting of a host of "historical territories" . . . In each of them the oppressive and at times choking atmosphere was counterbalanced by a certain pious submission and the sense of a historical solidity, all of which was more conducive to speculation, introspection, contemplation, and the development of local idiosyncrasies than to coming to grips with the practical and the real in a spirit of determination and with an awareness of greater contexts and more extensive territories. The origins of German Historism clearly show the impress of the conditions under which it was formed. Justus Möser based his ideas on his penetrating study of the historical development of a very restricted territory, that of the cathedral chapter of Osnabrück. Herder, on the other hand, saw the historical in its broadest and most general implications, yet at the same time in its profound particularity; but he represented it so little concretely that he is no help toward a grasp of reality. The work of these men already announces the tendencies which German Historism was long to retain: local particularism and popular traditionalism on the one hand, and all-inclusive speculation on the other. Both these tendencies are far more concerned with the extra-temporal spirit of history and the completed evolution

of what is in existence than with the presently visible germs of the concrete future. Such, in all essentials, the position remained down to Karl Marx.

Under such general conditions even Goethe's vivid impressiveness and lively sense of sensuous particularity—his "realism"—refused to be extended to an equally realistic apprehension and depiction of the individual grappling with history and the social forces at work in contemporary society.[23] He felt history, especially contemporary history, to be a threat, and when he presented contemporary events and movements in the course of his autobiographical works, "The real interest—manifest in dynamic and genetic treatment—attaches especially to personal matters and the intellectual movements in which Goethe participated, while public conditions are seen, though often graphically and vividly, as established and quiescent."[24] This lack of ability or desire to cope realistically with contemporary historical forces was a widely shared characteristic. If any one among the writers at the very end of the eighteenth century could have transcended it, it would have been Goethe.

THE FAILURE OF REALISM

In smaller compass and more particular focus, biblical interpretation quite unsurprisingly underwent the same fate. Even though its putative historicity and its narrative characteristics were usually recognized, the Bible failed to evoke clear appreciation of the significance of its narrative realism among commentators, finally even among those like Herder who, on asthetic and historicist grounds, might have been expected to explore such an interpretive option. In England, realistic narrative had begun to develop into a novelistic tradition of great power, accompanied by the beginnings of a critical appraisal of the differences and similarities between history and realistic fiction. For a variety of technical and cultural reasons this tradition made no impact on either English scholarly or edifying biblical commentary. When the realistic quality of the religiously central biblical stories was acknowledged, it was simply cited as evidence in favor of their veracity as historical reports. These stories were taken to be facts, allegories, or falsehoods, and never realistic narratives. There was, moveover, little interest in the biblical writings as writings. In Germany on the other hand, where there was strong interest in the Bible as writing, there was no strong tradition of realistic narrative. Thus, despite a far more vigorous appreciation than in England of literary and literary-historical analysis of the Bible as written sources, including its realistic features, the final upshot was the same as in England: it was never subjected to a reading in which the meaning of the realistic stories was taken to be the realistic, fact-like depictions themselves, regardless of their reference, of the question of their factual truth or falsity, or of the "spirit" pervading the writing.

In Germany, in contrast to England, there was strong, continuing interest in the Bible not only as true or false report but in addition as a large series of written sources with their own literary history, an interest augmented by the hallowed tradition of belief in the text's inspiration. In the pursuit of such matters, the narrative features of many of the biblical writings were not ignored, and interest in them was strengthened by the developing quest for a manageable view of the Bible's unity through the development of a single history traced in its pages. As we have seen, there were some for whom the narrative feature actually looked realistic, even though they finally always put it in a larger and therefore different interpretive context.

The development of historical criticism initiated critical inquiry into the literary history and character of individual biblical writings and its bearing on the claims made in them. Historical-critical investigation, we recall, was concerned with the character and reliability of individual writings. Hermeneutical interest, which came to have as strong a bearing as historical criticism on the fate of biblical authority for religious belief, concentrated on inquiry into the possible unity or unitary interpretation not only of each of the two Testaments but of the Bible as a whole. This was also the announced task of those diverse groups who called themselves biblical theologians.

The meaning of biblical statements came to be identified with the putative state of affairs and course of events to which they were thought to refer, the referents being logically distinct from and ultimately governing the linguistic sense of the text. But at the same time, the meaning of the statements came to be the spirit expressed in them, a sense which among Pietists merged at once indiscernibly and indissolubly with the mysterious or mystical sense that the Holy Spirit had imparted to at least some of the words over and above their literal meaning. For Pietists, the reader's converted heart was the indispensable condition or self-positioning without which neither the spirit of the text nor its inspiration by the Holy Spirit could be understood. Among idealistically influenced interpreters the cognate condition for understanding the Bible became the distinctive mode of reflection on the self and its relation to its world, sharply differentiated from ordinary empirical or theoretical ratiocination. The two shared the problem of relating two quite different notions of meaning in one comprehensive concept.

Clearly, reading or making sense of a narrative biblical text at a verbal or referential level was different from the self-positioning involved in understanding the spirit of the text, whether "spirit" was understood in a low-keyed or in a more strenuous and theological mode. Increasingly, therefore, a sharp distinction came to be made between understanding as making mere verbal or referential sense, and understanding as a profound inner exercise, at once mental and more—either religiously or aesthetically. How to relate or correlate the two things, denotative or connotative verbal sense and historical reference on the one hand, and inner understanding seeking its mental or spiritual counterpart in the text on the other hand, was to become a monumental preoccupation among Idealist and post-Idealist interpreters for the next two centuries, long after the demise of Pietism as a major intellectual and cultural (though not religious) force. More rationalistically inclined commentators for whom ideas tended to be supratemporal mental entities, and "understanding" them no problem, had an easier time choosing between fact and idea as the meaning of a statement.

Narrative interpretation of single stories and its extension into figural interpretation of the whole Bible appeared on the surface to find congenial successors in the Pietists and budding historicist Idealists like Herder, men who would never agree with the Deists' crude identification of meaning with ostensive, predictive reference in the argument over the fulfillment of prophecy. But in the final analysis the precritical cohesion of historical reference with literal sense, rendering directly accessible the world literally depicted, came apart just as completely through dissolution into meaning as reference to the immanent development of events, and meaning as the development of a religious, interpretive stance and tradition. No matter to which side one gave priority, the meaning of the text was no longer the text's depiction, even if it was agreed that the text was indeed realistic in character. Its realistic character was identified either with its factual reliability or with a unique realistic spirit in the tradition that produced the text. These identifications, due to logical confusion between meaning and reference on the one hand and to religious-apologetical interests on the other, prevented the possibility of a straightforward appreciation of the narrative features of the biblical stories in their own right. Obviously, then, once the question of a unitary meaning of the Bible as a whole came to be tackled, figural reading as an extension of literal-depictive reading could likewise never be an option. The complex heritage of Pietism, Idealism, and *heilsgeschichtliche Schule*, which we have described, finally became the chief ingredients in the twentieth-century version of biblical theology which developed in the train of theological neo-orthodoxy.

What drive there was for utilizing the realistic features of biblical narratives in interpretation—and it was by no means lacking—always ended up by encompassing them in a larger framework or category of explanation. If that interpretive framework was itself realistic it involved a historical reconstruction of the specific occurrences or the general conditions from which the text arose. Realistic interpretation was historical interpretation. It meant bringing the world as a network of naturally explicable and undisrupted physical, mental, and social connections to bear on the text, on the assumption that this was indeed the real world into which the world of the text could be ranged by the appropriate reconstruction of the explicative sense.

In addition to this interpretive procedure there might indeed be others, the shape of which would depend on the philosophical and religious outlook of the interpreter. He might or might not also wish to include the text in another interpretive framework, for example that of a common human structure of immediate self-consciousness of which all language—primitive, ancient, or modern—is a symbolic expression. But this was an exercise over and above the procedure of ranging the text into the agreed-upon "real" world of natural, explanatory connections which all men inhabit, whether they know it or not, no matter what additional interpretive perspectives might be open. This alone was realistic interpretation, and it was in effect the reconstruction of the true from the literal sense by referring the latter to its proper subject matter in that real world, either in the form of a specific occurrence or in the form of some nonspecific aspects of the historical conditions in which it arose.

The inherited texts crucial for religious belief were of course the realistic biblical stories, around which swirled the growing, unprecedented controversy about the status of their factual claims, and the issue of whether they made such claims at all. It was increasingly taken for granted that their meaning was either ostensively referential, i.e. that they made fact claims, or that they were nonrealistic in character, i.e. either the expressions of one kind of consciousness or the sensuous representation of a moral or religious teaching.

Inevitably, the growing concentration of analysis and interpretation on the meaning of the fact-like character and the factual reliability of these history-like stories came to focus on the story of

Jesus, especially as it was told in the synoptic gospels. Friends and enemies of inherited Christian belief alike came to agree that that belief stood or fell with the historicity of the reports concerning the chief events of Jesus' life. The essence of unrevised Christian orthodoxy was held to be the truth claim concerning these events, particularly the system of his teachings, his death, and resurrection. This was as true for those who wanted to vindicate this belief as it was for those who wanted to do away with it, whether by abandoning it completely or by championing the religion *of* Jesus instead of the religion *about* him. The reports about Jesus, it was held, demonstrated or failed to demonstrate that he stood in that unique and absolute relation to God which made him the very revelation in history of God himself. The center of traditional Christian belief was taken to be christology or the unique revelation in history of God himself in the person and teaching of Jesus. This was the position of right-wing as well as mediating theologians, in particular German Neologians such as Semler.

Those who interpreted the gospel texts realistically, and sought most vigorously for the reliable historical referents or origins of the written reports (most prominent and controversial among them was D. F. Strauss) were convinced that this was an accurate appraisal of the interpretive situation for orthodox as well as mediating theologians. In their view, the vindication or overthrow of the christological claims was equivalent to showing that the texts depicting Jesus' story did or did not refer ostensively. Part of the consternation caused by Strauss's *Life of Jesus* (1835) among scholars was due to its tenacious exploitation of their own consensus, from theological right to theological left, that traditional Christian religious or "faith" claims, though not limited to historical fact claims based on ostensively-referential textual interpretation, nonetheless had them for their indispensable (if insufficient) basis. And the most important of these supposed fact claims turned out, in Strauss's view, to be myths instead. In short, the general theological and interpretive problem of relating historical-critical judgment to traditional or even moderately revised Christian belief came to focus on the literal or reconstructed depiction of the story of Jesus Christ. The relation of history and faith was chiefly embodied in the relation of the historically factual "Jesus of history" to "the Christ of faith" who was or was not properly consonant with that historical figure.

What realistic narrative interpretation of individual biblical texts there was, since it did not exist in its own right, rose to the level of historical-critical interpretation. Realistic interpretation came in fact to be identical with the putative historical reconstruction of the events depicted in the story, either as Jesus' continuous life story or, more modestly, as historical confirmation of some crucial aspects of his teaching and career. In this fashion a form of realism, in the shape of historical-critical judgment, became crucial to the discussion over the relation between faith and history. The argument was carried on over generations in university settings by scholars and professors, in university lecture halls, learned journals, and books. No matter that the fruits of the discussion trenched directly on the faith of ordinary churchgoers and, until the second half of the nineteenth century, on the interests of cultured nonprofessionals like Lessing: this particular thought movement was and remained largely an adacemic one. And the level of realism attained in it was as incomplete as that we noted in connection with the major literary movement in the latter part of the eighteenth century. Narrative interpretation had given way to the ostensively referencing and reconstructive procedure of historical criticism. And its reconstruction of the ostensible events that began Christianity generally echoed a very modest depictive evocation of the relation of men, events, and historical forces.

Frequently the realistic, i.e. critically reconstructive analysis of the gospels, was transcended for broader and more ultimate interpretive purposes and cast into a spiritualizing, idealist framework. But to the extent that it was not, the depicted world was honorable, nonmiraculous, and highly personalized. On the one hand a bourgeois historical realism, seeking to reconstruct the personal "facts," and on the other a sweepingly romantic Idealism concerned with religious meaning, converged on the figure caught in the scholarly discussion of the relation between "historical" and "faith" judgments.

EPILOGUE: "FAITH," "HISTORY," AND THE
"HISTORICAL JESUS"

While the complex of technical issues in the relation of hermeneutics, biblical criticism, and theology have remained much the same since the late eighteenth century, the cultural significance of post-narrative, post-figural interpretation, especially in connection with the question of Jesus and revelation, remains in doubt. Speculation on the matter has been endless. In 1844 Karl Marx was able to write, in words that have since become famous: "For Germany the criticism of religion is in the main complete, and criticism of religion is the premise of all criticism." [25] The criticism to which he referred had largely centered around the question whether the meaning of human salvation or reconciliation, the realization of true human freedom, is necessarily connected with the occurrence of a specific and saving historical event, i.e. Jesus Christ. Among those who argued it critically and philosophically, the answer had in turn depended heavily on the fruits of historical criticism, since all but the most firmly committed Idealists thought that dogma could not contradict exegesis, and exegesis meant at least in part historical criticism. Well before the first half of the nineteenth century was over, Strauss had demonstrated to the satisfaction of young radicals that historical exegesis of the gospels does not justify basing the dogma of divine–human reconciliation on the historical factuality of Jesus' story. He effectively subverted what was agreed by all shades of theological opinion to be an indispensable tenet of conservative and mediating theology. Feuerbach had gone on from there to suggest that the real meaning or interpretation of the dogma of reconciliation or freedom is the divine self-reconciling power of the human race. This, he said, is in any case the real and only religious force left to the dogma in an age when its literal form has ceased to appeal to sensibility or self-consciousness, remaining only as a fossil of a moribund superstructure among men and society. Marx in turn radicalized and transcended this criticism as still too much bound to the situation and forms of thought it criticized.

However correct or incorrect Marx's remark about the criticism of religion, those to whom his description applied even partially ceased to have any further interest in pursuing the theological version of the question of the reconciliation of man from his own alienated state. This development, together with a wave of anti-Hegelian positivist reaction that swept German intellectual (including theological) circles in the middle of the nineteenth century, restricted the discussion of the relation of faith and history more and more to specialists in theological faculties. Marx had judged rightly—whether or not for the right technical reasons—for the vast majority of German intellectuals, and not only for his few followers in their midst. They went on to other business. The criticism of religion, at least in the form it had assumed in the piety of the confessional churches and in the theological heritage that asserted an indispensable divine–human historical starting point for a saving reconciling faith, was indeed complete as a broadly engaging cultural issue.

Marx's own small but increasingly important band of followers found that the real, secular meaning of religion, including the true meaning of Feuerbach's criticism of religion, emerges only in the process of social criticism. For all thought about religion, whether affirmative or negative, really takes shape as a response to the actual socioeconomic structure, which is only mirrored in the ideological—including the religious—superstructure. Reflection about religion is not a response to an eternal and intrinsic factor given in and with human nature. "The basis of irreligious criticism is: Man makes religion, religion does not make man," Marx had said.[26] Religion is a strictly social and historical phenomenon. Feuerbach had still conceived of the essence of the human species as in some sense self-reflective or spiritual. Hence for him the change of the species from error to truth had to be initiated by spiritual insight into the properly demythologized, anthropological rather than theological meaning of Christian discourse. In Marx's view this was not only a remnant of religious rather than irreligious criticism of religion but also an example of intellectualist or spiritualist heresy in the analysis of social change.

Marx went on to say that one had to realize that all critical thought, even the irreligious socioeconomic criticism of society, is no more than preliminary analysis of dialectical, changing reality—a reality encompassing even the very analysis itself. To think that critical insight into, or true criticism of society is by itself the major initiating step toward correcting the distorted social structure, with all its tyrannical injustice over oppressed peoples, is self-deception to the point of acquiescence in the wrong. This is precisely the intellectualist, spiritualist error which religion and philosophy were bound to commit, both in their constructive or speculative and in their critical roles. In the words of the culminating and most famous of Marx's "Theses on Feuerbach," "The philosophers have only interpreted the world, in various ways; the point, however, is to change it." [27] The remark represents, in Marx's view, not only a practical but a philosophical criticism of philosophy as well. Without the implementation of socioeconomic change, the secularizing interpretation or criticism is itself abstract to the point of being erroneous.

Marx was convinced that society itself was becoming secular— indeed had long since become secular except in the palest aspects of its ideological superstructure—by virtue of the social and economic conditions which modern industrial forces of production were bringing about. And now even the remotest, most deeply entrenched elements in the superstructure of thought were rapidly becoming secular along with it. On that assumption he was able to make his prophecy that criticism of religion was complete. He would have believed his view confirmed just as much by those who simply shrugged off traditional religious issues positivistically as by those who agreed with him that the secularizing process was the result of the dialectic of history espied by historical materialism.

A secular critique had had to be made of the supposedly

indispensable theological form or basis of historical salvation. The historic task of the historical-critical analysis of the gospels had been to have an historically brief and specialized part in this critique. Once this was done the historical dialectic, both in reality and in thought, could go on to its proper new business, the irreligious criticism of society in the service of such revolutionary social change as would implement true historical salvation. In the context of our topic, the upshot of Marx's view of the criticism of religion was that the very development of historical-critical investigation into the gospels, whether in support or denial of Christian belief in Jesus Christ, was itself already one of the signs that the christological belief or doctrine under investigation had ceased to be of historic significance. First the belief and then its scientific critique had had their day and ceased to be, the former after a long and majestic career, the latter after a recent brief moment of topicality and usefulness in the dialectic of cultural thought. The very exercise of historical criticism of the gospels, whether positive or negative, was to this outlook an admission of the discernment that the real world in which we ineluctably exist is not the biblical stories' world, no matter whether or not some of that world's individual components may be demonstrated to be real in terms of the world of history which we now accept as our real world. In the light of the completed "criticism of religion," the historical-critical investigation of the gospels is an admission of the fundamental cultural uninterest of the notion of christological salvation in history and of the notion of a relation between history and faith.

And indeed, after the publication of Strauss's *Life of Jesus* not only critical exegesis of the Bible but, more significantly, the topic of relating such historical exegesis to dogma or religious belief became increasingly the exclusive domain of technical biblical and theological scholars. From Lessing's days to those of Strauss it had been otherwise, although even then the inquiry had taken on the shape of a highly specialized study. But from now on few other intellectuals, within or outside the universities, any longer paid much attention. Theological scholars published lives of the historical Jesus, intended to rejoin the marriage that Strauss had put asunder between historical facts and a faith supposedly indispensable for salvation. Theological scholars likewise published the plethora of essays arguing that such a life could not or need not be written in support of the christological faith. And they also published numberless works on the general relation between faith and history, of which one's perspective on Jesus would be the crucial instance. Some of them conscientiously published the fruits of their labor, especially about Jesus, not only in learned volumes but also in books *für das Volk dargestellt*. But it is not recorded that *das Volk* became deeply involved in the matter; and it is certain that these professors' fellow intellectuals inside and outside university walls took virtually no part in the discussion.

The critical-life-of-Jesus movement and the cognate vast literature on the relation (or lack of it) between faith and history possess a certain intrinsic fascination, even if they did turn out to be largely tracts written by specialists for other specialists. Indeed, it is their great intrinsic interest and their mirroring of the cultural situation of which they were the product that make them fascinating, and not the very small cultural or religious effect they have had. Moreover, the whole development of this literature is not without a certain pathos. There is pathos in the discovery of each succeeding study of the "historical Jesus" that what its immediate predecessors had thought to be a path for genuine access to the figure turned out to be just another blind alley. There is pathos in the late twentieth-century revival of the topic, in the hope that historically reliable access, significant also for christological conviction, might be obtained—not indeed any longer to the self-consciousness of Jesus, nor to the sequence of his life, but to his unique identity. This, it is said, may be done by showing the likelihood that certain words attributed to him are indeed his own, and that they, in their uniqueness and distinctiveness, are the very essence of his own unique and distinctive being. This coherence of words and being, and the accessibility of being through discourse, are in turn explained by a complex ontology of language in which historical events, language, and being are all united, and words from the past become the historical event which is their speaker because being is linguistic. It is not merely a hidden substructure which is then linguistically "ex-pressed." There is pathos here too. It lies in the increasingly difficult and specialized conceptual apparatus that has to be invoked in this and cognate schemes in order to rescue the meaningfulness, the intelligibility of a supposedly universal claim at once religious and historical, a claim said to be of the utmost importance for all sorts and conditions of men.

There is pathos likewise in the constant escape from anything that might be termed historical realism in the depictions of Jesus or faith, and in the schemes relating "faith" and historical-critical judgment. The reality of the mundane world, the reality of the "random individual," and the reality and interrelation of locatable, natural, and historical events are indeed very much part of the apperceptive mass of the academic writers on our topics. Indeed, the conviction of that real world and the task of reconciling Christian faith to the changing forms in which that world is to be depicted often constitute the main motivation for doing the writing. But the failure of that reconciliation, the lack of historical realism and of any real world into which the stance of faith would fit, is evident in the privatizing of what becomes a specifically religious stance toward the (or a) world; it is evident in the purely ethical or existential manner in which Jesus, or the man of faith, is related to the public world in which he lives. The frequently depicted radical hope, radical faith, radical obedience, or radically authentic being of Jesus or the man of faith bear witness to this ethicizing, existentializing, privatizing stance— especially as each stance is often portrayed as "radical" beyond having any fit special object, since any such object would supposedly deradicalize or "objectivize" it. There is no fit relation between the stance and any public world in which it would be at home.

There is in such a stance, adopted by theologian, historian, or critic on behalf of his protagonist, at the very most a highly tenuous apprehension of a genuine, public, determinate and real world which is capable of significant depiction and of significant impact on the identity and destiny of the individuals engulfed in it. Lacking is the sense of a depictively rendered coordination of historical forces, specific circumstances, and individuals, which would allow the last to be at once specific selves and yet identifiably rooted in a determinate, societal type. While there is a real historical world for the modern writers on faith and history, the outlook they generally adopt in behalf of their protagonist, Jesus or the man of faith, is that of a vector perspective upon his real world, so that its reality is genuinely actuated only through his stance toward or his response to it.

The alternative to this dismissal of Jesus from the context of any and every real world seems to be to turn his life, teaching, and destiny into a figural representation. In that case, though it is argued that he is a real historical person in his own right, his real significance lies in his being placed in another depicted historical world than that into which literal and figural interpretation had cast him in precritical days. By something like figuration in reverse, he is now entered into another story. It may be a historically rendered world in which there is also an element of transcendence, or one in which there is not. It may be the "progressive" world rendered by Karl Marx's dialectical depiction, or a world of which the real substance is "salvation history." In any event, the reinterpretation means that the reversal which started in the late seventeenth century has been fully effected. The elements of the story that figural interpretation had originally woven into one single narrative have now been transposed into another framework. Their meaning, detached from their narrative setting, is now their reference to some other story, some other world, some other context of interpretation.

The movements of historical criticism and historical theology, considering with immense seriousness the relation between faith and history both methodologically and in substantive depiction, especially in the instance of Jesus, have been enterprises undertaken by academic specialists. Moreover, the sense of a world as well as of the individual's relation to it, rendered in such depictions, has usually reflected not only the academic specialist but also the member of the middle class with his this-worldly and yet idealizing sense of reality and human existence. One may speak of the fascinating quality of this enterprise, both intrinsically and as a matter of the culture it mirrored, and also of a genuine pathos in the course of its development since the later eighteenth century. But given this very character of the enterprise, it was surely a considerable exaggeration when Albert Schweitzer wrote in 1906, in the dramatic opening of *The Quest of the Historical Jesus*:[28]

> When, at some future day, our period of civilization shall lie, closed and completed before the eyes of later generations, German theology will stand out as a great, a unique phenomenon in the mental and spiritual world of our time. For nowhere save in the German temperament can there be found in the same perfection the living complex of conditions and factors—of philosophical thought, critical acumen, historical insight, and religious feeling—without which no deep theology is possible.
>
> And the greatest achievement of German theology is the critical investigation of the life of Jesus. What is accomplished here has laid down the conditions and determined the course of the religious thinking of the future.

The investigation Schweitzer spoke about into the documentary sources of the synoptic gospels and into the life of Jesus began its most intense period at the very time when Marx claimed that the criticism of religion was in the main complete. Nearly three generations after Schweitzer's prophecy the most striking thing about it is its lack of perspective on the scope, the spiritual power, and the cultural achievement of the historiography of the lives of Jesus. Schweitzer thought that he himself was providing both a climactic end and a monument to the tradition; and indeed his book came as close as any to accomplishing both tasks. But Schweitzer notwithstanding, it is doubtful that the reality he celebrated equaled in loftiness his retrospective celebration of it. While depiction of the life and thought of Jesus gained no greater historical credibility in his hands than in those of his predecessors, he set it forth with a dramatic power paralleled neither before nor since among historical critics. His judgment of the importance of the movement as a whole fits his own work more accurately than that of his predecessors or successors.

The close of the period Schweitzer had in mind may or may not have come; but so far Marx seems to have been the shrewder judge of the long-range cultural significance of the tradition both men talked about—the tradition of inquiry into the bearing of critical-historical investigation on the theological form of the dogma of historical salvation, focused in particular on our knowledge of Jesus of Nazareth.

12 Strauss's Perfection of the "Mythical" Option

The endeavor to relate faith and history came to an early but decisive climax in D. F. Strauss's *Life of Jesus*, published in 1835. All the endeavors to solve this issue in respect of the story of Jesus of Nazareth take their ultimate point of departure from Strauss's setting of the problem: (1) Is the meaning (and therefore the truth) of the gospels necessarily connected with reliable historical knowledge of Jesus as uniquely related to God? (2) If one answers affirmatively, can one actually demonstrate that the most plausible historical explanation of the "supernatural" elements in the accounts, the elements indicating the uniqueness of Jesus, is that they are factually probable?

Strauss thought that historical examination would return a negative answer to both questions. The answer to the first depended for him on the reply returned to the second. Unlike Reimarus, unlike "Naturalists" and "Supernaturalists" he insisted that one cannot obtain a proper explanation of the historical origin of the content of the gospel stories by asking the question: Were the evangelists giving honest reports, whether accurate or mistaken, or were they lying, whether in the interests of religious allegorizing or of their own self-aggrandizement? The explanation of the origin of the stories and the clue to their meaning is rather to be found in their authors' consciousness, which was historically conditioned to the level of their cultural and religious context. It is finally the phenomenon of a premodern cultural outlook that serves both as historical explanation and hermeneutical clue in the reading of the gospels. This is the climactic reading of eighteenth-century inquiry, for which hermeneutics, and therefore explication, was theory of exegesis—the text, and whatever its subject matter, being accessible to straightforward scrutiny by the properly trained investigator.

Strauss is properly identified with the "mythical" school which represented with greatest consistency one hermeneutical extreme —that of the completely historical understanding of an author. (The opposite extreme was that of biblical literalism.) Like all the other members of the school, he was basically concerned with the narrative portions of scripture: myths, whatever else they are, are sensuous accounts, and where there are no stories, myth as an interpretive device obviously isn't applicable. Theologically, the school quite evidently pushed in the direction of a denial of the positivity of revelation. After all, that issue was, as we have seen, the reason for examining the miraculous narratives in the first place, and for concentrating on narrative sequences rather than individual miracles. Strauss was no exception on this point. As he himself stated later, the dogmatic or rather antidogmatic issue had been the motive for his work all along.[1] It was his conviction that "the critical examination of the life of Jesus is the test of the dogma of the person of Christ," [2] and his conclusion was that the "historical Jesus" has neither historically nor theologically (or philosophically) any connection with the "Christ of faith."

But the theological position of Strauss or other members of the mythical school is not of primary significance in the present context because it does not necessarily coincide with what one might think to be the cognate hermeneutical stance, and it was the latter rather than theology that governed their biblical writings. Theologically, some members of the school (G. L. Bauer, for instance) [3] could be counted among the Neologians, while Strauss's own theology when he wrote The Life of Jesus was as vaguely pantheistic as only a young Hegelian's could be at that time.[4] The important polarization was over the hermeneutical and exegetical issues of the gospel story. Strauss, as a consistent mythophile, opted for a completely historical explanation of its origins which would at the same time constitute the clue to a complete explanation of its meaning. In that way all other possible interpretations would be eliminated, and certain criteria for the evaluation of the claims of positivity in theology would be established. His aim was to show that the writers' intention was indeed literal—destroying such mediating positions as the Neologians' accommodation theory—but that this intention itself has to be understood historically, viz. within the context of the general thought world of their times. Hence, even where the narrative contains some factual echoes, as Strauss had no doubt it does, that is not its meaning. Its meaning is the time-conditioned consciousness from which it was written and which it expresses.

The outcry against Strauss's epoch-making work was due to three of his claims. First, the upshot of his study seemed to him to be that the truth of the Christian claim, the idea of reconciliation or of the unity of the infinite and finite in man and his history, is philosophical (or dogmatic; the two things were the same to him) in nature and, therefore, has no essential, indispensable connection with any single historical occurrence or series of occurrences. In other words, it is not dependent for its truth on the claims that a God-man once existed and that Jesus Christ was that God-man. In this respect, and probably in this respect only, Strauss was and remained a "left-wing Hegelian." He denied the indispensability of the gospel's "positivity" for the truth content of dogmatic claims.

Second, not only are Christian truth claims not dependent on the assessment of what is factual in the story of Jesus of Nazareth: The investigation and assessment of the supposed historical facts ought in any case to be separated completely from all a priori philosophical or theological affirmations about the truth contained in these writings and its relation to the "facts." In other words, even if it could be shown that Christian meaning and truth-claims depend on the factuality of reports about a supernatural person, the investigation of the historical veracity of the reports is a completely distinct undertaking; it is historical and not theological. Indeed, if the meaning and truth of Christianity depend on historical veracity, historical-critical exegesis must be completely prior to dogma and the latter based on its independent findings. This was the gist of Strauss's break with Hegel, whom he found obscure and indecisive on the distinction and relation between positive fact and dogmatic truth, between historical-critical and speculative (religious and philosophical) procedures. Hegel and his school were ambiguous on the issues of the dispensability or indispensability of a factual occurrence to the truth of Christian faith, and on the possibility or impossibility of deriving factual assessments from speculative or ontological claims.[5]

Third, the key to assessing the factual value of the gospel reports and to their meaning, especially those involving supernatural elements, is neither an explanation trying to demonstrate the literal veracity of the reports nor yet one attempting to prove that natural occurrences underlay the reports of miracles, and that they were reported distortedly, mistakenly, or in deliberate accommodation by the authors to the intellectual milieu of their time. The key, rather, to understanding the meaning and assessing the historical reliability of the gospel story, including its crucial (as they appeared to Strauss) supernatural ingredients, is the mythical outlook which the authors shared with their time and culture in the Near East. To say that their outlook is mythical is, among other things, to include it in the group process spoken of as "unconscious folk poetizing." In this way the authors are absolved from the possible accusation that they were practicing deliberate deception in the supposed cause of right and truth—an accusation that is at least implied whenever the miracle stories of the Bible are classified as allegories or individually invented fables.[6]

Strauss had no intention of reducing the whole gospel, including the very existence of Jesus himself, to a mythical tale. But the category did help him render an explanation of the origin of stories that look as if they might have had external and literal, or internal psychic (but in either case factual and in principle datable), occurrences for their origin, and which the authors had then apparently embellished with supernatural decoration. Without having to search for the no longer recoverable natural, factual datum in each instance, whether external or psychic, one could account for the rise of such reports simply by referring them to the general mythical consciousness of the time.

Before Strauss, Herder had already used the spirit or group consciousness of a period as an explanatory device, making it so pervasive that he explained even the philological structure and usage of a group's language as a function of its distinctive collective consciousness. On the issues with which we are concerned, there were two essential differences between the two men. First, Herder used spirit not only as a category for understanding but simultaneously as a common bond between any given past and its present interpreter. The notion of group consciousness functioned for him at an aesthetically empathetic level rather than in a critical or normative fashion. By contrast Strauss, who was much more of a Rationalist, used folk consciousness as a critical-analytical instrument enabling him to render a technical explanation of the origin and genre of certain ancient writings. Second, Herder thought that the group consciousness expressed in the biblical writings was simple and realistic, whether or not given texts could be taken to refer ostensively to specific events. Strauss on the other hand thought that even where a text was simple and realistic, indeed when it happened accidentally to refer, its real meaning was the presentation of primitive Christian ideas in history-like form shaped by unpremeditatingly poetizing saga. In other words, the real meaning of the narrative biblical texts for Strauss was the mythical rather than realistic consciousness they expressed, a consciousness they had in common with other ancient primitive groups.

Storied texts of this sort, Strauss said, were generally current, and they were the natural expressions of reflection for that particular group culture which had not yet risen to the level of abstract conceptualization. The stories were bound to be applied to charismatic personalities who seemed to fit the stereotype—prophetic, messianic, or whatever. The stories of Jesus' temptation and transfiguration are striking instances of events that are naturally incredible as well as full of contradictions if taken as external occurrences. On the other hand, to interpret them as psychic events is highly dubious speculation about what took place inside Jesus, and what he might have told his disciples.

Besides, it goes against the obvious grain of the authors' intentions in telling these stories. In the face of all such unsatisfactory explanations of the origin of the stories, the most economical and reasonable account is that they do not stem from Jesus at all but were "formed about him; that is, they are primitive Christian sagas. . . . Robbed of all historical basis, we are directed for the tracing back of this tale [the Temptation] solely to thoughts, to Jewish and primitive Christian representations; and here we are fortunately able to say that there is no strain in the narrative which cannot be explained from Old Testament examples or from contemporary concepts of the Messiah and of Satan." [7] To find parallel stories or ideas in the atmosphere of their day is to have the most reasonable explanation for the appropriation of this tale to any given charismatic personality. This would seem to be the proper inference to be drawn from the appeal to a common group mind or consciousness and its representational process, expressive of the culture of that time and area. This common process is the genetic source and thus to Strauss the sufficient historical explanation of the individual applications of the story.

If a certain narrative or pericope can be shown to be mythical in character, particularly by comparison with other similar stories in another part of the Bible or elsewhere, especially in the same cultural context, this fact is to the most consistent mythophile either a sufficient historical explanation of the report's origin or it obviates the necessity, and even the possibility, of getting back to the supposedly underlying facts. Wherever historical explanation of any sort is clearly unnecessary because the story really functions as a general explanation, one speaks of "philosophical myth." Wherever further historical explanation might be desirable because the saga tradition of the mythical account may go back to an actual event, but one extremely hard to come by, one speaks of "historical myth." In a third case yet, poetic myth, nothing but the free and spontaneous imagination is at play. In all three subtypes, the real significance lies in the expression of the sensuous, childlike consciousness represented, not yet capable of rising to abstract conceptualization and verbal form. That is the

substance of myth. It comes in the form of a sensuous or
history-like account of divine and human miraculous actions, in
which the gods appear without mediation directly in the finite
world as agents. Like allegory, its meaning—what it represents—
is obviously different from the representation of it. But its
meaning, unlike that of allegory, is not a directly statable idea,
deliberately clothed in story form. Rather, the meaning of the
representation is the consciousness doing the representing. As a
technical critical tool for analysis, myth is a psychological-genetic
category which serves to explain the meaning and account for the
origin of miraculous stories. Even if some factual material lies
back of a given mythical account, that is not its real sense but
only its accidental occasion or evocation. Myths refer not to
specific events but to general cultural conditions and kinds of
group consciousness.

Supernaturally tinged individual reports in the gospel story
Strauss usually explained as philosophical myths. The synoptic
gospels as a whole he characterized more nearly as historical
myth. Thus in reply to critics who claimed he had turned the
whole story of Jesus into myth, he said at the end of the
introduction to the second edition of his book: "The author of this
work protests expressly against having imputed to him the
assertion that he knows that nothing happened, when he actually
explained that he does not know *what* happened." But if the
mythical hypothesis is thus indecisive as a *total* explanation of the
synoptic gospels' historical origin—largely because "the boundary
line between the mythical and the historical must always remain
fluctuating and fluid in reports which include the former
element" [8]—it is certainly helpful in explaining from a general
atmosphere instead of a specific occurrence the origin of individual instances of supernatural tales throughout the length and
breadth of the gospels; and this, of course, has a cumulative effect
on our understanding of the origin of these narratives as a whole.[9]
And even where it is likely that a mythical account involves traces
of actual occurrences, this is quite accidental to its real meaning.

Strauss himself was chiefly interested in historical assessment, that is, in investigating the credibility of the gospel accounts as factual reports, rather than in their abiding sense. The category of myth chiefly served this end for him.[10] In his own words in the introduction: "Now in relation to the gospels, with which alone we are dealing here, the whole of the following work has no other purpose than to investigate on internal grounds in individual detail the credibility of their reports, and thereby also the probability or improbability of their origin from eye witness or otherwise accurately informed sources." [11] The reason for internal procedure in this matter is obvious. Not only is this by now the German in contrast to the English tradition for examining the factual reliability of biblical reports, but external evidence concerning the life of Jesus or the early date and reliability of these writings (nonbiblical written witness either of contemporary or slightly later date than Jesus, to say nothing of archaeological material) is also much too sparse to be very useful in deciding the question.

In its absence, internal grounds for assessment will have to serve almost exclusively for the evaluation of the reliability of the reports.[12] The writings themselves have to be examined on the basis of three criteria. (1) Are the stories supposedly covering the same sequence of events mutually as well as internally consistent? This question explains the sharp rise in the number of gospel "harmonies" in the eighteenth century. (2) Are they intrinsically reliable when judged by the criteria of our general experience of natural, historical, and psychic occurrences? On both scores Strauss, it goes without saying, thought that the gospels came out very poorly indeed. The reasons for this conclusion, which he adduces from an analysis of our natural experience, have become standard explanation of the criteria that go into making unprejudiced ("presuppositionless") assessments of what is likely to have taken place in the past, and what is not.[13] (3) Literarily, i.e. in their character as writings, are these writings historical or nonhistorical in kind? Are they of a fact-reporting or of a mythical sort?

The answer to the last question is obviously central for Strauss; for if he can indicate that the genre of many parts of these writings is actually that of myth, he will have answered a large portion of his own overriding question concerning their historical reliability through a positive hypothesis about their likeliest historical origin. This would reinforce, indeed it would crown, the prior negative moves demonstrating the unlikelihood of such occurrences, on the grounds of their inherent incredibility and (therefore) of the inadequacy of the exegetical moves explaining them as historical. And this is in fact the sequence of Strauss's actual procedure. Having done the negative criticism in line with the first two criteria, he then turns to the positive question in the case of each pericope: What kind of writing do we actually have here, and what bearing does this have on the issue of the writing's origin and reliability? And the answer usually is, of course, that the writings are mythical in character. Therefore, no factual historical occurrence need be postulated for the origin of a given supernaturally tinged story. Not only, therefore, is the literal hypothesis incredible and unnecessary for explaining its origins, but the claim that there was instead a natural rather than the reported supernatural occurrence in back of the account is also as unnecessary as it is usually absurd.

It is clear, then, why Strauss made use of the category of myth. The literary-psychological analysis it allowed him to make of the genre of the gospel accounts served to supply him with an answer to the question of the status of their putative factual claims. Nor was he alone in wishing to assess the gospels' historical reliability with the help of the category. Hartlich and Sachs have shown decisively that the roots of the mythical school of interpretation to which Strauss belonged are deeply embedded in the soil of late eighteenth-century biblical study and its quest for historical explanation, and in the slightly earlier classical philology of C. G. Heyne (1729–1812).[14] Strauss was the most extreme heir to the tradition of interpretation chiefly interested in a technical, historical assessment of fact-like stories in the Bible. Strauss's

Hegelian antecedents have comparatively little to do with his understanding and use of myth, at least as a literary-historical category.[15]

It is indeed true that Strauss's use of myth, unlike Hegel's, served the quest for historical-factual explanation rather than for the discovery of the "notion" or "idea" which myth foreshadowed "representationally." It is likewise true that he derived it from eighteenth-century sources rather than from Hegel. However, the category of myth itself, as an explanatory device, is something of a transitional concept between eighteenth- and nineteenth-century historical understanding, partaking of some of the qualities we usually think characteristic of both eras. To the mythical school, myth was largely a technical category of explanation. To the budding romantic view, myth was largely important for its content, such as the role it played in mirroring the transition from innocence to self-awareness. The Romantics saw many things in myth, and if they were religiously inclined (as they usually were) they saw it as a form of the self-revelation of transcendent or divine to human spirit, and an indirect, externalized self-reflection of the human spirit.

All this means that the thesis of Hartlich and Sachs has to be modified to some extent. The authors tend to minimize the common elements in the understanding of myth in the mythical school and the budding romantic and idealist traditions which were there, for all their differences, and hence the common impact these traditions may have had on Strauss, as well as on the rather different "historicism" of nineteenth-century historians. Among such common features in the historical–critical and the romantic–idealist understanding of myth, one may mention the use of "consciousness"—at once in its universal human scope and in its particular, culturally determinate expressions—as a datum for historical inquiry; hence the need which both traditions emphasize for a certain empathy into something that lies beyond the deliberate reasoning prevalent in a given past era, empathy into its unitive, internal source of thinking, feeling, imagining, and acting in both the collective group and the particular individual. We have noted this way of thinking in Herder and others at the end of the eighteenth century.

There is a phrase, made famous by Schleiermacher's hermeneutics, to the effect that the interpreter must understand an author "better than he understands himself." [16] Both the historical-critical and the more philosophical (romantic, idealistic, and historicist) users of myth could agree with this claim. They believed themselves able to grasp, as it were from within, a mythological writer's necessary and unconscious belonging to, and expression of, the particular primitive consciousness of his era, its preconceptual and childlike sensuous level in inception, conception, and expression. Both traditions stressed the enormous difference between this early mythical mind-set and that of modernity, though the romantic-idealist in contrast to the historical-critical mythical school also emphasized the continuity between "myth-making" man and "modern" man.[17] Though Hartlich and Sachs quite evidently do not stress with sufficient vigor the common elements in the influence of the mythical and the romantic-idealist schools on endeavors in biblical interpretation such as that of Strauss, their great merit is that they recognize the difference between these two traditions. We may single out two such differences.

First, the mythical school was, from beginning to end, confined to a rationalist stance toward the data under examination, despite its claims to quasi-internal understanding of mythical consciousness. No matter what mythophiles may have thought of the permanent (if any) "content" or "truth" in ancient myths—some had a high, others a low estimate of it—they did not finally consider themselves in the same world of thought, sensibility, or discourse as the writers they were examining, at least not so long as they were estimating from a historical perspective the worth of their supposedly factual reports and the status of their world views. This is, of course, the essence of the critical stance. Hartlich and Sachs rightly emphasize that the mythophiles, in contrast to someone like Herder, thought of "empathy" with the ancient consciousness in the very spirit of its own time as only the first step

in coming to an understanding of myth.[18] The second step was
that of impartial rational assessment of the cultural situation from
which myths arose, and of its archaic forms of life awareness. This
critical stance the mythophiles shared with all the other technical
hermeneutical schools of their day. It is odd but nonetheless true
that in respect of this rationalist stance toward the historical data,
the mythophiles, including Strauss, had more in common with
their opponents, the literalistic Supernaturalists than with the
Romantics together with whom they developed the very concept
of myth.[19]

Second, we may extend this difference in stance between
mythophiles and Romantics to the very aim of interpretation.
Where the Romantics sought *immediate* access to the spirit of
ancient myth-forming consciousness, the mythophiles thought
that understanding or explanation of the ancient writings was
finally synonymous with the assessment of their reliability as
reports of factual occurrences and of their usefulness for explaining the origin of the traditions they express. The governing
explanatory or hermeneutical questions for the mythophiles are:
What actually happened, and how is one to account for the
writings? Once again it is perfectly obvious why, with these issues
foremost in their minds, the narrative portions of the Old and
New Testaments formed their hermeneutical preoccupations.
Like Strauss, their late and climactic representative in biblical
interpretation, the mythophiles believed the answer to these
questions lies in the simple disjunctive alternative: either the
meaning of the miraculous narrative refers to outward miraculous
facts, or it does not, because the narrative originates from and
expresses the myth-making consciousness of the times in which the
oral or saga tradition, later written down, first arose. There is no
other choice.

13 Hermeneutical Options at the Turn of the Century

Largely because the "fact" question provided one of the aims, if not the overriding end, for interpretation, mythophiles and others for whom historical questions had become crucial drew a sharp distinction between two stages of interpretation. The first was the determination of the literal or grammatical sense of a document, the second its historical assessment. At the first level, the pure mythophile might also want to appeal to the sense of empathy with the writer. But the important consideration remained the second step. If one raised the further question of the abiding meaning, significance, or religious content of the writing, the answer would have to await the solution to the second problem.

But even for Strauss, the issue of the abiding meaning or application of the narrative texts was confusing. No factual claims made in the texts can come close to that meaning. On the other hand, the more one looks for "abiding" meaning in the consciousness expressed in the text, the more it has to be focused on the mind of the era that produced the text. And to the mythophiles, unlike the Romantics, that era in its preconceptual, sensuous naiveté is so different from our own that a common bond between the two modes of consciousness would be difficult to establish or express. Small wonder that by 1817 Friedrich Lücke could take for granted the justice of the complaint about all the historical critics, and not only the mythophiles, that they seemed to know nothing about the "inner" or religious meaning or applicability of texts. The problem was to become grim in twentieth-century hermeneutics. In the early nineteenth century it signaled the end of what had hitherto always been taken for granted: no matter what the meaning of a text, its explication and application were technically or formally rather than substantively distinct tasks, because what a text meant formerly and in itself and what it means now are one and the same thing in principle. For example, Keil and Stäudlin, who argued about the scope of historical criticism in estimating the meaning of biblical texts, were quite agreed on this point. To the mythophiles, however, this affirmation has become impossible. Explication has shown the vast difference between ancient and modern consciousness, the mythical shape of the former and the critical shape of the latter. What then is the applicative meaning of an ancient biblical text? At this point Strauss, in the conclusion of *The Life of Jesus*, chose the Hegelian path which he was later to forsake. The mythical consciousness bodies forth in representational form the idea of reconciliation, the universal unity of the ideal and the real which develops throughout the long history of human consciousness. It is difficult to say whether this does not put Strauss finally in the camp of a certain type of allegorizing interpretation. In any case, he gave it up after a fairly short time.[1]

The earlier mythophiles could admit no such stark series of disjunctions as those between the explicative and applicative meaning of the biblical narrative, between meaning as positivity and totally nonpositive meaning. The result of their ambiguous stance on all these issues was thoroughgoing ambiguity in the estimate of the abiding meaning of texts. To some extent they became Naturalists, stipulating some sort of nonmiraculous occurrence in back of a mythical account which constituted its meaning.[2] To some extent they drew banal rationalist lessons in religious philosophy from the narratives, in effect reducing them to vivid expressions of an anthropomorphic teleological theism without specific divine intervention in the world.[3] All they could be sure of was that the second or historical stage of interpretation must come before the estimate of abiding meaning.

In fact, this understanding of what it is to interpret a narrative text already involved a fateful decision concerning the relation of the written text to what it is "about." This decision had in principle been made by Semler, who was the original spokesman for the gathering consensus of biblical historical scholars. While both Ernesti and Semler are regarded as fathers to "general" biblical hermeneutics, Semler was the pioneer in historical interpretation. Both men's analysis typified the disruption of all dogmatically or pietistically founded unity of the canon, simply because both investigated individual writings in their particular character. Both sought to do so by drawing up general rules for the interpretation of all writings, including, of course, the Bible. Both acknowledged the importance of following philological principles in order to master the use of language in particular writings.

But there the agreement ended. Semler and most of the critics who came after him insisted in addition that interpretation must be historical. And this meant, of course, not only understanding the use of words in their particular historical linguistic context— which would be a purely lexicographical procedure—but also the authors' and their first readers' thought in their particular cultural milieu, in its distinction from that of others, including ours. This, together with careful fact assessment, constituted historical understanding and, indeed, the major part (if not the whole) of the hermeneutical task in the case of narratives. Semler himself did not always distinguish clearly the historical-interpretive hermeneutical task from a theological-hermeneutical one (we recall his use of the accommodation theory!), as later historical critics tried to do; but his intention is no less clear for all that, especially in view of such cognate distinctions as his very sharp one between non-normative, historically changing theology and the unchanging, authoritative Christian religion. He summed up the rules of interpretation as follows: "The most important thing, in short, in hermeneutical skill depends upon one's knowing the Bible's use of language properly and precisely, as well as distinguishing and representing to oneself the historical circumstances of a biblical discourse; and on one's being able to speak today of these matters in such a way as the changed times and circumstances of our fellow-men demand. . . . All the rest of hermeneutics can be reduced to these two things." [4]

By contrast, Ernesti and the few who followed him on this score insisted that general hermeneutics reaches no further than the words of texts, i.e. the grammatical meaning and the rules of speech, either literal or figurative.[5] The fateful difference between these two hermeneutical schools was not simply that the one wanted to confine hermeneutics to grammatical meaning while the other included historical interpretation. It was a broader disagreement; for historical interpretation is only one example— though perhaps for that era the crucial one—of the understanding of general hermeneutics as extending to the *subject matter* as distinct from the *words* of a text. This crucial distinction was drawn equally sharply by both sides; and for each it involved a priority choice. For Ernesti, interpreting the subject matter (*res*; the common German terms were to be *Sache, Gehalt,* or *Sachverhalt*) is a separate issue, no longer a general hermeneutical but a theological task, and one to be undertaken only on the basis of, and in harmony with prior determination of the verbal meaning. For those who followed Semler, on the other hand, the priority of grammatical or textual understanding was a merely chronological or procedural matter. The words themselves were not really understood until they were understood on the basis of a grasp of the subject matter which they expressed or represented.

What we have here, then, is a fundamental disagreement over the scope of hermeneutics, i.e. the range of the applicability of general, theologically nonprivileged principles of interpretation. For Ernesti and those who followed him, this range was confined to or identical with the words, or verbal configurations. For Semler, and the vast majority who followed him, meaning intelligible on general rules extended to the subject matter of a text which was, at least partially, distinct from its words.

The contrast is evident in an essay by J. P. Gabler written in deliberate opposition to Ernesti's views; it exemplifies Semler's historical approach, and the quest for the explanation of the subject matter (*Sacherklärung*). The essay is instructive because it illustrates the kind of unstable, mediating point of view concerning subject matter which, if pursued further, could only move to the consistently mythophile extreme. And indeed, though evidently "naturalistic" in this essay in the apparent hope of rescuing some sense of nonmiraculous positivity from his text, Gabler was at other times clearly among the mythophiles.[6]

In the essay, "Concerning the differences between exegesis and explanation, elucidated through the differing ways of treating the narrative of Jesus' temptation",[7] Gabler's wider problem is obviously that of miracle. If one cannot believe in it, as he obviously cannot, what is the status or meaning of a story such as this? The temptation narrative speaks of an external effect and appearance of Satan. How can we interpret this, given on the one hand the difficulty of believing it, but on the other the evangelists' belief that the events had happened just the way they reported them? Gabler rejected the option that the evangelists were deliberate allegorizers. They understood the story literally: even a cursory examination of the text showed that the most natural sense of the story's beginning is that Jesus actually journeyed into the desert; the writers therefore took it that they were reporting an actual event that had happened in the desert. "And with that," says Gabler, "the business of the grammatical exegete, who needs only to be concerned with the true sense of his writer, comes to an end."

But in our day and time this does not get us very far. Now comes the turn of historical and philosophical criticism, which Gabler called *Sacherklärung*, in contrast to *Wortauslegung* or discovery of grammatical meaning. This is the difference between exegesis (investigation of the text's sense) and explanation (elucidation of the subject matter itself). It is not enough to be content with the fact that an ancient writer related a certain event, believing it to be true. It is necessary to ask, was it true indeed? And if it cannot have happened in this way, one has to go on investigating: "How did the writer happen on the story? Is there something true at the base of it? What? How did the additions originate? Or is the whole story fiction? Intentional—that of a deceiver or enthusiast—or only well-intentioned fiction? Philosophical or poetic myth?"

Quoting another commentator with approval, Gabler goes on to say that Ernesti's rule—that in interpretation only what is

written and not what is true is at stake—is correct only where
there is no quarrel about the subject matter. But in disputed cases,
"where something can be genuinely explained as myth or history,
it is indeed important which explanation makes truly appropriate
sense." He ends by warning that one must not overlook the
differing interests of philologist and theologian. "The philologist is
interested only in exegesis, the theologian on the contrary in
explanation of the Bible. The genuine exegete combines both. He
begins with exegesis, and explanation is his goal."

The two stages are quite distinct, and Gabler's interest is clearly
in the second. The preoccupation with miracle and positivity
involves Gabler in identifying the true meaning with the subject
matter rather than the words of the text; and the subject matter
here, and wherever possible, means first assessing the historical
origin of the text in order to see if it refers to a factual state of
affairs, before its meaning is assigned to some other subject
matter. (In this instance, Gabler's movement of explanation is not
from myth but from a natural or nonmiraculous event, viz. a
vision on the part of Jesus, by way of Jesus' own mistaken or
deliberately "accommodated" report of the event as having
occurred externally, to the evangelists who put down correctly
what they had heard and believed.)

As for the applicative meaning of the story, Gabler does not
tackle it. What would he have done if he had done anything at all
on this score? Obviously not the words but the subject matter
would have governed meaning in this sense also. The fact that he
can even momentarily entertain the notion of allegory or
accommodation in connection with this story makes it clear. So
does his affirmation elsewhere of myth in the New Testament,[8] for
it means that he must look beyond the author's literal intention to
the subject matter. However, neither he nor any other mythophile—except for Strauss's half-hearted Hegelian attempts—tries
seriously to tell us what the truth or abiding meaning in myths
might be. For that one must look to the Romantics and their
successors. But then the question will arise afresh whether a text
can at the same time have a mythically, i.e. supernaturally and

positively expressed religious content for its applicative subject matter, and positivity for its explicative subject matter. However, this was not Gabler's concern.

Gabler and Ernesti would have agreed on the two clearly distinct stages of interpretation (though for Gabler there should logically, in nonostensive or mythical texts, have been a third stage, whereas for Ernesti the third or applicative stage would have been a purely practical, perhaps homiletical task). But they would have disagreed vigorously on the scope of general, theologically neutral, and nonprivileged hermeneutics. Ernesti confined it to philological or verbal rather than "subject matter" meaning. It must be remembered that Ernesti wrote to safeguard exegesis against what he regarded as the arbitrary vagaries of pietistic interpreters who had claimed the direct coincidence of the Holy Spirit's presence in the words of the Bible with their own equally inspired reading of them. Being a convinced orthodox Lutheran himself, he did not press the use of a general theologically neutral, critical interpretive method any further than against this claim to an inspired philological interpretation. He did not think that substantive doctrinal matters, truths, or "contents" in the Bible could be adjudicated by appeal to natural, rational analysis. And this proscription included the "facts" of positive revelation, i.e. their occurrence as well as their qualitative meaning.[9]

Ernesti—whom Emanuel Hirsch calls the founder of "purely profane-scientific biblical exegesis" [10]—insisted that (1) the use of words, (2) historical circumstances governing their use, and (3) the author's intention are the only criteria for establishing the meaning of any text. Grammatical exegesis is therefore sufficient for exegetical purposes. His point of view is strikingly reminiscent of some of the linguistic analysts of our day. He declared that "the sense of words depends on the *usus loquendi*. This must be the case, because the sense of words is conventional and regulated wholly by usage. Usage then being understood, the sense of words is of course understood." Again, like interpreters of the common language-analysis sort, he warned against taking etymology as a guide to the meaning of words and denied any difference between the grammatical and logical senses of words. The use of language may be either literal or metaphoric ("tropical").[11] To the latter, Ernesti subjoined rather vaguely the allegorical use. His vagueness need not surprise us, for he could not have been happy with any independent allegorical sense of a text over and above a metaphoric one. For metaphoric sense is obvious from the language, whereas allegorical meaning demands either a knowledge of the author's intention as distinct from his words, or a sense of the text disregarding the author's intention altogether. In either case, the analysis of meaning would trench upon subject matter rather than philological or grammatical interpretation. Wherever possible, Ernesti insisted, the literal sense ought to prevail because it is the primary use of words. Hence the three criteria cited earlier—use of words, the historical circumstances governing their use, and the author's intention—are really three aspects of one principle. Again like some present-day philosophical analysts, Ernesti does not think of the author's intention as a privileged realm beyond his words, to which either he or we, the exegetes, have special access. The words constitute the intention, and any meaning beyond them is a special subject matter which is not within the confines of general hermeneutics, but a "res" specially revealed by the Holy Spirit. Against pietistic interpreters he asserted vigorously—and here he agreed with Semler and his descendants—that one must not assign more than one meaning to a text. Ernesti, unlike Semler, confined that meaning to the author's own.

There was irony in this stand. He meant it, as well as other strictures against the Pietists, to apply to the mystical or spiritual interpretation which they added freely to the literal sense of texts, and which Ernesti, and most other commentators, identified with typological reading. We recall that a typological (not spiritual) reading had been the main stream of precritical Protestant interpretation. Indeed, a basic typological pattern of interpretation had furnished the scheme for the crucial claim that the Bible, particularly both testaments, forms a unity. The typological scheme had been conceived as based on a literal and historical-factual, rather than either mystical or allegorical, understanding of the text. Far from contradicting such an understanding or adding another meaning to the text, typology was thought by the classical Protestant theologians to connect into a significant sequence pattern a series of two or more events, at once literally describable and affirmed as factual occurrences.

This is the irony of Ernesti's argument against typology. That very notion had in part played the role of protecting the literal meaning of words, for which Ernesti was so concerned. It is not surprising, then, that he, as a conservative confessional Lutheran who wants to stress the literal use of words, does not push the argument against typology all the way. He simply says that it is, in any event, not proper exegesis (of a general sort), because it is not derived from the meaning of the text which is accessible to all readers. It cannot be deduced from the words or from the intention of the author which, we recall, coincides for the most part with his words. Clearly, then, the assignation of typological meaning is made by meaning derived rather from the subject matter than from the words of a text. Where prophecy has actually been fulfilled, and a later event is a clear teleological referent of an earlier one so that the two constitute a special series within the space–time continuum, there one may speak of typological meaning derived from the actual subject matter, that is, the events themselves or the Word of God. Otherwise, meaning is verbal and, more often than not, literal. In that case, typology may be read only where the author clearly and intentionally indicates it to be his purpose ("then was fulfilled that which was spoken"). Ernesti is firm that no subject matter whatever, be it occurrences, intentions of authors distinct or separable from their words, or general ideas allegorically represented by the words of the text, can subvert the verbal meaning of the text, to which alone general hermeneutics extends.

Subject-matter meaning, independent of the author's intention and connected with the subject rather than the words of a text, can only be that of the Holy Spirit working autonomously in the Bible as well as in believers. Or else it is the ignorant invention of human fanaticism. In most cases of individual in contrast to confessional interpretations, Ernesti inclined to the latter opinion: once a man regards the subject matter of scripture to be the divinely appointed fulfillment of foreshadowed events, and the communication of such "facts" to be saving truth to which he is privy, he will find the subject covertly present everywhere in the Bible and in control of every text. And the guarantee of the rightness of his interpretation will be his own illumination by the same Spirit who governs Holy Writ. Against this sort of procedure Ernesti warned that since "types are not words but things, which God has designated as signs of future events," we should be careful never to exceed the instructions of the Holy Spirit concerning subject-matter affirmations. Further or more specific instructions Ernesti did not give (except for cursory, possibly contradictory appeals to the *analogia fidei,* the dogmatic instrument for apprehending and interpreting the unity of canonical subject matter), beyond deprecating those who intrude typology arbitrarily into every part of the Bible.[12]

Just how little he thought of this procedure in exegesis is indicated by the fact that shortly after the passage just cited, in which he at least seemed to allow the practice under properly authorized auspices, he proceeded to reject it altogether. He warned his readers that "the method of gathering the sense of words from things is altogether deceptive and fallacious; since things are rather to be known from pointing out the sense of words in a proper way. It is by the words of the Holy Spirit only that we are led to understand what we ought to think respecting things." [13]

Here was the issue that pitted Ernesti and his school against the whole field: everyone else from Supernaturalist to historical critic was convinced that the scope of hermeneutics extends to the subject matter; and unlike the Pietists everyone else (once again, of course, Ernesti excepted) affirmed that it is general hermeneutics that extends to the subject matter. The choice of the logical priority of the subject matter over the words is the fateful decision of late eighteenth century hermeneutics.

Let us recall the hermeneutical polarity concerning biblical narratives, corresponding to, and largely occasioned by, the issue of the positivity of revelation. The mediating positions tended to be pushed either toward a specific, ostensive, or referential interpretation, i.e. the affirmation of biblical literalism and the factual reliability of the accounts, or toward a completely historical, nonostensive understanding of the narratives. Strauss was the most consistent example of the latter position. He adopted it, we recall, to demonstrate the unreliability of the narratives as factual reports. Semler had won out over Ernesti, who would have detached such questions of the true subject matter from the investigation of the generally accessible meaning of narrative texts. Given the overriding concern with demonstrating the historicity or nonhistoricity of the contents of the accounts, this result is hardly surprising. The choice of subject matter finally came to be between the two extremes of literally intended accounts which are reliable factual reports, and historically understood mythical accounts which have no essential connection with fact reporting.

THE RANGE OF SUBJECT MATTER PROPOSALS

A variety of positions went down the drain of incredibility as a result of this centrifugal pressure, though the reader is apt to find echoes of some of them in certain present-day hermeneutical stances. The basic decision over the scope of general hermeneutics having been made, we can simply sketch out the spectrum of positions at the turn of the century, before the triumph of the romantic–idealistic revolution in theology, which reinforced the victory of the mythophiles in hermeneutics. Thereafter, the debate changed titles and the issues about revelation or positivity and biblical interpretation reappeared under the heading of "the relation between faith and history." But at the turn of the century this was still in the future, and the choice of subject matter constituting the meaning of the biblical narratives was fairly wide. Three distinct positions may be identified on this issue, though it must be added that some of them could be (and were) held in combination.

1. There were, first of all, those who believed that the subject matter must be ostensive, i.e. the meaning of the narratives is the state of affairs in the spatiotemporal world to which they refer. This state of affairs would usually be extramental. In regard to some narratives it could be mental, but even then its status would be determined by its connection with extramental, datable occurrences. (With regard to the gospels, either the ministry or the resurrection of Jesus was the crucial instance of an extramental occurrence for most interpreters, while his temptation and transfiguration were much more easily conceded to have been mental events.) Theologically, the men adopting some version of the ostensive meaning theory were (with the one obvious and notable exception of Reimarus) committed to the positivity of revelation, whether they focused it on the narrated events or on the character of the historical Jesus. For these proponents of ostensive meaning there were three options.

(i) There were the so-called Supernaturalists, who took the narratives literally. (The German word is *eigentlich*, the meaning of which hovers ambiguously between literally and actually, a fact that introduced considerable confusion into the debate.) For them, the meaning of the narratives was bound up with the credibility of their miracle reports, and with that of the narrative transactions generally.

These supernaturalistic literalists were very much on the defensive, for they were arguing on their opponents' terms. Like them, they asserted that the subject matter is the meaning of the narratives, but unlike them, of course, they asserted that all of a narrative, including the miracles, is to be taken literally. To understand the words is to understand the subject matter. At the same time, however, the words must be understood *through* the subject matter. The contradiction is apparent rather than real, because we know these words in the same way we know all those used in ostensive descriptions. In other words, the subject matter in this instance is sufficiently like others we are acquainted with (spatiotemporal events pictured or mirrored by words) that its similarity guarantees the meaning of the words. Philosophically and theologically, this stand meant that the Supernaturalists had to argue in the court of natural reason that miracle is both a coherent and, therefore, meaningful notion and a possibly real occurrence. Actual rather than possible truth, in other words credibility in actual instances, is the only point where the issue is raised beyond the level of general argument to that of faith, and even here the matter is doubtful because "evidence" counts in raising or lowering credibility.

Hermeneutically, the Supernaturalists argued that the meaning of the narratives corresponds to their authors' intention, and that the intention is literal. The words themselves express the authors' design. But once again they were arguing on their opponents' grounds. For they were in effect equating identity of intention and words with identity of intention and subject matter, i.e. with the authors' intention to give a reliable report of spatiotemporal occurrences. In effect, their literalism is quite different from that of Ernesti, for whom the meaning of the text is the use of words, and the intention of the author counts only as coinciding with the words, not as an independent factor behind the words, pointing to the subject matter beyond them. But for all subject-matter interpretation, the intention of the author is sufficiently independent of the words that their meaning is really his intended reference to the subject matter, i.e. (for the ostensivists) external occurrences. The German word for literal, *eigentlich*, covered this ambiguity, so that one could never know if it meant that a series of words made sense literally rather than (say) allegorically or symbolically, or if it meant that the sequence of words "meant" by fulfilling the author's supposed intention to describe the external world.

A typical instance of this ambiguity may be found in the writing of the supernaturalist theologian most frequently cited as opposing the mythophiles, Johann Jakob Hess.[14] In his essay, "Gränzenbestimmung dessen, was in der Bibel Mythus, Anthropathie, personifizierte Darstellung, Poesie, Vision und was würkliche Geschichte ist," [15] he notes in the preface the curious biblical combination of religion with "narrated history." The word he uses is *Geschichte,* and it is often quite impossible to tell if he is using it in the sense of story or sequence of actual events. This ambiguity parallels the other, concerning the meaning of *eigentlich.* His critical opponents automatically assumed that he was speaking of the subject matter, that he was making a case for ostensive meaning. And this is, of course, what he was doing theologically. Whether or not this was also his hermeneutical stance is an open question, on which one can only say he manifested considerable inconsistency and confusion. Neither this nor his opponents' automatic assignation of his hermeneutics to ostensive meaning is surprising: it was in the atmosphere of the day, once general hermeneutics was automatically assumed to be dealing with subject matter.

Hess wanted to distinguish sharply between the meaning and the credibility of history-like biblical accounts. The task of *Gränzenbestimmung* between literal and mythical meanings in the Bible is not to be confused with their credibility. But one of his criteria for the distinction is appeal to the author's intention. "They meant much of the miraculous material they related to be understood literally." To this the mythophiles, as Schelling, Strauss, and Hartlich and Sachs have pointed out in turn, had an irrefutable answer: of course the authors meant their descriptions to be taken literally, since they themselves partook both unconsciously and necessarily of the mythological thought mode of their culture. All that Hess could properly claim, therefore, was that the authors were not allegorists.

Hess deliberately cited Ernesti's words: "in interpretatione nihil aliud quaeritur, quam quid dictum sit, non quale fit aut quam vere dictum." The influence of Ernesti on him was strong indeed. He wanted to undertake a kind of surface reading (*kursorische Lesart*) which would permit him to pay attention to the narrative mode (*Erzählungsweise*), and obviously to the verbal or grammatical meaning. Nonetheless, between this and the discussion of the credibility of the narratives, he stipulates another level of the quest for the meaning of the narratives, and this involves the apprehension of the subject matter (*Sache*). This subject matter is identical with the ostensive meaning of the words, and he is bound to have the authors' intention brought into line with the correspondence between their description and the external events. But why, ask the mythophiles, should we assume identity between the meaning of the words and the intention of the authors, seeing that the authors are of a mythological mind-set and the events so incredible? In the words of Hartlich and Sachs: "it is not the intention of the mythographer but objective criteria . . . which determine whether a narrative is mythical." One can hardly be surprised by the same commentators' adoption, under these circumstances, of the disjunctive alternative, excluding all other options about subject matter, which we have seen to be the outcome of the pressure toward outright rejection or defense of positivity: these narratives mean either literally, i.e. ostensively, or they mean mythically. "For orthodoxy," say Hartlich and Sachs, "when it can no longer hold rigidly to the dogma of immediate inspiration, everything depends on a sure criterion for the delimitation of what in the Bible is to be understood literally, and what mythically." [16]

It is apparent that "historical understanding" of the consciousness of the authors and of their time has made it impossible to find such a "sure" criterion in the case of all narratives of miraculous or inexperienceable character. Just what are the two authors asking for in this statement, so triumphalist for one side, so pathos-ridden for the other? What is wanted is demonstrable identity between subject matter and words or description in some scriptural texts, so that one may be able to affirm it as possible in others. But as long as a distinct subject matter (governing the words) and privileged access to the author's intention (distinct from the words) dictate the reading of the words, the only way one can demonstrate this identity is by external evidence. And this is not easy to come by.

Ernesti had fought dogmatic Supernaturalism in hermeneutics, but adopted a very conservative, confessional stance in dogmatic theology. It was ironic that within a short period his theological position should have been defended by the very hermeneutical approach he himself had rejected because he considered it far too sweeping—that the subject matter is the meaning of the text to which general hermeneutics has access. This is what the literalistic Supernaturalists, like their scientific-historical opponents, were saying.

(ii) The second group for whom the subject matter or meaning of biblical narratives must be ostensive were the so-called Naturalists, of whom H. E. G. Paulus was the most distinguished. Unable to believe in miracles, they dropped the literalistic interpretation of individual miraculous reports and, of course, the promise-fulfillment scheme with respect to the Bible as a whole. But they still believed that the meanings of the narratives are the occurrences in the spatiotemporal world to which they refer. For them, as for the Supernaturalists, the specifically narrative character also drops out of the understanding of the narratives, together with promise-fulfillment. Instead, a vindication of the possibility of some sort of nonmiraculous historical occurrence in back of individual reported incidents becomes the primary intention of interpretation. The subject and hence the meaning of biblical narrative statements are the historically reconstructible nonmiraculous or natural occurrences erroneously reported as direct supernatural interventions.

While this position was not important in itself, it was a significant if not indispensable ancillary argument for those who wanted to uphold the positivity of christocentric revelation in more moderate form than the revelatory meaning of the sheer occurrence character of the narrated events. We recall those for whom positivity was a matter of nonphysical miracle, to be found in the teaching and bearing of Jesus, bespeaking his uniqueness. The Neologians generally were close to this position, and so at times were mythophiles like Gabler and Bauer. All those who, like Semler, wanted to distinguish between something like the moral and the public, statutory aspects of Christian religion, but without losing all hold on positivity, veered at times into the naturalist position.

(iii) Finally, there were some (Reimarus is the classical instance) who believed that the gospel accounts, especially those of the resurrection, did indeed mean ostensively. But the real event to which they refer is a plot to deceive people. The real intention of the evangelists is the very opposite of what they reported. They lied when they related the miracle of the resurrection. The tale was designed to enable them to perpetrate a spiritual power grab.

2. The second group were those who rejected the notion that the subject matter or meaning of biblical narratives is ostensive. For them, the subject of the narratives consisted of the ideas or moral and religious truths (*Gehalt*) stated in them in narrative form. We may call them allegorists or rationalists. They believed that the narratives refer ideally rather than ostensively. There were two versions of this view.

(i) Some thought these ideas or truths were inseparable from the authors' intentions. As a result, the interpreters understood the narratives as deliberately contrived allegories or fables, by means of which the writers had communicated ideal truths in the impartation of which they had accommodated themselves to the thought pattern of their contemporaries. This was really the only hermeneutical position for which the intention of the writer as something completely distinct from what he actually said played the crucial role. Ernesti, and before him the Supernaturalists and Anthony Collins, had also stressed that texts must be interpreted in harmony with the authors' intentions; but the point for all of them was that in the reading of texts precisely the identity, not the opposition, between authors' words and their intentions, is decisive. The reverse was the case for the allegorical interpreters.

This was a popular notion among nonsupernaturalist interpreters in the late eighteenth century. But it appeared comparatively rarely in pure form. Instead, it was usually found uneasily yoked with one of the ostensivist positions: the idea contained in the allegory is the religious meaning of the reported occurrences which nonetheless did happen, either in natural or literal, miraculous form. G. T. Zachariä's position is an instance of this combination. In purer form—that the allegory alone is the meaning because it was the intention of the author, and that the question of the occurrence of the events is either an error or simply beside the point—one finds this position in theologians like K. F. Bahrdt, J. B. Basedow, and, to a lesser extent, J. A. Eberhard and S. Steinbart. In matters of biblical interpretation these men corresponded to the more general rationalism of such better-known figures as Moses Mendelssohn, Friedrich Nicolai, and the poet C. M. Wieland. They all represented in Germany the adherence to that pure rationalism or natural religion which had made much more rapid gains in France and England. As noted, in its less pure or consistent form this was the favorite position of many mediating theologians or Neologians.[17]

(ii) Others (actually Kant seems to have been the only important figure in the late eighteenth century) detached the allegorically shaped subject matter wholly from the author's intention, and also from any endeavor to understand the thought forms of his day, and from all inquiry into the relation of possible occurrences to the allegorical narrative. For Kant the meaning of the biblical narratives was strictly a matter of understanding the ideas they represent in story form. Any historiographical considerations are strictly irrelevant to the interpretation of the subject matter, which is the foundation and advancement of a pure moral disposition in the inner man and its connection with the ideal realm of ends.

Eichhorn's objection that one can determine on historical grounds that the biblical writers in fact did not intend to allegorize, while decisive against the previous variant of the allegorist position, would not have fazed Kant one whit. The meaning of a text, the proper interpretation of its subject matter, must be in accordance with general canons of reason. Hence it is quite independent of its author's intention as well as other historical or historiographical considerations. But it is instructive of the strength of historical interpretation at that time that everybody rejected Kant's view on grounds similar to those of Eichhorn. Kant had the privilege of seeing almost everyone, no matter from what hermeneutical school, united against him. One hundred years later, Wilhelm Dilthey could still speak of the notoriety of Kant's hermeneutical position.

Immanuel Kant's *Religion Within the Limits of Reason Alone*[18] is a very difficult book, and it is best not to analyze it at all rather than do so cursorily. But one thing must be pointed out. It is often said that Kant's is the archetypical example of dissolving the unique biblical message into general, rational ideas, i.e. historical faith and salvation into a moral disposition, allegorically set forth in historical and ecclesiological terms. But this is an oversimplification of Kant's stand. One of the most interesting features of this fascinating book is the fact that it renders an account of the process of conversion which has been such a preoccupation of liberal Protestant theologians. They have always posed the question of the way in which one may meaningfully describe the transition from the possibility to the actual occurrence of faith, or, alternatively, the transition from a state of sin ("radical evil" in Kant's equivalent term) to one of grace. They have always wanted to find the coherence between a descriptively universal human situation (such as that of sin) and the contingent free historic act (and/or miracle) of faith. The moral-religious parallel to this endeavor is Kant's preoccupation, at least in the earlier part of the book: and in Book Two he describes the rationale of the transition from one state, that of radical evil, to the other, that of the dominance of a good will. In the process he does his best to reinterpret, into the terms appropriate to this transition, the concepts and stories derived from biblical and traditional Christian usage.

The interesting result of this endeavor is a characteristic which Dilthey alone among commentators has noted, at least in part.[19] Kant is one of the few major thinkers of his day—Herder and the biblical theologians aside—to claim once again the unity of the canon. This is, however, only partly due to the fact that he

detached the meaning of the books from their authors' intentions
and imposed the same framework of moral interpretation on all of
them. In part, and Dilthey did not see this, the recovery of the
unity of the canon is due to the recovery of the significance of
narrative shape which Kant takes seriously. He takes it seriously
at once in the description of the individual's radical moral
change, and in the description of life in the service of the kingdom
of ends. This stress on the narrative feature and its mirroring of an
actual moral process makes Kant's "subject matter" in the New
Testament far more than a simple, abstractly statable moral idea.
It enables him, among other things, to take seriously those
elements of meaning in the gospel accounts that were traditionally closely connected with, indeed derived from, the event
sequence of the story. Thus Kant can deal far more positively
than any other Rationalist with one of the doctrines that was most
troublesome to the Neologians, the doctrine of substitutionary
satisfaction.[20] Certainly he can do far greater justice to it than any
other Rationalist. He can, in fact, evaluate it far more positively
than Neologians like Toellner or Semler.

All of this indicates why Kant is rightly called an allegorical
interpreter. The term is admittedly used loosely in this connection. None of the allegorical interpreters are strictly speaking
employing allegory, if one means by that the personification of
general qualities such as courage, virtue, pride, or melancholy.
Further, Kant is no allegorical interpreter of the gospels if the
definition of allegory involves claiming that the author's deliberate intention is to clothe general ideas in story form. On the
contrary! But he fits the case more nearly than the others
mentioned under this general rubric, if allegory involves a
description of a stage-by-stage process, in which the stages of the
narrative are paralleled by similar stages in the real subject
matter to which the narrative points, and which we know
independently of the narrative.[21]

3. Finally there were the mythophiles. They did not believe
that the meaning of narratives was in any sense ostensive, even

when the tales accidentally rendered a degree of information about past occurrences. Equally decisive was their rejection of both variants of the allegorist position. The first practically dishonored the authors; the second (Kant's position) ignored them and imported meaning into the Bible from the outside. There were times when the mythophiles were forced to think about the "content" of myths, but their tentative motion at such times toward the allegorist position was confused and even muted. For their main emphasis was to see the subject matter of biblical narratives neither in the events to which they referred nor in the ideas supposedly stated in them in narrative form, but in the consciousness they represented. The mythophiles' sharp distinction between representation and what is represented is the same as that between the authors' literal intention and the actual state of their minds which is one of necessary and unconscious mythologizing. The latter is the subject matter, and it is the critical historian who has access to it and the ability to evaluate it properly for what it is. As noted earlier, as a technical tool for explanation "myth" is a genetic-psychological category employed in the process of critical-historical understanding

In one important respect the hermeneutical principles of the mythophiles were similar to those of Herder. He too saw the subject matter of the narratives in the historical group consciousness they represented or embodied. But he persistently claimed that there is perfect harmony between that consciousness and what he believed to be the realistic representation in which it was embodied. Hence he did not share the mythophiles' muted tendencies toward allegorizing the abiding meaning of the narratives, or their more general affirmation of the distance between the narratives' subject matter and their story form. In part for these, in part for other reasons he took a dim view of the mythophiles' (and other scholars') view that technical, historical-critical procedure can reach the actual subject matter of the narratives. And, again unlike the mythophiles, Herder's beliefs in the coherence between consciousness and realistic representation led him to affirm that the meaning of some (though by no means all) of the biblical stories is as much their ostensive reference as the consciousness they embody.

This was the variety of hermeneutical positions concerning biblical narratives which prevailed at the turn from the eighteenth to the nineteenth century. I have stressed several times that the pressure of the problem of positivity weakened the mediating positions both theologically and hermeneutically. The Naturalists had to have recourse to ludicrous postulations of natural occurrences to account for miraculous tales. The deception theory of Reimarus stirred a brief flurry of excitement, but little more. The Allegorists (first variety) had little or no evidence from the writers to support the entirely speculative and unlikely hypothesis about the writers' intentions and their self-accommodation to their readers' supposedly lower level of insight. Kant's decision to ignore that intention in apprehending the meaning of narratives might have worked in an earlier, ecclesiastical-theological day when biblical meaning could be taken to be independent both of authors' intentions and the words of the text. But this kind of miraculous status had to be guaranteed by something like the independent authority and direct agency of the Spirit in the writing of the Bible. In a day of rising historical consciousness this would hardly do; Kant might have won some assent if he had argued the one option or the other—either to ignore the words or to abandon the author and his historical context. To do both simultaneously was too much for his contemporaries. As for the various syntheses, compromises and vacillations between allegorist and naturalist positions, between Naturalism and Mythophilism, etc., they all suffered from theological and hermeneutical ambiguity or inconsistency with regard to the question of the positivity of revelation. Given that overriding theological issue, and given also the one hermeneutical agreement among all schools except that of Ernesti—that the meaning of a text is its subject matter—the hermeneutical choice had to be between literalistic Supernaturalism and the mythical school.

14 Myth and Narrative Meaning: A Question of Categories

> For orthodoxy, when it can no longer cling rigidly to the
> dogma of immediate inspiration, everything depends on a
> sure criterion for delimiting what should be understood
> literally in the Bible, and what mythically.[1]

It would appear at first glance that the rise of critical historical
inquiry into the biblical writings, and the debate over their
miraculous factual claims describing direct divine intervention in
the sequence of finite events, forced a neat and tidy dilemma on
the theologian.

On the one hand, he would have to acknowledge the natural,
human origin of these writings. He would have to admit that they
were factually unreliable as well as fallible and time-conditioned
in their ideational content, and hence (finally) relative rather
than absolute in any truth claims they might make. All this would
mean that they were only relatively "inspired," i.e. to a degree
compatible with the natural-historical development of the race at
the time of their inception. Hence they occupy no qualitatively
unique or special truth-revealing status in comparison with other
sacred writings or with the reflective products of wise and
well-informed men of any time. Scriptural revelation is equivalent
to the historical development of the consciousness of the race. This
is the lesson Lessing and (in more conservative form) Herder drew
from the struggles over biblical narratives.

On the other hand, if the theologian did not want to move in
this direction, he would have to insist that the biblical writings
were not only inspired and, therefore, absolutely coherent, but
also factually reliable, their guaranteed and infallibly true
ostensive character at one with the infallible truth and coherence
of their language and message. In this view, the nature of the
biblical writings is truth as well as fact communicating, except

267

where it is indicated to be figurative (or "tropical") by unmistakable internal evidence. In other words, in the face of Deists and other critics, questioning the reliability and inspired character of the writings, one would have to show (1) the credibility, if not probability, of the "facts" asserted in the writings; (2) the ostensive character or sense of a large and crucial segment of the writings, especially descriptions of divine intervention (i.e. that they either had no other meaning than their ostensive character, or had such other meaning only in addition to, but not contravention of, their ostensive character); and (3) criteria for distinguishing fairly between those portions of the writings that possess literal meaning and ostensive character, and those that do not.

Concerning the hermeneutical issue, as it arose especially in German biblical scholarship, mainly under the pressure of the question of the positivity of revelation, the basic problem was simply this: Was the sense of the writings ostensive? If not, just what was their meaning? The basic issue in hermeneutics appeared to be that of covering the gap between statements that appeared sufficiently history-like to warrant their being considered historical, and their "real" meaning if they were not. We have seen the range of suggestions proposed for closing the gap. Whatever they were, they depended on the tacit or explicit acceptance of this hiatus between the statements and their meaning. Even the Supernaturalists argued that the narratives "mean" by reference to something beyond themselves, to wit, events in the external world. To close the gap between the words or narrative and the "real" meaning, one had to appeal to one or more of the following: historical occurrences; the mind of the author as distinct from his words; ideas independent of both, as well as of the words of the text. In all three cases, the meaning is the subject matter as distinct from the words. Furthermore, except for the third instance (Kant), the estimate of meaning involves historical assessment. In the first, this is obvious. In the second it takes the form of appeal to the author's intention, followed by an estimate of the value of his intention by means of historical understanding of the cultural setting of his mind.

The triumph and increasing dominance of the mythical school was due to its making a credible proposal for bridging the gap between words and meaning, and showing how the texts mean if they are neither ostensive nor yet allegorical. The connection between the narrative form and the consciousness represented by it (which is their meaning) is made by the device of historical understanding, using the genetic-psychological category of myth in order to show the distinct consciousness of which myth is a product. Between this and ostensive meaning of the literal sort the mythical school saw no cogent position. Hence the disjunctive and apparently exhaustive alternative quoted in the epigraph at the head of this chapter. It represents the theme of the mythophiles' claim. They thought that the literalists had the most appropriate alternative to their own view. It made better sense of the narratives than any of the compromising positions. But how could the Supernaturalists or literalists make good on the claim that a certain writing is not explained better by the mythological hypothesis?

Now, as long as this question challenged the literalists to show that a narrative is not only meant literally by its writer but should also be taken as, in fact, literally ostensive and therefore nonmythical, the mythophiles' case seems to be secure.

But is this really the only set of alternatives concerning narrative meaning? There is one particular way of understanding narratives which could not be caught in so wide-meshed a net. Commentators of the mythical school were vaguely, yet evidently and, one may add, uncomfortably aware of it. Nor was it seriously considered by any of the mediating hermeneutical positions. Hess was trying to adumbrate it, but could not get it in focus. The reason for this is obvious, for the suggestion involves the claim that the hiatus posited between narrative and subject matter is misleading, if not wrong. In regard to the meaning of biblical narratives, Ernesti was far closer to the mark than his opponents, no matter what their place in the range of subject matter proposals, when he insisted on distinguishing words from subject matter but confined hermeneutics to the sense of the words. As for those for whom general hermeneutics extends to the subject matter of the text, a subject matter that is distinct from and governs the meaning of the words, they could obviously find no room for a proposal claiming that the narrative itself is the meaning of the text, that it refers to no other "subject matter," and that the meaning, to the extent that one does think of it as at all distinct from the text, emerges cumulatively from the text itself. Such a proposal would be more than wrong; it would finally be unintelligible in the spectrum of differing hermeneutical advocates (excluding Ernesti). All of them would immediately mistake it for a suggestion concerning the ostensive character of the narratives, or they would ask how one can understand any description apart from the historical situation of the writer and of the historically conditioned character of his ideas and language.

On the other hand, if they are wrong, such a proposal is at least viable, and the dilemma concerning the question of the significance of the Bible (or at least its narrative portions), stated in the epigraph at the beginning of this chapter, is misleading and insufficiently complex, for it rests on the assumption that there must be an organic connection, if not identity, between literal meaning of the narratives and the literal-ostensive claim that they were accurate descriptions of external events. Otherwise, this assumption entails, literal meaning makes no sense.

The mythophiles were evidently uneasy over the appropriate classification of, as well as assignation of meaning to, the narrative form or structure of the biblical stories, especially Genesis 1–3 and the synoptic gospels. To what genre, if any, do stories of this sort belong, and how does one determine the classification? Indeed, in their eyes one of the advantages of their own hermeneutical device, in contrast to more rationalist procedures, lay in the fact that it did not explain away the narrative structure as a peripheral item but sought instead to interpret it. What must be questioned is the effectiveness of this interpretation. This was also

Hess's point, and the reason he tried hard to make room for a distinct category of *Erzählungsweise* in his adumbration of hermeneutical principles. But he did not make his point, since he argued that the narrative mode is an expression of the author's intention to make ostensive claims. If one cannot argue that the author's intention is identical with the words or the descriptive shape of the narrative (and Hess either did not or left the issue confused), one had best leave the question of the author's intention aside altogether in figuring out the sense of a narrative text. This was Ernesti's point. It was a good point to make in connection with the biblical narratives, but it went almost totally against the hermeneutical grain of the day.

The mythophiles recognized a distinctive phenomenon in the narrative texts, but every time they tried to set forth its specifying differentia they failed because, in effect, they explained that what they had just acknowledged to be there wasn't really there after all. Their interpretive device or category was simply not fitted to the task. All the mythophiles acknowledged that some "myths" were more "history-like" than others. Sometimes it was said that they were simpler, less decorative than others; but the previous way of putting the matter is perhaps better. Once again, Strauss, by virtue of his consistent, astute, and at the same time simple-minded reductionism on this matter may serve as the best representative of the school. The simplest and commonly accepted definition of myth is that it is the history of the gods. Right there Strauss had to modify if not abandon the term, because it does not fit much, if anything, in the Bible. The best criterion for myth that would also include the appropriate biblical tales, he found, was the direct intercourse of the divine with men, especially with men of heroic, almost divine stature. Compared to certain other myths, especially classical myths, the status of biblical heroes may be somewhat less than perfectly fitting. Nonetheless, the other part of the description certainly fits. In actual fact Strauss seems to equate myth, inclusive of biblical myth, first of all with miracle. It is "a happening in which the divine enters without mediation into the human, ideas manifest themselves without mediation in embodied form." Second, following Heyne, Eichhorn, Schelling, Gabler, and Bauer, he specified as myth any narrative which tells "in history-like fashion either absolutely inexperienceable matters, such as facts of the supernatural world, or relatively inexperienceable ones, where due to the circumstances no one could have been a witness." [2] Biblical myth in this general sense, slightly different from miracle, is simply identical with "the sacred history" of creation, promise, salvation, and consummation.

Whether the "content" of myth is a thought—i.e. an inchoate explanation or general idea not yet risen to the level of abstract generalization (philosophical myth), or the detailing of a past occurrence handed down through oral tradition or saga (historical myth), or the spontaneous exuberance of verbal decoration behind which neither of the two previous elements is visible (poetic myth)—the content is presented "in historical form, but a form determined by the sensuous and fantasizing mode of thought and speech of antiquity." [3]

The meaning or content of the myth and its form of depiction, what is represented and the representation, are obviously separable things, though each is worthy of consideration. Biblical myth must obviously fit this pattern.

And yet Strauss and the earlier mythophiles were aware that the fit is at least not precise. The difference, as already suggested, seemed to have something to do with greater history-likeness or simplicity, not necessarily with greater credibility. After all, there is no intrinsic reason why a simple miracle—say, a raising from the dead with no details given—should be any more credible as an actual occurrence than an embellished miracle. The fact that this puzzle over classification should have arisen in connection with *biblical* "myth" is almost irrelevant. The point is really the broader question of the effectiveness of myth as a general hermeneutical category.[4] And back of that lies the issue of the degree to which any single category of interpretation is adequate to the inquiry into the meaning of ancient narrative documents involving miracles. In other words, the chief issue that haunts the debate over myth in the Bible is not merely the applicability of the category to its various narrative portions, nor whether these portions of the Bible are unique in meaning and, therefore, subject only to a completely special hermeneutics; the heart of the matter is the question whether ancient narratives of doubtful ostensive value but realistic or history-like form, exemplifying a close relation between narrative form and meaning, no matter where they are found, can be unlocked by the identical interpretive device—that of myth and, more broadly, any category separating the meaning from the depictive shape. The lingering qualms of the mythophiles concerning the classification of the biblical narratives as myths were or should have been qualms about the adequacy of this procedure. The members of this school should have been uneasy about the extension of general hermeneutics (and myth as its particular instrument) to the subject matter of texts, for it forced them to read the words in line with the subject matter postulated by their general hermeneutical device. It is at least possible that in regard to realistic narrative literature, the function of general hermeneutics should be formal rather than material; it should be confined to identifying a piece of literature as belonging to that particular genre rather than some other, rather than claim to interpret its meaning or subject matter.

As for the latter task, there may be no single interpretive device to satisfy it (nor is there necessarily any need for such a weighty interpretive device!), due to the nature of this type of literature. And it does not matter whether it is found in the Bible or elsewhere. In a sense, every narrative of the sort in which story and meaning are closely related may have its own special hermeneutics. While such a distinction between general and special hermeneutics, corresponding to the distinction (in narratives) between genre specification and understanding of meaning, is not the same as Ernesti's distinction between understanding the sense of the words and understanding the subject matter and confining the task of interpretation to the former, there is no denying an affinity between the two suggestions.

The mythophiles noted that the gap between representation

and what is represented, between narrative shape and meaning, is not so great in the simpler history-like biblical myths as in some others. They noted this feature quite obviously at points in the Bible where miracles and inexperienceable data are being narrated. Hence the difference they sensed between biblical and other myths is obviously not the same for them as the difference between historical fact and fiction. Since all miraculous and inexperienceable features were obviously fictional for them, the difference between the simple and the embellished, the more and the less "history-like," should in fact have been for them nothing other than a difference between one kind of narrative writing and another. They had a literary or hermeneutical distinction on their hands, and they sensed it, but they could not handle it. They had no category for dealing with the meaning of biblical narratives other than the disjunctive device that assigned either ostensive or mythical status to them. It was a case of obvious category confusion: "myth," a genetic-psychological category, became confused with a literary-analytical device, and so had to do duty for both. The failure in literary or hermeneutical analysis became inevitable. As soon as a literary analysis loomed, indicating the distinction between biblical and other myths, it was immediately transformed into—because it was thought to be part of—a historical analysis. The analysis of the history-likeness of the narratives was thought to be an analysis of their possibly ostensive meaning, and, therefore, part of an assessment of their historical reliability.

About the "Mosaic" creation story, Gabler wrote: "Concerning the main subject matter, there is no denying . . . that none of the ancient cosmogonies, be they myths or philosophical constructions, can be even vaguely compared with the Mosaic cosmogony. It is the simplest and loftiest conception, and the one most nearly appropriate to even the most penetrating modern observations about the course of nature." [5] Bauer, one of the more consistent mythophiles in the generation before Strauss, conceded the lack of variety in the later shaping and embellishing of original myths among Hebrew in contrast to Greek and Roman authors. He also thought that Hebrew mythology differed advantageously from others by its lack of the weird if not the miraculous, its monotheism, its creationism, and its consistently religious character.[6]

But it was Strauss who was most vividly aware of the differences between biblical and other narratives and proceeded to resolve them immediately by a reduction to the historical issue of fact vs. fiction, and to the corresponding hermeneutical issue of literal-ostensive vs. mythical meaning or subject matter. He said, in effect, that he had discerned a difference and then, instead of trying to see systematically what it was, went on to say that actually it wasn't there at all. He analyzed the differences as follows.

1. Like most commentators since the second-century apologists, he claimed a higher moral plane on behalf of the biblical, especially the New Testament concepts of God and of sacred history than for other ancient traditions. He added immediately that this fact has no demonstrative power in favor of the historical factuality of the biblical narratives: "An immoral history of the gods *must* be, but even the most moral *may* be fiction." The real subject matter, the real meaning in other words, is either ostensive or mythical. The words just quoted are indicative of his whole approach. He confused hermeneutical and historical issues as soon as he saw a distinctive literary genre, and he reduced literary meaning to the status of possible (as distinct from likely or actual) historical factuality.

2. He agreed that the element of the weird is much less pronounced in biblical narratives than pagan myths, reiterating that this quality is a sign that the latter must be fiction, but not that the former need be true. He has an imaginary interlocutor say: "But of things unbelievable and unthinkable there is all too much in the pagan fables, whereas nothing of the sort is to be found in the biblical story, if only one presupposes the immediate operation of God." To which the author responds: "Indeed, if one presupposes this." [7] The distinction between the simple and history-like and the embellished and weird is there once more.

But it is lost as a cutting difference immediately, because the two different types of story "mean" in relation to the same subject matter: it must be either myth or fact. And so a difference in meaning that has nothing to do with the fact–fiction issue is lost.

3. Strauss claimed that the assertion that the Bible contains no myths finally rests on the difference in character between pagan myths, in which the gods themselves have an all-too-human history, and the contrasting affinity of biblical narrative with what we think metaphysically and morally worthy of the idea of God. It is not only pagan polytheism and the character of the gods' desires and acts, but the very fact that they have a history at all (being born, growing up, marrying, begetting children, etc.) that is offensive to our notion of the Absolute. We recognize myths wherever the Absolute is conceived of as subject to time and change, affects and passion.[8] By contrast, Strauss suggested, the biblical narratives guard the distinction between the divine and the human. Particularly in connection with the metaphysical question, even the New Testament which lays such stress on the divine–human relation asserts that divine being is related to temporal being only in a way that does not impair divine unchangeability and immutability.

It is puzzling that Strauss should have used such clearly metaphysical (nonmythological) notions as arguments for the greater historical-factual possibility of the biblical stories, instead of arguing their metaphysical superiority over other myths. But the fact is that he did it in the present context. Once more, therefore, one may note that he saw nonmythical or at least distinctive features in the biblical narratives, this time in their metaphysical "character portrayal" of deity and of the divine–finite relationship. Again, it was a case of a much closer relationship (if not downright identity) between description and what is described than in other myths, with their history of the gods. And once more he turned the issue into a historical one, confining the "meaning" options to the disjunctive myth–ostensivity alternative. (One should add that he thought, of course, that this nonmythical feature in the Bible was balanced by much more weighty arguments on the other side, so that he could assign the meaning of the biblical tales to myth after all: he simply shifted the weight of the definition of myth from history of the gods to direct intervention of deity on the finite plane, and the Bible immediately turned into myth.)

Like other mythophiles, Strauss was ambiguous about what he thought was the subject matter of the texts. He wanted to affirm both the mythological hypothesis and a distinct ideational "content," in the process hopefully avoiding both versions of the allegorist position. Whether he succeeded in this combination is not the point of our present discussion. In the context of debate with the ostensivist position he argued that the subject matter of biblical narratives is the distinctively sensuous, preconceptual consciousness which they express. Doing so, he failed to consider the significance for the meaning of these narratives of the fact which he himself had come close to noting—that their character- istics as writings were quite different from those of other stories supposedly of the same sort. Those others he could much more easily characterize as myths because of the hiatus in their case between what is represented in them and the representation. In the case of the biblical narratives, this was at best a much more difficult task. But instead of utilizing the difference for purposes of understanding the hermeneutical issue involved—the meaning of the texts—he turned it into a fact–fiction question. Since both types of stories, biblical and other myths, were to him obviously fictional, he ended by denying the very difference he had discerned between them.

Why this confusion of a hermeneutical with a historical issue, this inability to treat an evidently hermeneutical factor, a distinctive feature in writing, on its own terms? It is only a repetition of previous statements to blame the oversimplification on the disjunctive proposal of the mythical school and their later sympathizers: either mythical or ostensive meaning. While this is indeed a factor, it is symptomatic rather than basic. One comes closer to the heart of the problem if one recalls that the mythical school, together with practically everybody else, affirmed that understanding the text's subject matter (*Sache*) has priority over understanding its words, indeed that the text's words have to be interpreted through the subject. Once this point has been made, it is quite secondary whether the subject is historical events, the general consciousness or form of life of an era, a system of ideas, the author's intention, the inward moral experience of individuals, the structure of human existence, or some combination of them; in any case, the meaning of the text is not identical with the text.

Back of all this, especially of the drive toward a general hermeneutics of the "subject matter" of biblical stories, and the resultant failure to consider as a hermeneutical option a narrative reading of these stories, there were the factors already enumerated at various points in this essay. There was the theological preoccupation with the "fact" question, i.e. the positivity of revelation. There was, further, the tendency of hermeneutics to become associated with left- or right-wing religious apologetics. Even Strauss, at the time he wrote *The Life of Jesus*, was apologetically inclined. Had he considered the narrative option seriously and explored the significance of the difference between biblical and other "myths" more determinedly, he would have had to face the possibility that the meaning of the gospel story is that very focus on the narrated enactment of the specific messiahship of Jesus which he found factually incredible and therefore religiously impossible. In that case the gospels would have had to be declared not only historically but also religiously anachronistic, and he would not have been able to write the concluding (apologetic) sections (150–51) of his book, in which he tells us that the dogma of the God-man, far from being meaningless, really means the eternal incarnation of the divine Idea in the human species as a whole and in its historically developing general consciousness. Whatever may have been true of Strauss in his late years when he wrote *The Old and the New Faith* (1872), the young author was unwilling to separate meaningful religion from Christianity and the Bible.

In addition to the issue of positivity and the apologetic

tendencies of hermeneutics, "subject matter" hermeneutics was influenced by the identification of theory of meaning with theory of knowledge, which meant (among other things) that the sense of a fact-like statement was almost automatically turned into its ideal or, more likely, ostensive reference. And hand in hand with that inclination went the general absence of a literary tradition of realistic narrative writing or interpretation, virtually ensuring that "realism" in the biblical stories would be equated with conservative or radical historical-critical "reality" reconstructions, while their meaning would be a species of human spiritual interiority, either with or without a coincident affirmation of the significance of their factuality.

Together with the increasingly unquestioned assumption of the priority of subject matter explanation over verbal exegesis went the affirmation that general hermeneutics has priority over any possible special hermeneutics. It was not only, indeed not even in the first place, the grammatical or literal sense that had to be understood by general canons of meaning, as Ernesti had urged, but also the subject matter, which he had claimed not to be a hermeneutical issue. The disagreement with Ernesti on this score was virtually unanimous, except among a few Supernaturalists. Now whenever the subject (no matter what it is defined as being) and the words are first severed, in order to be joined again thereafter by interpreting the words through the subject (to which general canons of logical as well as religious meaning are applicable), it will be very difficult indeed to do justice to that form of writing in which the verbal form coheres with the meaning. Yet precisely this was the case in certain narratives, including some of the more important biblical narratives. Indeed, ironically enough, this peculiar, literary-literal narrative shape was almost universally admitted. The mythical school, in contrast to Allegorists and Naturalists, came close to discerning this distinctive quality in its own right, but they finally could not analyze it because like so many others since Anthony Collins' day, they confused the claim to the close, intimate relation between the sense of a story and its narrative shape with the claim to the identity between sense of story and reliability or unreliability of its reports.

This was hardly surprising, for the literary parallel between history writing and history-like writing is perfectly clear: in each case narrative form and meaning are inseparable, precisely because in both cases meaning is in large part a function of the interaction of character and circumstances. It is not going too far to say that the story is the meaning or, alternatively, that the meaning emerges from the story form, rather than being merely illustrated by it, as would be the case in allegory and in a different way, in myth. A great theme in literature of the novelistic type, like a pattern in a historical sequence, cannot be paraphrased by a general statement. To do so would approach reducing it to meaninglessness. In each case the theme has meaning only to the extent that it is instantiated and hence narrated; and this meaning through instantiation is not *illustrated* (as though it were an intellectually presubsisting or preconceived archetype or ideal essence) but *constituted* through the mutual, specific determination of agents, speech, social context, and circumstances that form the indispensable narrative web.

If one uses the metaphorical expression "location of meaning," one would want to say that the location of meaning in narrative of the realistic sort is the text, the narrative structure or sequence itself. If one asks if it is the subject matter or the verbal sense that ought to have priority in the quest for understanding, the answer would be that the question is illegitimate or redundant. For whatever the situation that may obtain in other types of texts, in narrative of the sort in which character, verbal communications, and circumstances are each determinative of the other end hence of the theme itself, the text, the verbal sense, and not a profound, buried stratum underneath constitutes or determines the subject matter itself.

Moreover, even though a "no author" theory of understanding any writing is absurd, as though the thoughts and projected actions had written themselves down through the medium of the author's pen—a curious area of agreement between advocates of a fundamentalist theory of biblical inspiration and implications of the more extreme among the "newer" literary critics—nonetheless, the author's intention is not a separable mental entity or action from the consecutive activity of working out his writing. An intention is an implicit action, an action an explicit intention; in the words of Gilbert Ryle, "to perform intelligently is to do one thing and not two things."[9] And this is as much to be remembered in the reading of texts as in understanding any other intelligent activity. If it is true, then neither from the side of paying attention to oneself nor from that of paying heed to what others are about is it necessary to enter a mysterious realm of being and meaning, or an equally mysterious private-subject world in order to discover what makes any intelligent action publicly or commonly intelligible. Especially in narrative, novelistic, or history-like form, where meaning is most nearly inseparable from the words—from the descriptive shape of the story as a pattern of enactment, there is neither need for nor use in looking for meaning in a more profound stratum underneath the structure (a separable "subject matter") or in a separable author's "intention," or in a combination of such behind-the-scenes projections.

15 The Hermeneutics of Understanding

All commentators are agreed that biblical hermeneutics underwent a sea change in the early nineteenth century.[1] The
transformation was, of course, the result of the romantic and
idealist revolution that was sweeping philosophy and historical
study as well as the literary arts and criticism. It was to be
expected that the interpretation of biblical texts, like that of
others, would be affected by the drastic new turn in the estimate
of the human spirit's place in the spiritual universe. It is therefore
rather surprising that, in comparison to previous decades, relatively little that was new was written under the title of hermeneutics. But once one notes the change in the meaning of the term
hermeneutics, from determination of the rules and principles of
interpreting texts to inquiry into the nature of understanding
discourse and what is manifest in it, this dearth of titles is not
really significant or surprising. Hermeneutical reflections, in fact,
reappeared under other headings and in combination with other
topics. Theological hermeneutics tended to reenter the scene
through writings discussing the relation between two types or
perspectives of understanding. Each of them is a methodological
procedure possessing its own integrity, perhaps even autonomy,
and is readily applicable to any subject matter or discourse
appropriate to it: there is critical-historical understanding, and
there is a "faith" perspective or understanding. And then there is
(presumably) a proper way of relating these two perspectives not
only in general but also in focusing them on the same object,
especially, in the instance of the Bible, on the story of Jesus of
Nazareth. Between them, these two or a cognate set of perspectives would, it was hoped, render the "essence" of Christianity,
once they were applied to its early history or to the whole history
of the Church.[2]

Additionally, however, the nineteenth century saw a temporary recession in actual hermeneutical inquiry, including bibilical hermeneutics, especially in connection with the gospels. This was due in large part to the enormous influence wielded almost single-handed by Strauss's *Life of Jesus*. While there had been a significantly developing movement of source criticism of the gospels long before Strauss,[3] his work forced the biblical aspect of the discussion concerning the positivity of revelation into this arena. That is to say, he forced the discussion away from hermeneutical and into historical questions, particularly the reliability or unreliability of the written sources for providing access to Jesus as he actually was and taught.[4] It appeared to most historians and theologians in the nineteenth century, until Martin Kähler,[5] that to reach a solution to this question one had to find out above all what were the earliest strata of the existing documents or their most primitive predecessors.

But even if there had been agreement on the so-called synoptic problem, it would have meant little without a proper determination of the nature and scope of faith, and its part in understanding the gospels and the figure of Jesus. Faith and its setting, not only in the practical context of life but within general inquiry into the nature of man, became a steady preoccupation among theologians. Theological inquiry was changing, gradually but drastically, in the decades after Kant's philosophical revolution with its strict division of "reason" into theoretical and practical functions and, above all, its transposition of inquiry into the scope of certainty from the transcendent or dogmatic arena of metaphysical objects to the arena of the transcendental structure of reason itself. Religious theory after Kant focused more and more on faith as a distinctive and self-conscious human stance which is reducible to no other. And faith in this sense qualifies whatever "reality" it is properly in touch with, analogous to the way in which for Kant the structure of reason qualifies the transcendental ego's contact with the objects of the sensible world, turning them from things-in-themselves into phenomena for human consciousness. It became a commonplace in nineteenth-century Protestant theology that we know God only under the qualification of a religious relation to him (be it revelation or some other), and not as he is in himself. The theoretical and practical exploration of this relationship became a consuming engrossment and all the more complex for the fact that somehow it had to be brought into contact with the positivity of Christianity, i.e. the historical fact of revelation in Jesus Christ, which was thought to be normative by most Protestants.

More than anyone else it was Schleiermacher who expounded this stance in theology and shaped it into a full theological system, for which every doctrine was normative only to the extent that it was a *Glaubensaussage*—a direct expression of faith or the living religious relation with God. He likewise pioneered in applying a parallel view to the interpretation of the Bible. For given its peculiarly central status for Protestants (with which he was at best only in partial agreement) and the task of adjusting critical analysis of the Bible with an ordinary and religious reading of it, it was all the more important to bring to bear on it the fruits of a more general investigation of just what is involved in understanding any instance of human speech and writing. "Faith" and "understanding" are not the same thing, but in that day both seemed to involve a step back into the inwardness of our own consciousness to find out what is going on there and how well it is equipped to perform its proper function.

Though Schleiermacher influenced philologists like August Böckh, the paths he explored for biblical hermeneutics were only lightly traveled until the end of the century. There were several reasons for this neglect. First, it was due to his own fairly strict distinction between hermeneutics and criticism, which tended to leave ambiguous their relation.[6] Second, though still connected with the first, his hermeneutical reflections were overshadowed by the impact of Strauss's *Life of Jesus*, moving the theological discussion toward historical-critical rather than hermeneutical issues.[7] Third, Schleiermacher's hermeneutics, much more than his theology, became caught in the mid-century reaction against idealistic modes of thought, which swept theology only a little less forcefully than other disciplines. Albrecht Ritschl, the most influential theologian of the later nineteenth century, was more positivistic and more moralistic than Schleiermacher in his approach to the interpretation of texts. He did not share Schleiermacher's concern over the subtle process by which one comes to understand or internalize the discourse of others and the being or consciousness out of which it arose.

After the turn of the century, the influence of Dilthey and then Heidegger in philosophy, and that of the early Barth and the later Bultmann in theological-biblical exegesis, reawakened interest in Schleiermacher's hermeneutics. The present inquiry is in no sense an investigation of the full scope or influence of Schleiermacher's hermeneutical reflections. My ultimate aim is simply to answer the question: What happens to narrative meaning in their wake?

Strauss's *Life of Jesus* was published after Schleiermacher's death. Nonetheless, Strauss was the climactic representative of a tradition, continuing into our day, that stems from the eighteenth century. By contrast, Schleiermacher's hermeneutical reflections, beginning with his translations of Plato, represent a later day, quite unlike his work in historical criticism which brought forth little that was new. For the tradition that Strauss typified, the most important functions of historical thinking are critical in the technical sense of that word: to assess the correspondence or lack of it between the accounts and the putative facts reported in them; to account for the fact that the reports came to be written in the first place; and at the hermeneutical as well as critical level, to adjudicate the question whether the subject matter of a given writing is ostensive or of some other sort.

Nineteenth-century history writing did not forsake this kind of critical inquiry, so representative of the eighteenth century, but added another, in which explanation tended much more nearly to merge into historical description or depiction. Together with it there arose an inquiry into the logic or rationale of this procedure, a hermeneutical undertaking covering history and historiography. What, it was asked, are the principles involved in the rendering of the distinct mode of consciousness, the individual thoughts, the collective presuppositions and tendencies of given eras of the past?

Furthermore, what are the principles involved in rendering the genesis and *developmental* sequence of ideational and cultural movements? The intellectual and cultural historian had to be artist and philosopher in addition to being a competent critical assessor. The description or narration of individual or collective idea sequences was raised to the status of self-conscious procedure. The historian was a narrator, but chiefly a narrator of ideas, attitudes, and tendencies, individual and collective. The influence of Herder on this development was unmistakable. The methods or principles of historical procedure were now thought to form a coherent whole. In the opinion of some thinkers, these were statable as a unified structure, rather similar to Kant's transcendental structures of reason.

Others would not have agreed. While they were eager to acknowledge and exhibit in operation the transcendental coherence of historiographical procedure, they did not believe in trying to state it and its logic abstractly or by itself. Writing the history of ideas and of cultures meant to them describing human being in its ideational and distinctively self-conscious embodiment in a specific past sequence. Historiography was the process of the writer's understanding shaping the material for description, even while he finds the shape inherent in the material. Subject matter and procedure had a natural affinity: both were born of spirit in its one yet constantly self-differentiated universal development, rather than being related to each other merely externally, accidentally, or by means of a "pragmatic" scheme (the term was denigratingly used in the idealist era).[8] But these thinkers did not believe in separating the procedure transcendentally from the material to which it was applied; to do so would have involved for them a false abstraction (and calcification) of history-writing from the historical process.

One of the most engrossing aspects of the romantic and idealist revolution is the pervasiveness of its chief themes through the whole of its intellectual spectrum. With the notable exception of the physical sciences, and those elements in other disciplines which demand a similar procedure, *Wissenschaft* meant to the

Idealists the same systematic and whole-making quest every-where. It is doubtful that philosophical speculation and literary and literary-critical activity were closer to each other in any other time and place than they were in Germany at the turn of the nineteenth century. More than one commentator has noted that Goethe's *Faust* (part 1) reads like the aesthetic scenario for Hegel's *Phenomenology of Spirit*;[9] and the latter work itself abounds with allusions to the spiritual condition of that and the previous era as mirrored in their literary artistry.[10] On the methodological side, the search for an overarching understanding of all the ages and genres of literature through their "inner forms," which motivated much of Friedrich Schlegel's writing, not only exercised a deep influence on Schleiermacher's hermeneutical reflections but in its own right was also typical of the intellectual undertakings of the day. Schlegel and Schiller (in contrast to Goethe) were character-istic of many writers of that time in trying to set forth the affinity of philosophical reflection and literary art.

SCHLEIERMACHER, HEGEL, AND THE
PROCESS OF UNDERSTANDING

Hermeneutics, so far as it was regarded as a self-conscious "art theory" (*Kunstlehre*, so called by Schleiermacher[11]) as well as practice, obviously bore a strong resemblance to both historio-graphical and literary theories. But its wider, indeed indefinite applicability would make it into an object of systematic inquiry in its own right. Like other systematic intellectual enterprises, it changed drastically in this era, both in subject matter and procedure. And as in history writing, there were those who thought that the hermeneutical procedure and its logic should not be abstracted from the process of its application, and, therefore, should not be stated by itself; others claimed this is a task that can and must be performed. Hegel was of the former opinion, whereas Schleiermacher, in part as a result of his understanding of man and consciousness, in part because of preoccupation with issues of biblical interpretation and authority, was the outstanding repre-sentative of the latter view. But there was no disagreement between them on the autonomous and (at least for Hegel) creative role of the interpreter (or to put it in a less individualistic mode: the role of "spirit") in the task of interpretation. Whatever is to be understood is refracted through the interpreter's understanding so that hermeneutics now turns from the rules or guidelines for interpreting texts, which it had been hitherto (and was still to be for Strauss), to the theory of the process of knowing or understanding. The aim of hermeneutical procedure must be to answer the question: What does it mean to understand? [12]

Unlike Schleiermacher, Hegel did not try to state the logic or structure of understanding by itself, apart from its application. Instead, he wrote a phenomenology, calling it a rendering, or systematic study, or science of "knowing in manifestation" (*Darstellung des erscheinenden Wissens, Wissenschaft des erscheinenden Wissens*).[13] He thought of *Wissen* (most nearly equivalent in his terminology to Schleiermacher's *Verstehen*[14]) as an autonomous undertaking, i.e. as not bound dogmatically to a fixed object, whether verbal configuration or the subject matter behind the words. Neither Schleiermacher nor Hegel could return in hermeneutics, any more than on any other issue, to a pre-Kantian stance, for which either knowing or understanding would be a merely isomorphic internal reproduction of given external data.

But Hegel differed from Schleiermacher in making no attempt to abstract understanding and its components into a separate, unitary, and determinate totality. Here as elsewhere, the contrast between them is illuminating. Schleiermacher denied the very possibility of a universal philosophy because there is no universal language.[15] But he affirmed the possibility of, indeed the necessity for, a separate, general, or comprehensive theory of understanding. The reverse was true for Hegel. Hermeneutics, separable from the full-fledged philosophical enterprise of the investigation of knowing and being, would have been impossible for him. For knowing or understanding not only takes place solely in application to a subject matter (Schleiermacher would have agreed to this) but is itself intelligible only in application. The reason for this is that understanding is for Hegel in constant motion or transition, changing reciprocally with its changing, contingent content or objects, of which one must say that they are given to and shape understanding, and yet are shaped by and are, therefore, the product of understanding. The process of this reciprocal change is one instance of that pervasive motion which Hegel calls mediation or dialectic. It is a process that begins immediately with the presence of consciousness and an object to which it is related;[16] and it is really intelligible only in its own uninterrupted thrust toward completing what has once been begun. In contrast to Schleiermacher, the understanding's unitariness or wholeness is simply not statable except by way of a systematic rendering or description of all the contents of consciousness in their coherence with consciousness as whole as it strains ineluctably toward its own completion.[17] This coherence—and the intelligibility of this coherence—between diversified, changing, yet unified content and diversified, changing, yet unified consciousness is an emerging process of mediation. There is no *immediate* union of consciousness and its contents. But even though it emerges, the coherence also encircles or encompasses the heterogeneity of its two sides: the process toward coherence of consciousness and its objects is the self-mediation of Spirit. When it is seen as such at the end of the phenomenological depiction[18] (and again at the end of the whole speculative inquiry, from logic to ontology, but at that point of course not merely in the form of phenomenology or manifestation of and for knowing, but rather as a reality judgment), the subject–object duality between knowing and what is known will be seen as a duality internal to Spirit itself, rather than a state of everlasting heterogeneity. And then, of course, the duality is seen in its own transcendence.

Then, and only then, can one really know what it means to know or understand; and this knowledge of understanding is one with, inseparable from, the purview of its application, i.e. from the ordered or understood sequence of its own contents. And so Hegel writes the following among the triumphant words that conclude the tortuous path of the *Phenomenology*:

> The aim, absolute knowing or Spirit knowing himself as Spirit, has as its path the remembrance of spirits as they are

in themselves and execute the organization of their realms. Their preservation in their aspect as free existents [*Dasein*] appearing in the form of contingency is history; but in the aspect of their comprehended [*begriffnen*] organization it is the science of knowing in manifestation. Both together, history comprehended, form the remembrance and the Golgotha [*Schädelstätte*] of absolute Spirit, the reality, truth and certitude of his throne, without which he would merely be the lifeless Alone.[19]

Under these circumstances it is not really appropriate to talk of Hegel's hermeneutics at all. If one does so nevertheless, it is doubtless sound to characterize his procedure, in the words of H.-G. Gadamer, as one of "integration," in contrast to Schleiermacher's hermeneutics of "reconstruction."[20]

SCHLEIERMACHER'S HERMENEUTICS

For Schleiermacher believed that one may take a given discourse, from the past as well as from the present—there is no difference in principle in the task of understanding them[21]—and reproduce the original in such a way that, far from being a merely mechanical copy, it is in the very act of reproduction, penetrated by the interpreter's understanding. This assertion the far more historicistic Hegel would have denied altogether. But Schleiermacher had a heavy stake in the claim. For him, the walls of time and of the historical transmission or mediation process disappear, and the two—the original and the interpreter—are directly and, therefore, in unaltered shape present to each other in a heterogeneity which is at the same time a mutual fitness, affinity, or even homogeneity.[22]

Through what Schleiermacher calls the technical or psychological aspect of the process of understanding (as distinguished from the equally indispensable "grammatical" aspect), and in particular through an immediately intuitive or "divinatory" move within the psychological endeavor (but only as the divinatory is qualified or modified by a countervailing "comparative" move), the interpreter equates himself directly with the original. He turns himself, Schleiermacher goes so far as to say, "as it were into the other, . . . and seeks to grasp the specific [das Individuelle] in him immediately."[23]

Hegel considered historical reproduction, without a showing forth of the process of mediation encompassing both the original and any consciousness to which it is made present, in no sense a genuinely appropriative understanding but a mere piece of intellectual mummification. If Schleiermacher had agreed, he would not have thought hermeneutics possible. The very possibility of the enterprise involved for Schleiermacher not merely that understanding and its object or content are given together in a direct and polar relation; additionally, he endowed each side of the relation with a kind of determinate, independently describable character. So it is that one may cull out and state by itself, at least in the abstract, the process of understanding and, likewise, the nature of discourse. As for the fact, on which Schleiermacher agreed with Hegel at least to some extent, that each of the two sides as well as their relation involves a process rather than a static datum for analysis, it seemed to Schleiermacher that in both cases genesis and development are encompassed within determinate, self-contained character. The task is to understand the individual totality in its development which comes to expression in a single work or discourse, but even more in the interconnection of the same author's total production. In other words, what is to be understood is the author in and as his self-expression.

Yet there is something incomplete or even misleading about this way of stating the hermeneutical task. It is not only the case that, for any interpreter's understanding the verbal artifact and the author's thought are inseparable, so that hermeneutics is confined to thought in the context of discourse and cannot deal with it as a separable entity.[24] In addition, individual discourse itself has to be understood as a point of complex dialectical coordination or intersection between universality and individuation: it is an individual focus of a common linguistic and cultural stock and also the self-expression of individual, self-developing spirit.[25]

This complex situation necessitates two distinct procedures in the hermeneutical operation and explains why the whole unitary act of understanding a discourse resembles an artistic more than a scientific undertaking. The "grammatical" moment in interpretation is directed toward understanding the discourse as a focus within a language as a whole, characterized by its relation to the total linguistic stock. The "psychological" or "technical" moment is directed toward understanding the discourse "as a fact in the thinker."

The unitary act of understanding, composed of both aspects, is more nearly an artistic than a systematic or scientific act because there is no further method or precise prescription for the way these two moments are united: a certain "oscillation" between them has to be involved.[26] Similarly, of course, there is no further statement concerning the unity of language and thought in the speaker. They are constituted into unity by himself in such a way that he himself is each moment and also the unity of both; there is no further statable factor or aspect of him that binds the two together. Unity of discourse and unity of understanding correspond: each involves something like a unity-in-duality, and hence the understanding's unitary grasp of the unity of the content is something like an artistic act. Moreover, interpretation is artistic rather than scientific because it involves, in regard to the discourse both as a sample of the universal and as an individual act, an infinite or indefinite approximation; understanding can therefore never be complete. Summarizing both the complex and approximative nature of the unitary act of understanding, Schleiermacher says: "If the grammatical aspect were to be completed for itself alone, there would have to be a complete knowledge of the language, and in the other case [the technical] a complete knowledge of the person. Since both can never be given, one must always pass from the one to the other; and for the way to do this there can be no rules." [27]

Discourse and understanding are made for each other. It is the marvelous and curious unity of their heterogeneity and affinity (which in turn, to Schleiermacher, involves a relation of hermeneutics to both ethics and dialectics) that is of greatest interest. Every discourse is the external aspect of thinking; and the act of understanding is a reversal of an act of discourse "in that there must come into consciousness the thought that was at the base of the discourse." [28] The act of understanding is indeed an act of reversal, for to understand any discourse one must proceed from its language to its thought. There is no technical understanding without grammatical understanding. And yet it is not only the case that one must "pass" from the one to the other, and that, furthermore, there is no rule by which to construe the process of the passage; finally it is also true that technical or psychological understanding involves a direct grasp of the thinker and thought in the discourse. There is a divinatory procedure in the psychological aspect of hermeneutical art, qualified though it always has to be by the contrasting comparative procedure. Because understanding necessarily involves a reversal in one's dealing with a given discourse, one may speak of heterogeneity between them; because it equally necessarily involves divination, turning one self "as it were into the other," one may also speak of their affinity.[29]

Some extraordinary consequences are involved in the notion of this affinity. It is a sense of homogeneity not only at the level of renewed and determinate thought or intention, it is also, indeed probably more significantly, a homogeneity at the level of basic humanity—a confrontation of one life in its inner particularity by another, and a penetration through reconstruction (*Nachbildung*) of the former by the latter.[30]

Important as this aspect of interpretation is for Schleiermacher, it must be held against its dialectical counterpart—understanding any work in its general linguistic setting. In his most detailed mature statements,[31] he spoke of linguistic and not merely grammatical interpretation, indicating the rich cultural and literary, not narrowly philological significance of such interpretation. Language to Schleiermacher is something like a form of life (to use Wittgenstein's phrase), and life is tied to language. And, therefore, he can suggest that the predominance of grammatical-linguistic interpretation can as well lead to genuine understanding as the predominance of technical-psychological understanding. It is important to stress this fact, since otherwise the aspect of which we are now speaking, the sense of homogeneity or affinity of one individual life with another at the level of basic humanity, can lead to a highly romantic view of the creation and understanding of discourse.

In one sense Schleiermacher held such a view; but some of his interpreters have gone to far greater lengths than he ever did when they treat the technical-psychological aspect of his theory of understanding undialectically, i.e. in relative isolation from the linguistic. Hence they constantly accuse him of "individualism," "psychologism," "subjectivism," and the like. For when taken by itself, the apex of the technical-psychological aspect of the theory of understanding is that of unconscious creation as the heart of individuality expressing itself in discourse. Schleiermacher moved in this direction when he said in a famous phrase that the hermeneutical task is that of "understanding the discourse first as well as and then better than its originator." [32] Why? one wants to ask. The answer is that a great deal of what the interpreter wants to understand about the genesis and development of a project must remain unconscious to its author, except to the extent that he becomes his own reader. And in that role, Schleiermacher hastened to add, the author is in no privileged position compared to any other interpreter.[33]

To this limited extent, then, the interpreter's reconstructive or recreative act of understanding is of a higher order than the author's and yet, of course, is homogeneous with it. The act of understanding corresponds to that of discourse and thought. But the interpreter sees, as the author does not, both the individual spontaneity and the organic development of the discourse, and its coherence with its cultural context. He sees, in the constant act of approximation which is understanding, the continuity or necessity of the process by which a production evolves from its genesis into its fully articulated final form, in which all its parts are ordered into a totality. And yet Schleiermacher always kept within bounds this bold stress on understanding discourse by understanding the author as it were immediately and from the inside. The other side of his view always remained that no thought is accessible except as speech; and in grammatical interpretation discourse is seen as a product of common language and culture.

SCHLEIERMACHER AND SCHELLING: A POSSIBLE PARALLEL

The affinity, in which the interpreter understands the author better than he understood himself, is reminiscent of some far more daring speculative moves which F. W. Schelling had made at the beginning of the century. It had seemed to Schelling[34] that the artist's creative insight, underlying and giving order to his work, is the sole and climactic instance of the full union between idea or thinking (subjectivity) and reality (objectivity), both in awareness and in actual representation. "Aesthetic intuition" involves a transcendence of the distinction between passivity and activity which marks all other forms of awareness. The artist's intuition is the one instance where the spontaneously active subject creatively penetrates the material he receives. The material is totally plastic to his intuition, so that his vision does more than merely supply form to it; he bestows actuality on it, even as he receives it. He is the organ of a creative process that comes to consciousness through him. And yet it does not attain *full* consciousness in him. Full consciousness is achieved only by the philosopher who understands what is happening; but he, though understanding it, does not participate in the creative process itself. So said Schelling in 1800. (One should add that the idea of unconscious or preconscious conceiving was one that Schelling shared with Fichte, though the latter did not focus it in aesthetic but moral activity.) Whether this view does not finally mean that the real work of art is the ideal rather than the actual work is a moot question. In any case, the focus of the real work of art must be the act of creating it, rather than the finished product. Furthermore, since in this essay aesthetic intuition is the crucial coordinate that links into one the vital parts of a complete philosophical system, Schelling's tendency at this time was to assign literary art a higher place in the total philosophical system than the plastic arts or painting.[35] More than a transcendence of the cleavage between subject and object in awareness, the artist's intuition, as exemplified chiefly in literary art, is at the same time the place where the heterogeneity between the real world of nature and the ideal world, the realm of freedom and subjecthood, is overcome.

Less than two years later Schelling claimed that this transcendence is not unconscious or partially unconscious, but that it is an immediately and self-consciously cognitive, intellectual act. In short, he now thought of it as intellectual rather than aesthetic intuition. Philosophy in effect is not only queen of the sciences because it is the most general form of reflection; it is also the most informative form of knowledge.[36]

Schleiermacher never aimed so high. He denied all epistemological and ontological claims to the intellectually intuitive knowledge of a point of indifference between nature and spirit— the Absolute which is neither object nor subject—or of the unity between the Absolute and individuated, particular being.[37] The latter was of course for him a matter of discovery in feeling or immediate, transintellective and transvolitional self-consciousness. He did not even claim immediate intellective apprehension of transsubjective finite reality. In other words, he laid no claims to a purely intellectual and, at the same time, informative transcendence of subject–object duality either in being or knowing. In this respect he was firmly on Kant's side. It is only in one subject's understanding of the spiritual activity of another subject in verbal self-expression (i.e. only in hermeneutics) that Schleiermacher spoke of divination or of an immediate intuition[38] that seems to resemble Schelling's intellectual intuition.

To this limited extent he paralleled Schelling's move of replacing an unconscious aesthetic intuition, in which the artist does not know what it really is that he intuits creatively, by conscious intellectual intuition. But whereas Schelling posited this move as the subordination of the aesthetic to the intellectual perspective (in principle) and, therefore, at least ideally as a hierarchical ordering within the same subject, Schleiermacher distributed the two stances between the two subjects, the author and the interpreter. There can be no unity between these two perspectives, even when an author becomes his own interpreter. An artful discourse (and artful discourse alone calls forth a corresponding hermeneutical act) is and remains to some extent an aesthetic intuition and presentation; and to that extent it is and remains incompletely intellectual and incompletely transparent to the author's own intuition and understanding. But the interpreter, in his reconstructive act, replicates the original act in conscious, intellective fashion, including a moment of immediate intellectual intuition or divination. And so he, more than the author, comes close to seeing the discourse in its spontaneous inception and its organic development, its individuality, and its connection with its cultural nexus, its organic wholeness, and its individual elements. Doing so, the interpreter in his divination as it were transcends his own individuality or subjectivity without losing it, and becomes the other in the form of understanding him intuitively.

Without going into the complex issue of Schleiermacher's thought about the relation between intuition and feeling, one must stress that while he believed in a living affinity between them, especially in his early years,[39] it is doubtful that a link of this sort exists in his hermeneutics.[40] For in understanding a person through his discourse, and the style he manifests in it, we do indeed pay heed to his being, but to his being in and as his intellectual and verbal self-expression; and we do this by virtue of a similar being and activity of our own. Indeed, our own act of understanding the author is more fully intellectual, cognitive, and conscious than the author's act. And the indispensable element of divination or immediate intuition on the interpreter's part is no exception to the intellectual character of this procedure. It seems, in short, to be at the very least a rough-and-ready equivalent to an intellectual intuition, the only instance in which Schleiermacher makes room for such a claim. Of course, Schleiermacher modified the intuitive element in understanding discourse by the moments of comparative (discursive) intellectual interpretation and linguistic (grammatical) interpretation. But these qualifications in no sense eliminate divination or immediate intellection. In short, in the interpreter's affinity with the author Schleiermacher noted an element of immediacy which is different from but no less real than one's immediacy to himself. Of myself, I am immediately self-conscious, but I am not intellectually or cognitively self-intuitive. I am related to myself in feeling or one may say that in feeling one is himself. I am not immediately conscious of another person in that same way. (So far as I know, Schleiermacher never used the term *Einfühlung* which Herder had coined.) On the other hand, my apprehension of him in his self-expression is no mere inference from, or indirect projection of, my self-consciousness. I apprehend his being in and as self-expression immediately (though, of course, also in other ways). My immediate apprehension of him through divinatory understanding, my equation of myself with him (*Gleichstellung, Hineinversetzung*) is an immediate intellective act rather than one of immediate self-consciousness or feeling. Similarly of course, someone else in understanding me immediately must do so intellectively, since my own self-consciousness or "feeling" is a more nearly aesthetic than intellective act: in short, no author or speaker can as such be his own interpreter, but another man may be; and genuine understanding of the author is by no means lost in the process, even though it must always be approximative. We understand the artful discourses of others better than they do themselves; they, in turn, understand ours better than we do ourselves.

An argument from silence is admittedly dangerous. But are we to account it accidental that Schleiermacher hardly mentioned the word feeling in his hermeneutical writings? Even when it occurs, it does so in a completely nonpregnant sense, scarcely signifying anything more than "hunch." [41] And this despite the fact that during much of the time he wrote on hermeneutics he was preoccupied with the notion of feeling as immediate self-consciousness. The most systematic, inclusive sketch of his hermeneutics (1819) was written while he was working on the first edition of the *Glaubenslehre*, in which the notion of feeling plays so large a part. Yet the sketch contains only two incidental references to the notion. By contrast, the term and its equivalents abound in the lectures on *Aesthetics*, in which Schleiermacher was perhaps at his most subjectivistic or romantic. Divinations or intuitions of real or ideal being play no part in the artist's perspective, which is the only one to which Schleiermacher pays significant attention in his *Aesthetics*.[42] In short, it seems unlikely that Schleiermacher in the *Hermeneutik* wanted to claim that one could describe a formal affinity between feeling and interpretation, and the notion of divination or intuition should not be taken to imply such a connection; it is quite distinct from feeling.

While one may doubt Gadamer's claims of a generic relation between Schleiermacher's hermeneutics and his theory of feeling, he is doubtless right that the act of understanding the author better than he understood himself refers in Schleiermacher's hands not to the subject matter of a discourse or to the author's deliberate intention, but to the act and process of its creation, and to its relation to the being of the author.[43] However, Gadamer exaggerates the significance of this climactic part of the psychological aspect of Schleiermacher's hermeneutics, and hence also the significance of unconscious creation for Schleiermacher's understanding of the art of interpretation. It is not only the case that the saying concerning understanding an author better than he does himself, and the motif it embodies, occurs (so far as I have been able to discover) only four times through the long span of Schleiermacher's writing about hermeneutics. Additionally, Schleiermacher made clear in connection with this formula that the psychological and technical sides of interpretation must be balanced by grammatical interpretation. He always remained true to his belief that the act of understanding is one of dialectical as well as aesthetic unity, and that both of its moments, grammatical and technical-psychological, are equal in value and importance.[44]

UNDERSTANDING AND CHANGE IN HERMENEUTICS

Let us sum up. As long as we remain sufficiently cautious and provisional not to press the matter to a rigid formulation Schleiermacher did not give it, we can reconstruct his hermeneutical position in some such way as this. *Understanding* a discourse involves a determinate, yet internally creative process, similar to the way in which the discourse itself must be understood. Following some leads provided by Friedrich Ast, who had written a hermeneutics heavily dependent on the early philosophy of Schelling,[45] Schleiermacher thought that the development of understanding is at once circular and explicative. (This was his version of the so-called hermeneutical circle which came to play a heavy role in the hermeneutics of understanding in the twentieth century.[46]) From an intimation (*Ahndung*) of the connectedness of the organic whole of a single work, or even a whole authorship, with its individual parts, understanding proceeds to the differentiated and clear grasp of precisely this same relation. In this, as in other respects, the interrelation of totality and individuality is extremely important. Understanding is an aesthetic as well as systematic (*wissenschaftlich*) process, and the discourse to be understood must likewise be seen as a process, in a sense therefore as a historical datum. It is to be understood, both in regard to its language and its thought, as a process in which individual style or concretion (to borrow an appropriate term from A. N. Whitehead) emerges within a broader totality. Hence both divination and comparison are indispensable tools for understanding at every stage of the way in linguistic or grammatical as well as in technical-psychological interpretation, although Schleiermacher adds that "in the psychological task a heavier stress on the divinatory is inevitable." (It should be added that the accent in grammatical-linguistic interpretation lies not only on language as a developing form of life but also as a specifically given general structure that is constant rather than developing in relation to a specific work under consideration. For that reason, all special hermeneutics are simply an abbreviated procedure for applying general hermeneutical rules.[47])

Simultaneously with this understanding of a discourse as a particular concretion in a wider process, one must also understand it as an individual, determinate, self-developing and, finally, completed act or process of creative construction. When one sees it this way in its individuality, one may distinguish, without separating, three aspects.

First, there is the inception, i.e. its origination in and from the individual life or spirit of the author. (*Keimentschluss*, germinal decision, is the term Schleiermacher used very late in life for this moment.[48])

Second, there is the development of the author's intentional thought and presentation. From this, Schleiermacher at times distinguished the theme, idea, or explicative sense (*Sinn*) of the discourse.[49] Nothing illustrates so well the break of his hermeneutics with those of the immediate past as the fact that he spent comparatively little time on this notion which had loomed so large in earlier reflections on interpretation. The reason is, of course, that for him the clue to interpretation was the reconstruction of the process of discourse by that of understanding. By contrast, the debate over the relation between the author's intention, or even his words, and the actual subject matter of a work presupposes that the significant unity of a work is its finished structure, to be seen quite apart from its genesis and development. However, Schleiermacher was clear that the theme of a work and its words or its expressed intent need not coincide. On the other hand, he did not fall prey to the common illusion generally known as the intentional fallacy, for which an author's purpose has to be reconstructed contextually, i.e. indirectly from the text and from other evidence, rather than being expressed directly in the text. If he did not move in the direction of this hiatus between intention and expression, it was in part due to the close relation he saw between an author's thought and his language, in part because he was concerned with other issues—chiefly how thought comes to be expressed in discourse—and in part because he saw language as an embodiment of the speaker or thinker himself and not merely of his specific intentions. Language is expressive or self-expressive, and not merely deliberately descriptive of specific subject matter and/or intention.

Third, because language is the distinctive self-expression or style of an author, one may see this feature as an inseparable and yet distinguishable aspect of the process of discourse. Despite the fact that language is an expression of the individual life of the speaker, either at a given moment or over a period of time, his language is not therefore a highly private, idiosyncratic instrument of self-transmission instead of an act of public communication. A man's style in artful discourse is his own, indeed it is he himself in verbal expression; and yet it is closely related to, indeed at times it is governed by, the stylistic and rhetorical forms of a common language tradition. Sometimes the two, self-expression and linguistic form, coincide completely. This is a lesson which Schleiermacher had learned well from his reading of F. A. Wolf, the noted philologist.[50]

To the first two aspects of this process at least, there corresponds in each instance a specific aspect of understanding: psychological to the first, technical to the second. Understanding the distinctive style of an author appears to be a matter for technical interpretation more than psychological, indeed a matter for both technical and grammatical interpretation.[51] Yet the issue in the third aspect is difficult to disentangle, since in a sense style is the nearest linguistic equivalent to the native self-expression of immediate self-consciousness, which is gesture rather than speech.

The "art" of interpretation, for the integrated unity of which there can ultimately be no rules, is the recapitulation in the understanding of the interconnected process, structure, and content of the discourse itself. There can be no ultimate, integrating rule for it; that is, it cannot be a "science," because when we describe the act of understanding we can never get beyond the rhythm of its linguistic-grammatical and its technical-psychological aspects. Again, we can never get beyond the dialectical motions of comparative and divinatory modes of understanding, in linguistic as well as psychological understanding. Finally, we can never get beyond the double movement of understanding as a reversal of the original—moving from discourse back to thought—and as a reconstructive or reproductive forward motion, especially in divination. But in each instance the two sides of the dialectic must remain together. This is especially true in the two largest contrasting elements in the act of interpretation, grammatical and psychological-technical interpretation, since otherwise one would be tempted to stress only the latter side of Schleiermacher's skillfully balanced view.

One of Schleiermacher's typically long and complicated sentences exhibits the scope as well as the balance between unity and diversity which he steadily held in view in his hermeneutical reflections:

> An art theory can doubtless . . . come about only when language in its objectivity, as well as the process of begetting thoughts as a function of the individual spiritual life, become so completely transparent in their relation to the nature of thinking itself, that from the mode of procedure in the connecting and communicating of thoughts, one may also render in its full connectedness the manner of procedure of understanding.[52]

For the thinkers examined earlier, understanding and explication were distinguishable; yet they were not only inseparable but equally important. Explication was the mode of interpretation most nearly appropriate to the rationale or sense of the work one read. Explication was the appropriate reproduction of the work as given, determinate structure. Application was a different matter because it is concerned with the significance, and possibly with the authority of the text in a context other than the original. Application becomes a significant hermeneutical issue only when the sense of time difference between the original and present time becomes an acute issue for a consciousness conceiving itself as possessing a uniquely present location. Moreover, this sense of being at present has to be joined to an ambiguity concerning meaning. Where "meaning" hovers between the explicative sense of a work and its significance for somebody, application becomes an important part of hermeneutics. Precisely this ambiguity, together with the sense of present location and of the difference between then and now, was developed in the hermeneutics of understanding, in contrast to the older procedure for which temporal perspective mattered little but the distraction between explicative and applicative sense was clear and pronounced. Once the aim of interpretation is to find the peculiar act of consciousness or understanding of the original in relation to that of the interpreter, to understand is already to apply, to have one's own pre-understanding or subjectivity, with which one enters into the interpretive process, modified or perhaps even reshaped decisively by the understanding one encounters there. Nor is it necessary to assume that the understanding encountered in the work is simply that of the author himself. All one has to say is that what one encounters corresponds to the pre-understanding with which one encounters it sufficiently to modify, develop, or reshape that pre-understanding. One can leave suspended the question of the ground of this common phenomenon of meaning-as-understanding which unites interpreter and work interpreted. No matter what that source, the sense of the work is now merging into its significance for the interpreter, and explication becomes identical with application.

The older interpreters distinguishing between explication and application, had tended to assign the latter to a secondary place. On the other hand, they had not emphasized very vigorously the distinction between understanding and explicating a work. The two activities form one common undertaking. If anything, *subtilitas explicandi* corresponded to the text even more than *subtilitas intelligendi*. It is, in fact, the focal aspect of interpretation, rendering as it does the fixed structure of meaning corresponding to the structure of the text itself.

But for Schleiermacher the process by which the verbal shape arises from the thought, and the thought from the life-moment of the author, formed the focus of technical-psychological interpretation. In other words, explication becomes secondary, in part because understanding is in principle a self-completing operation or process, of which explication is merely the external expression, and in part because a fixed relation of unvarying subject matter and words is no longer the aim of interpretation. Verbal exegesis together with subject-matter explanation (whether it referred to ostensive data or something else) did not add up to meaning for him, as they did for the earlier interpreters. The activity of understanding must correspond to the process by which the discourse has come into being. The writer's conscious intention need not be, indeed is not likely to be, the meaning of a discourse, nor is it the words (though they may come closer to disclosing the sense than the writer's intention). For Schleiermacher, even after the work of *Wortauslegung, Sinnverstand,* and *Sacherklärung* has been done, the task of hermeneutics must be taken up again. It is there before historical criticism has begun, and after it is finished. The meaning of a discourse is the connection of all these things with the origin of the process in the spirit of the individual author as well as the spirit of his age. The hermeneutical task reaches to the complex unitary source of discourse, whence conscious intentional idea, true sense, individual self-expression, and style all originate. This, rather than the determinate or normative structure of a work alone is the goal of understanding, and when this is comprehended, explication is seen to be merely part of the interpreter's concern.

"Only so much is clear," said Schleiermacher near the end of his two academy lectures on hermeneutics,

> that word and subject matter explanation are not yet exegesis but only its elements, and that hermeneutics really begins with the determination of the sense, though of course by means of these elements. And similarly that the explanation (as determination of the sense) will never be correct if it does not pass the test of measurement by the spirit of the author as

well as [the spirit] of antiquity . . . (This Herr Ast also says when, in speaking of the explanation of the sense, he says that whoever has not grasped the spirit of an author is not in a position to uncover the true sense of individual passages, and that only that [sense] is true which agrees with that spirit.)[53]

When one considers a passage of this sort, its emphasis on the spirit of the individual author as well as of his time, and sees that, in addition to grammatical interpretation, this spirit, together with the process of consciousness and with the similar process of the interpreter's understanding, is now the focus of hermeneutics, one can discern how thorough a change has been wrought in hermeneutics. The convergence of understanding and application, the recession of subject matter explication are but technical expressions of this transformation. In hermeneutics, as in the consideration of other functions of reasoning, there was no going back to the precritical stance, for which the understanding process itself had no contribution to make to the object to be interpreted or to the interpretive results but was simply a picture of a normative subject matter.

16 "Understanding" and Narrative Continuity

Scarcely a stone of interpretive procedure has remained unturned. At first it hardly seems possible to compare the meaning of interpretive art for Schleiermacher and the earlier thinkers even for purposes of contrast, to say nothing of similarity. And yet finally, no matter how sharp the break between them, in the estimate of the meaning of narrative texts the idealist and romantic revolution simply reinforced the tendencies we observed earlier. For the newer hermeneuticians as for their predecessors, general hermeneutics extended beyond the words and the descriptive shape of a narrative to a more profound level whence meaning and the apprehension of meaning originate, even if it is not a simple, clearly identifiable subject matter as it had been for the earlier commentators.

In short, for Schleiermacher, as for his predecessors, the sense of a narrative could in no way be either the narrative itself or its descriptive shape or its narrative structure. For the earlier writers, configurations of words and sentences, and finally total configurations such as a connected passage or work "mean" by being included under the more general heading of statements of the same type. This was general hermeneutics, of which special hermeneutics was merely a special instance. Moreover, the meaning of words, sentences, and finally of larger configurations was secondary to the meaning of the subject matter; indeed it was to be understood through the subject matter. The narrative "meant"—by referring to or stating a subject matter quite distinct from itself—external occurrences, ideas, a distinctive type of primitive consciousness called mythical, or some combination of the three. And behind these factors there lay the larger nonhermeneutical factors which had brought biblical hermeneutics into being in the first place: the question of the authority and truth of the Bible, particularly of history-like biblical narratives, and hence the issue of the positivity of revelation, which Christian apologists had chosen to identify with the essence of Christianity. On the matter of general hermeneutics, Schleiermacher firmly agreed with his predecessors. Though he substituted a hermeneutics of understanding or consciousness for that of subject matter, he thought of all hermeneutics as a fully coherent and articulated theory of interpretation, equally applicable to every discourse. On the question of subject-matter reference, Schleiermacher was more ambiguous since subject matter was not the core of the structure of meaning for him, and he was eager not to destroy the connection between the words and what the words expressed. As for the larger nonhermeneutical issues, for Schleiermacher they loomed as large as they had done for his predecessors.

The issue concerning the relation between words, descriptive shape and what they express is a subtle one. His success in keeping the two things coherent depended in turn on his success in making two different moves. First, he would have to provide sure cohesion between technical-psychological interpretation, for which the clue to a discourse lies mainly in thought and individual spirit, and grammatical-linguistic interpretation, which treats discourse as a function of a common linguistic stock. But Schleiermacher admitted that there is no specifiable relation between them except one of "oscillation." Their unity became a sheer dogma, the basis of which could only be the assumed unitariness of the interpreter's consciousness. The interpreter, or rather the assumption of the unique as well as unitary stance of his understanding, alone unifies meaning and the two interpretive approaches.

Second, Schleiermacher's success in keeping words and what they express coherent depended on his ability to describe the process of discourse coming into being in such a way that it did not break apart into two unlinked aspects—that of thought or individual spirit, and that of speech or self-expression. He was not threatened, as so many other thinkers after Descartes were, by the division of intentional action into two parts, one internal and real, the other external and peripheral. Intention did not play that large a part in his hermeneutics, but he was threatened by the equivalent division of the self into consciousness and self-expression in word. In his defense one must observe that discourse or words never became a secondary expression of a putatively more real internality for him.[1] He was no mere subjectivist in his hermeneutics. But the unity of the two aspects of individuality gave him grave trouble. The genetic or process-like description to which he was committed in the technical aspect of his hermeneutics could work only if he could find a way for understanding to do justice to the author's self in the actual moment or act of external self-revelation, of passing over from consciousness to self-expression. His last hermeneutical reflections concentrate precisely on this problem, but they are no more than hints of his awareness of it.[2] The feat is a notoriously difficult one, which has been tackled repeatedly by thinkers from Hegel to the present under the general topic: Is there a "nonobjectivist" and yet equally "nonsubjectivist" way of thinking, to grasp this actual aspect of self-hood—the self as subject in the act of its own self-actualization or external self-expression? In his hermeneutics, at any rate, Schleiermacher gave no sign of going beyond Kant in this matter. Like Kant, he did not forsake the canons of ordinary "objectifying" thought in the description of the understanding and the discourse to be understood. Divination may be such a further step, but on the other hand it may not be. There is in any case no sign that Schleiermacher thought it incompatible with the exercise of such thoroughly mundane objectifying means of understanding as comparative interpretation. And both are needed, in his view, to describe the process of discourse as self-expression. But given the difficulty of understanding the actual point of cohesion between consciousness and overt self-expression in the interpretation of discourse, the focus of meaning would tend to shift constantly, though subtly, from the discourse as such to the consciousness, understanding, or spirit which is expressed in the discourse. In any case, the strain on the cohesion between words or descriptive shape and the consciousness of which it is the product was too great, just as the unity of grammatical and technical-psychological interpretations also proved to be extremely tenuous.

Meaning, therefore, was "located" at once in what we might call the external shape and the internal form of a given discourse. Apart from the tenuousness of the cohesion between these two, the question of the meaning of a text, including a narrative text, involves the issue of its continuity, of the relation of the parts to the whole. Now Schleiermacher and Hegel both reflected on this issue. And here also, indeed on this matter quite decisively for our particular purposes, both men were disinclined to see the meaning of narrative as the narrative structure itself. Unlike at least some of their predecessors, Hegel and Schleiermacher did not posit the unity or continuity of narrative texts either in general ideas or in ostensiveness, i.e. in a sequence in the spatiotemporal world to which the narratives supposedly refer. (However, the connected "biographical" nature of the Fourth Gospel, in contrast to the disconnected "aggregational" shape of the synoptics, seemed to Schleiermacher to constitute an argument for the historical reliability of the Fourth Gospel.[3])

Where, then, is the continuity of narrative to be found? The answer is that it does not lie in the narrative sequence of character and incident shaping each other through their interaction, but in consciousness, and this in at least a twofold sense. First of all there is the author. It is his spirit that must be grasped. Dilthey was absolutely right in his comment on Schleiermacher's technical-psychological procedure, that "in the unitary intuition of the genesis of work lies also the total unity of the exegetical operations." [4] Hence Schleiermacher's tendency to push histori-cal-critical considerations to a secondary position in hermeneu-tics, to presuppose them as peripheral in the comprehension of the author's uniqueness, and even to argue, in the case of such works as the Fourth Gospel, that there is a connection between spiritual unity manifest in literary unity and historical reliability. It was the lack of a determining or controlling scheme that bothered him in the synoptic gospels, as well as their failure to show any connected temporal sequence or development. He saw them as aggregative rather than organic, their sequence disconnected and merely ranged together, one incident or group of sayings to the next. Much as twentieth-century form critics, he saw the individual pericopes and their groupings as the prevailing literary synoptic units. With his penchant for discovering organic unity in writings, he would have welcomed redaction criticism, though he was not aware of the procedure. Obviously, non-narrative works expressing the author's spirit directly were far better than fictional expressions or historical accounts in manifesting his specific consciousness. Dilthey correctly remarks that Schleiermacher's interpretive efforts succeeded far better with the Platonic dialogues and the epistolary literature of the New Testament than with the synoptic gospels[5]—not even to mention the narrative works of the Old Testament, to which Schleiermacher very wisely paid scant attention.

Second, continuity in narratives is to be found in their inner form or organic connection which must obviously be compatible with but is not simply the same as the spirit of the author. In the gospel narratives, this inner form is the consciousness of Jesus, who is their chief character. Indeed, it was the pervasive presence or effusion of his consciousness, communicating itself to the variety of the New Testament writers' individual perspectives, which alone constituted the unity of the New Testament canon. And here it was again obvious that he would prefer the Gospel of John to the others.[6] For its biographical, in contrast to their disjunctive character, provides a genuine bond which is nothing other than the unbroken consciousness of Jesus woven into a continuous series of self-manifestations. The bond is the consciousness itself and, at the same time, the organic sequence or order of its self-expressions. The mystery of their unity is the mystery of human being itself, developing through its temporal continuity— thought and discourse in one, consciousness and self-expression in one.

Whether one views a discourse as the process of the author's self-expression or as the process in which a character is rendered, the narrative continuity lies in consciousness. And that location of continuity of course precludes locating it in the interaction of character, context and circumstance. Schleiermacher's predilection for the Fourth Gospel, in which narrative is reduced more to self-manifestation than to significant incident, is perfectly coherent with his general hermeneutical outlook. Another point of view could not have entered his horizon. He did not have the conceptual tools to locate the structure or continuity of the narrative in the narrative sequence itself, if that sequence is made up of the interaction of incident and character which meticulously gives precedence of meaning to neither one nor the other.

Similarly, he could not have made the cognate move of defining character and significant social context by reference to each other, preference once again being given neither to one nor the other. For that move would have meant investing the surface mores and behavior patterns of society with genuine importance in their own right, allowing the individual to define himself (or be defined) sharply by his relation to this particular context. But just this was the sort of characteristic which romantic or idealistic literary commentators like Friedrich Schlegel deplored about the contemporary social, realistic novel in England.[7]

Where hermeneutics and interpretation are governed by the conviction that the interpreter's unique stance and process of understanding are face to face with that same motion within the discourse to be interpreted, and that this affinity alone (apart from the "linguistic stock") is the ground for understanding what is being said, such "surface" reading, finding character and society firmly related—a reading, moreover, which discovers the continuity of the narrative in its very contingency—must be viewed as superficial or worse.

In short, the perspective for which narrative meaning is identical with the dynamics of its descriptive shape—for which the characters, their social context, the circumstances or incidents, and the theme or themes are all interdependent—was as impossible for Schleiermacher's hermeneutics of understanding as that same outlook had been for the earlier hermeneutical writers. At that time the search for the subject matter beyond the text had obscured narrative meaning. Now it was the quest for narrative unity or continuity in the consciousness of the author, or in the inner form as represented by the characters' consciousness, which prevented the descriptive or narrative shape from assuming its rightful place. In regard to the hermeneutical status of biblical narratives, which Hess and Strauss came close to but finally failed to discern, the new hermeneutics, produced by the romantic and idealist revolution, brought about no change whatever. How could it? Once consciousness becomes the basic element characterizing human being, the bond between society and individual being loosened, the mutual fitness of character with the suffering or doing of significant action or incident likewise becoming increasingly tenuous, the significance of narrative (other than biography or autobiography for which the focus of the human person lies beyond doing and suffering) is bound to be minimal.

Consciousness and Narrative: The Gospels

What is so striking and revealing about Schleiermacher's inference that Jesus probably underwent only a *Scheintod* on the cross is not his disbelief in the resurrection.[8] Skepticism about physical miracles, especially that one, is, after all, a typically modern attitude. Far more remarkable is the fact that, no matter what he may have chosen to believe about the facts of the case, it never occurred to him that there is something unfitting, indeed ludicrous, about rendering the story of Jesus in a way that makes such a thundering anticlimax possible. But the fact, of course, is that it becomes possible, indeed perfectly fitting, if the crucial continuity of the story (and hence by derivation the crucial historical facts also) lies in the inner being of Jesus—his consciousness as manifest in a connected pattern. In that case the traditional climactic occurrences of the story become more or less irrelevant. It is a typical maneuver of the ostensivist-naturalist sort, of which we spoke earlier, and would have done justice to H. E. G. Paulus. But then one has to recall that to a rationalist age it seemed fitting to alter the ending of *King Lear* in order to bring it into harmony with more advanced moral ideas. Why not, then, alter the end of a story about the presumably historical basis of which we have such confusing information but which we may hope to make historically more credible than its unrevised form? [9]

Indeed, Schleiermacher was far more consistent than other commentators who have approached Jesus in the same characterological manner. Like Schleiermacher, they tried to connect the death of Jesus with his self-consciousness, making it the fitting outer expression of his self-consciousness or character (I use these rather disparate words synonymously for the present), always careful (at least until Schweitzer's rather reckless account in *The Quest of the Historical Jesus*) to stop short of implying suicidal tendencies in Jesus. Yet they also affirmed the death as a factual historical occurrence: he really did die! And thereby they brought two incongruous elements within the hermeneutical horizon. First, they were in fact suggesting that the actual occurrence of the death (in the story, rather than in fact, even though it was of course with history in mind that they usually affirmed it), as distinct from the intention or consciousness of Jesus (i.e. his willingness to die if necessary) constituted part of the meaning complex of the story. This meant, of course, the threat that an element quite heterogeneous to the character or consciousness of Jesus formed part of the bond of the story.

In the second place, they were, of course, confronted then, as Schleiermacher was not, with the question of the significance of the resurrection within the narrative. For while the death of Jesus might still be linked with his character or consciousness as an outward manifestation, the resurrection could hardly be regarded that way. No matter what one might do with it as a historical fact claim, placing it hermeneutically was an awkward problem because it was so heterogeneous from the rest of the narrative's bond. At that point, all one could do was to break with and go beyond the purely characterological interpretive framework, or invoke a new character-in-manifestation, that of God, whose perspective (we could even say "consciousness") would now become projected into the story like a deus ex machina. Under this latter option, the resurrection (no matter what its claims to historical veracity) is simply a mythical or shorthand name for the admittedly puzzling self-manifestation of this new self-consciousness, imposing itself from here on the whole story, and giving the whole characterological development a new perspective.

Whatever the resurrection as a historical or fictional claim, its status *in the story* is then not that of reference to an occurrence but simply the affirmation that the whole of Jesus' self-manifestation is in fact the self-manifestation of God, a disclosure that cannot be seen until the end of the story and thence covers all of it in retrospect. And the story's bond becomes not that of Jesus' self-consciousness in expression, but God's. Horace Bushnell was a distinguished representative of this point of view in the last century, Rudolf Bultmann and some of his followers in the present—with suitable allowances, of course, being made for the present age's greater historical skepticism and more complex "phenomenological" view of *Dasein*, self-understanding, and (finally) of being, compared to the understanding of consciousness-in-manifestation of the last century. But there is no need to single out names among the adherents of this view; their name is legion.

It appears that Schleiermacher's move was more economical and consistent than this, heading off as he did the threat of a heterogeneous intrusion into hermeneutical continuity by placing the meaning and continuity of the narrative firmly in the *being* of Jesus, rather than in the interaction of his being with contingent occurrences quite heterogeneous from his consciousness, such as actual death and, especially, resurrection. If the being or consciousness-in-manifestation of Jesus is at the same time the being of God in him—in other words, if one abides by the terms of the characterological alternative in the hermeneutics of the gospel story—it is obviously best if one avoids altogether such heterogeneous elements as the resurrection, which have to be reworked so hard to make them fit this framework of interpretation.

If one is committed to the positivity of historical revelation as belonging to the very essence of the Christian faith (and Schleiermacher was fairly clear that he was so committed, especially in his second *Sendschreiben an Lücke*),[10] it is best if one tries to make his critical-historical claims consistent with his hermeneutical and theological claims. Schleiermacher was always a thinker of extraordinary subtlety and consistency. He was never more consistent than in the perfect correlation of the critical-historical hypothesis concerning the possibility of Jesus' *Scheintod* with the claim, at once part of his hermeneutical stance toward the gospel story and of his systematic theological perspective on christology, that the deliverances of scripture about the resurrection are not an immediate expression of Christian pious self-consciousness. The personal dignity of Jesus Christ as redeemer is known quite apart from the occurrence or nonoccurrence of the resurrection.[11] Others, though like-minded, did not practice the same economy and consistency in coordinating historical-critical, hermeneutical, and dogmatic affirmations. Commentators often suggest that Schleiermacher's rationalistic or naturalistic reconstructions of miraculous reports (like the resurrection) are at odds with the romantic tenor of his theology (and hermeneutics). Whatever may be true at a very general level, in regard to biblical narrative, especially that of Jesus, and therefore in regard to christology, these two strains in his outlook fit together perfectly.

Unlike Schleiermacher, Hegel did not have to worry about the confluence of historical fact claims with the meaning of the gospel narrative. Whatever his final position on the issue of the positivity of revelation—whether (as seems more likely) his left-wing followers were correct that the notion was never more than the sensuous representation of the idea of reconciliation for him, or whether his right-wing followers were correct that he believed the positive event embodies an actual and indispensable stage on the way to the full self-realization of truth—he had no ultimate apologetical stake in the notion. For that reason alone he was able to do greater justice than Schleiermacher to the narrative shape of biblical stories: He could interpret them narratively while casting aside the ultimacy of narrated occurrence as historical revelation. Moreover, he always considered Christianity as the crucial historical exemplification of the fact that truth must be seen in specific, contingent, and representational form. Unlike Schleiermacher (but very much like Herder) he was able to take very seriously the accounts of creation and the fall in Genesis, and he was able to do far greater justice than Schleiermacher to the death–resurrection sequence as the focus and climax of the gospel story. In this instance, as in so many others, he applied the hermeneutical principle, already clear from his *Phenomenology*, that objective elements such as putative occurrences bear an absolutely essential formative relation to the receiving and shaping consciousness. However, for him also, the continuity of a story which provides its intelligibility was not the interaction of character and incident, i.e. the realistic narrative shape. It was, instead, the integration of the consciousness-event interaction into the history of consciousness, or the stages by which Spirit becomes himself. The story of the death and resurrection of Jesus Christ marks the transition of Spirit from the stage of individual consciousness to that of general consciousness. Though Hegel came closer than Schleiermacher to seeing narrative as its own continuity and meaning, it was finally the case for him that the meaning is the common framework into which the interaction of incident and character is taken up, so that the interaction may be seen to be more than a contingent external relation. And that framework, at the phenomenological or interpretive rather than ontological level, is that of consciousness or knowing. Of things past, we remember, Hegel said: "Their preservation in their aspect as free existents appearing in the form of contingency is history." If one of the chief characteristics of biblical narratives, distinguishing them from myth, is their history-like character, it is precisely this character that is denied or rather transcended, just like history itself, by the form- or meaning-bestowing capacity of knowing. "In the aspect of their comprehended organization," Hegel went on to say of the preservation of things past, "it is the science of knowing in manifestation." In other words, narrative sequence is understood only as that sequence itself is overcome or comprehended by being ranged into a consciousness sequence, even though that sequence is wider than Schleiermacher's individual consciousness. The narrative sequence of Jesus' death and resurrection is finally both a stage of transition in the process of consciousness and a representational picture, i.e. a mythical or historical representation, for consciousness. (There is for Hegel finally no difference between mythical and historical forms of consciousness since they are both representational rather than notional or purely rational. Hence he did not have to worry, as Christian theologians and Strauss did, over harmonizing historical fact judgments with interpretive judgments about the meaning of the putative facts.) The meaning of the narrative is that it represents the negation of individual consciousness (death) and the negation of that negation, i.e. the passage of individual consciousness into the general spirit which is the community-consciousness (resurrection).[12]

The hermeneutics of understanding—in the form of Schleiermacher's individual understanding penetrating the "thou" meeting him in discourse, or in the form of Hegel's phenomenological procedure, ranging contingent positive occurrences together with consciousness into the horizon of Spirit—simply cannot deal with narrative continuity, and narrative meaning as a function of this continuity. The bond of continuity, the meaning of the narrative, has to be discovered at a level more remote than that of depiction or cumulative rendering through the interaction of character and incident. The meaning of the narrative is something other than the narrative shape itself. There is, for this whole point of view, simply no way of dealing with descriptive or narrative shape without shifting its meaning to a more profound stratum. The documents mean something other than what they say.

The charge of subjectivism, individualism and psychologism raised against Schleiermacher will not hold without large qualifications. Concerning the first, it has to be said that he always insisted that grammatical interpretation is as important as technical-psychological interpretation. About the second, one may note that grammatical interpretation sees even the spirit of the author, to say nothing of the equally important language stock he uses, as instances of broader cultural and not merely individual expression. Concerning the third, it must be reiterated that he always kept consciousness or thought and discourse together as the datum for interpretive understanding. What needs to be said, rather, is that the unity at which Schleiermacher aimed is in grave jeopardy. Regarding the cohesiveness of psychological with grammatical interpretation, Schleiermacher simply admitted the issue, but he was obviously never concerned with it. As for the unity of the self as thought and as expression in language, he never even raised the question. Given the fact of the unity which the interpreter himself constitutes; given, further, that understanding takes place in, with, and through his own activity moving toward the datum under his interpretive glance; and given, finally, that he finds in the other a "thou" both like and unlike himself, he really did not need to worry about such matters as the cohesiveness of the two modes of interpretation.

If, on the other hand, this a priori unity of the subject, and the a priori conceptual scheme of subject–object correlation and transcendence cannot be taken for granted as bases for every possible interpretation of texts, Schleiermacher's procedure is more hazardous. Apart from dogmatism, what is there to tell us that two interpretive devices so different as grammatical and technical-psychological must be united in one common framework? If they are not, it still does not necessarily follow that grammatical interpretation can do justice to the obviously narrative features of such realistic texts as the biblical stories. But it does follow that of these two it alone is a candidate, since it alone is concerned with verbal connections, whereas technical-psychological interpretation obviously is concerned with finding something in the discourse that corresponds in affinity as well as in difference to the structure of meaning or understanding that informs (or is) the interpreter.

Technical-psychological interpretation is clearly confined to a task set within the limits of such a conceptual scheme. Thus, it might well be one interpretive mode among others, doing one particular and limited task. One might even say that to the extent that some narrative (or better yet, because more nearly fit for the method, non-narrative) texts allow the sort of analysis that technical-psychological hermeneutics undertakes, there are some admirable even though always tentative interpretive results to be achieved by this means—tentative, because inevitably relative to the consciousness or structure of self-hood presupposed in the interpretive approach. But given this limitation, such technical-psychological interpretation of the "meaning structure" discerned in a text may well be useful. (Understanding hortative texts, parables, etc. may perhaps be explained best by some such device as psychological interpretation or its later derivatives, for which the text becomes an event "confronting" the hearer. But locating the identity of a person in a story is surely another matter.)

However, as soon as it is forgotten that the unity of the two modes of interpretation, grammatical and psychological, depends on the philosophical scheme of the necessary, indissoluble subject–object correlation and its hermeneutical transcendence, and the scheme is automatically made absolute for every kind of interpretation, fearful and wonderful things begin to happen to those texts that do not easily lend themselves to this sort of interpretation. And of this kind, narratives in which incident and character in their contingent interaction form the meaning are the prime example. They are simply not amenable to this sort of treatment, or rather this conceptual apparatus simply cannot do justice to their structure. It can do so no better than Strauss's critical category of myth.

Given a relative or limited, rather than absolute applicability of the conceptual scheme of subject–object correlation, there is no reason to assume the unity between psychological and grammatical interpretation which Schleiermacher claimed so casually. They are simply two different procedures, and their unity remains a speculative, tentative matter. There is no need to assume the unitary consciousness, for hermeneutical purposes, of the understanding doing the interpreting. There may, in short, be a variety of hermeneutical procedures, with none of them (including the one that starts from "consciousness") in a privileged position.

Likewise, there is no need to assume the normativeness of the model of human being which is selected for hermeneutical purposes by this particular hermeneutical scheme: that of the nonobjectifiable subject and its public ingredience in (either objectified or nonobjectified) speech and event. We have noted that the model tends to break up into its two component parts. But even if not, even if such questionable concepts as the "linguisticality of being," designed to overcome that particular hiatus and other problems internal to the point of view, turn out to be intelligible, there is no need to assume, except on the prior assumption of the normativeness and inescapability of the conceptual scheme of subject–object correlation, that this particular model of human being is normative. If, in another conceptual scheme and another hermeneutical context, a model functions better for which the human situation is characterized by intentional agency ingredient in external, "objective" contingent circumstances and social contexts and is, in turn, shaped by them, why should one not choose that model instead for the understanding of narrative texts, and perhaps even texts of another sort?

But this was not even a possible or envisaged alternative among those who followed the hermeneutics of understanding, whether in Schleiermacher's or Hegel's form.* The conceptual scheme underlying it had achieved the status of an unquestioned and absolute assumption. Yet even within this scheme itself there is reason to wonder if the various hermeneutical procedures to which it lends itself can all be held together in one superstructure.

---

* The exception to this monolithic front is of course the Marxist revision of the Hegelian version of the scheme into a form of historical and narrative realism: but even here one wants to raise the question whether the contingent interaction of character, social context, and circumstance is taken into full account. One always wonders whether the dialectical historical movement does not finally undercut the necessity of a narrative rendering of the real historical world. Furthermore, the suspicion lingers that the systematic character of "dialectical" explanation may, despite the materialist trappings, owe a considerable debt to the idealist notion that group consciousness constitutes the continuity and meaning of realistic narratives.

Schleiermacher's grammatical interpretation does not really fit the scheme at all, except on the assumption of the unitariness of the interpreter himself constituting the unity of the two interpretive modes. But what of those that do fit? Hegel claimed that the unique place in time of the interpreting consciousness, one's "historical horizon," and the transmission process by which a text comes to the present consciousness, make a difference in the understanding of a text's meaning; they transform the text's original horizon. Surely, one may say, there is something to that. Schleiermacher, on the other hand, claimed that given the context of the historicity of the original discourse as well as one's own, one is nonetheless confronted directly, through the text, by the spirit manifest in it. Again, most of us who have ever said of an author from the past, "I do understand him," will want to agree with Schleiermacher's assertion, without denying the justice of Hegel's claim. Finally (though the relation of this claim to the conceptual scheme is less obvious than that of the other two), one may feel that one understands how a particular text makes explicative sense, i.e. what its subject matter or formal structure is, without relating it to the author's spirit and without paying heed at the same time to its changing meaning over a long stretch of time—and yet this does not mean one denies that the other things are also true! But to explain them all as part of the same hermeneutical structure (to which at least the first two obviously belong), and to trace their interrelation in understanding under the unifying subject–object correlation scheme, may well be impossible. When we interpret a text in one of these three ways, we simply do not interpret it in the other two ways.

But most important in our general context is that the whole procedure—whether in the form that Schleiermacher and his later followers gave it or in that which Hegel and his followers gave it—simply undercuts all realistic narrative. As soon as one's perspective, i.e. the process of understanding itself, schematically sets the terms on which the text is to be interpreted, the meaning of the text is bound to be similar to the structure of understanding or "linguisticality" or some other special structure of human self-and-other apprehension. What this does to narratives we have seen in the instance of Schleiermacher on the death and resurrection of Jesus. Whatever cannot be ranged into this structure becomes meaningless, or at best forced back into it by way of a reinterpretation of its "objectified" form. The text itself, not as self-expressions or "word events," but simply as the formal narrative shape of a story, cannot be the meaning or the subject matter of the narrative. And yet precisely this history-likeness (the direct interaction of character, descriptively communicative words, social context and circumstance, whether miraculous or not), in which descriptive shape and meaning cohere, was, by common agreement, a distinguishing characteristic of much biblical narrative.

There is no doubt that biblical hermeneutics underwent a radical transformation between late eighteenth-century subject-matter interpretation and early nineteenth-century hermeneutics of understanding. Both had in common the subsumption of biblical under more general canons of explicative sense as well as religious or moral applicative meaning. Beyond that they had little in common. The earlier scholars had been confident that the text is directly accessible, and therefore a science of interpretation is no more than a codification of principles and rules of procedure. The later commentators stood in the shadow of Kant's Copernican revolution in philosophy and of his successors. The hermeneutical upshot of the transformation was that the focus of inquiry now became the unitary structure of understanding rather than the written text as such. Sometimes the inquiry was undertaken with the natural confidence that the text, and more particularly its (distinguishable) meaning, is truly present to the interpretive procedure. But there was increasing unease that this might not be the case and that there was a gap between the interpreting "subject" and what can be known of the meaning of the text from the past. The endeavor to bridge that gap and gain a normative interpretation of texts—one that would do justice both to technical philological and historical-critical work, and to broader human reading—became increasingly frequent, complex, and uneasy.

This has been especially true in the study of the biblical narratives. All the more fascinating, in view of this hermeneutical revolution and its large effect on biblical interpretation, is the continuity of the fate of a narrative reading of biblical stories, a continuity that remained unbroken from the days of Deism through the first third of the nineteenth century—unchanged by whatever else happened in biblical study. The realistic narrative reading of biblical stories, the gospels in particular, went into eclipse throughout the period. Whether anything has changed in this respect since the days of Schleiermacher and Hegel is a question for another day.

Notes

CHAPTER 1

1. Erich Auerbach, *Mimesis* (Princeton: Princeton Univ. Press, 1968), pp. 48f, 73ff, 194ff, 555. See also Auerbach's essay "Figura" in his *Scenes from the Drama of European Literature* (New York: Meridian Books, 1959), pp. 11–76. Auerbach's are the most illuminating analyses available of the figural or typological procedure. (I use the two terms synonymously in this essay.)

2. Auerbach, *Mimesis*, p. 15.

3. "An Essay on the Allegorical and Literal Interpretation of the Creation and Fall of Man," Conyers Middleton, *Miscellaneous Works* (1752), vol. 2, p. 131.

4. "The Art of Fiction," reprinted in Henry James, *The Future of the Novel*, ed. and introd. by Leon Edel (New York: Vintage Books, 1956), pp. 15f.

5. For discussions of the role of narrative in historical accounts and explanations, see Michael Scriven, "Truisms as the Grounds for Historical Explanation," in Patrick Gardiner (ed.), *Theories of History* (Glencoe, Ill.: Free Press, 1959), esp. pp. 470f; Arthur C. Danto, *Analytical Philosophy of History* (Cambridge: Cambridge Univ. Press, 1965), esp. chs. 7, 10, 11; W. B. Gallie, *Philosophy and the Historical Understanding* (2nd ed., New York: Schocken Books, 1968), chs. 1–5; Louis O. Mink, "The Autonomy of Historical Understanding," *History and Theory* 5 (1), 1966, 24–47, esp. 38ff; I have also been helped on this topic by the unpublished Yale Ph.D. dissertation (1968) of Charles L. Lloyd, Jr., "The Role of Narrative Form in Historical and Theological Explanation."

6. Auerbach, *Mimesis*, p. 44.

7. For the importance of "type" in literary realism of Marxist persuasion, see Georg Lukács, *Studies in European Realism* (New York: Grosset and Dunlap, 1964), p. 6. For Marxist literary analysis as an "extrinsic" approach to literature, see René Wellek and Austin Warren, *Theory of Literature* (New York: Harcourt, Brace and World, 1956), ch. 9.

CHAPTER 2

1. For an argument that the roots of biblical-historical criticism and historical-critical theology go back to the seventeenth century see Klaus Scholder, *Ursprünge und Probleme der Bibelkritik im 17. Jahrhundert*, Forschungen zur Geschichte und Lehre des Protestantismus (Munich: Kaiser, 1966), vol. 10, p. xxxiii. See also Scholder's review of other scholars' opinions on the same question, ibid., pp. 7ff.

2. M. Luther, "Assertio omnium articulorum," *Werke* (Weimar: Böhlau, 1883–), vol. 7, pp. 96ff.

3. Luther, "Auf das überchristlich, übergeistlich und überkünstlich Buch Bock Emsers zu Leipzig Antwort," *Werke*, pp. 650–52.

4. John Calvin, *Institutes of the Christian Religion*, trans. by John Allen (7th American ed., Philadelphia: Presbyterian Board of Christian Education, 1936), Book 2, chs. 7, 8.

5. Ibid., Book 2, ch. 9, ¶4. On the other hand for a distinction between promise and law see 2.11.10; also 2.10.2.

6. H.-J. Kraus, "Calvins exegetische Prinzipien," *Zeitschrift für Kirchengeschichte* 79–80, 1968–69, 331.

7. *Institutes*, 1.7.4, 5.

8. Kraus, p. 333.

9. *Institutes*, 1.2.

10. *Institutes*, 4.17.3, 21 passim.

11. John Calvin, *Commentaries on the First Book of Moses, called Genesis* (Edinburgh: Calvin Translation Society, 1847), vol. 1, p. 170.

12. John Calvin, *Commentary on the Book of the Prophet Isaiah* (Edinburgh: Calvin Translation Society, 1850) vol. 1, pp. 244ff.

13. See above, ch. 1.

14. Auerbach, *Mimesis*, pp. 73, 555.

15. Auerbach, *Mimesis*, p. 73.

16. *Institutes*, 2.11.1.

17. Sixth ed., 1764. For a powerful exposition of pietistic views of the Bible and their sometimes paradoxical effect, see Emanuel Hirsch, *Geschichte der neuern evangelischen Theologie* (Gütersloh: Bertelsmann, 1949–54), vol. 2, pp. 169–86.

18. *The Chief Works of Benedict de Spinoza* (hereafter *Works*), trans. and introd. by R. H. M. Elwes (New York: Dover, 1951), vol. 1, pp. 99, 100.

19. *Works*, p. 186; cf. p. 104 passim.

20. *Works*, pp. 170f; cf. p. 106.

21. Johannes Cocceius, *Summa doctrinae de foedere et testamento Dei* (1648; 6th ed. Amsterdam, 1691), e.g. pp. 266ff, 283ff. A detailed exposition of this essay is given by Gottlob Schrenk, *Gottesreich und Bund im älteren Protestantismus, vornehmlich bei Johannes Cocceius* (Gütersloh: Bertelsmann, 1923), pp. 82–115.

22. Schrenk, p. 29.

CHAPTER 3

1. The standard account is still Sir Leslie Stephen, *English Thought in the Eighteenth Century* (1876; New York: Harcourt, Brace and World, 1962), 2 vols. Written in the firm conviction that the nearer religious thought comes to any kind of orthodoxy the more deeply it is enmeshed in obscurantism, this learned work does not have the spaciousness and brilliance of the great essay that inspired it, Mark Pattison's "Tendencies of Religious Thought in England, 1688 to 1750," published in the intensely controversial *Essays and Reviews* (1860), reprinted in

Pattison, *Essays*, ed. Henry Nettleship (Oxford: Clarendon Press, 1889), vol. 2, pp. 43–118. Among several later studies in English theology of the eighteenth century, the most helpful are G. R. Cragg, *Reason and Authority in the Eighteenth Century* (Cambridge: Cambridge Univ. Press, 1964) and E. Hirsch, *Geschichte der neuern . . . Theologie*, vol. 1, chs. 13–17, vol. 3, ch. 27. For the English Enlightenment in the context of the general critical movement in European religious thought, see Ernst Cassirer, *The Philosophy of the Enlightenment* (Boston: Beacon Press, 1955), ch. 4, esp. pp. 171ff; Peter Gay, *The Enlightenment, an Interpretation: The Rise of Modern Paganism* (New York: Knopf, 1966), esp. chs. 5–7; also Paul Hazard, *The European Mind: The Critical Years (1680–1715)* (New Haven: Yale Univ. Press, 1953), pt. 3, chs. 1, 2; *European Thought in the Eighteenth Century from Montesquieu to Lessing* (New Haven: Yale Univ. Press, 1954), pt. 1, chs. 3–7; pt. 3, Book 3, ch. 1.

2. *Spectator Papers*, nos. 411–21, in *Works* (London: Bell and Daldy, 1872), vol. 3, pp. 395–430; cf. John Locke, *An Essay Concerning Human Understanding* (New York and London: Everyman's Library, 1965), vol. 1, pp. 123f (Book 2, ch. 11 no. 2). Locke opposes "judgment," i.e. carefully distinguishing ideas from one another, to metaphor or allusion that strikes "the fancy" and demands "no labour of thought to examine what truth or reason there is in it."

3. Joseph Butler, *The Analogy of Religion Natural and Revealed* (Everyman's Library, London: Dent, 1917), p. 9.

4. L. C. Knights suggests that Francis Bacon's prose style is an early sign of the coming change in sensibility. See Knights, "Bacon and the Seventeenth-Century Dissociation of Sensibility," in *Explorations* (New York: New York Univ. Press, 1964), esp. pp. 112ff.

5. For some discussions lending credence to this claim, see Wolfhart Pannenberg (ed.), *Revelation as History* (New York: Macmillan, 1968); F. Gerald Downing, *Has Christianity a Revelation?* (London: SCM Press, 1964); James Barr, *Old and New in Interpretation* (London: SCM Press, 1966) chs. 1, 3.

6. Larger works including analyses of the deistic controversy are G. R. Cragg and Leslie Stephen (both, n. 1 above); Frank Manuel, *The Eighteenth Century Confronts the Gods* (Cambridge: Harvard Univ. Press, 1959); Ernest C. Mossner, *Bishop Butler and the Age of Reason* (New York: Macmillan, 1936); Roland N. Stromberg, *Religious Liberalism in Eighteenth-Century England* (London: Oxford Univ. Press, 1954). Useful excerpts from the chief deistic writings, accompanied by brief commentaries, may be found in Peter Gay, *Deism; an anthology* (Princeton, N.J.: Van Nostrand, 1968). The best brief statement in English of the concept of revelation and related notions at the end of the eighteenth century is J. M. Creed, *The Divinity of Jesus Christ* (Cambridge, Cambridge Univ. Press, 1938), chs. 1, 2.

7. This in effect was the summation of Christianity in John Locke's enormously influential *The Reasonableness of Christianity* (Chicago: Regnery, 1965), which charted a latitudinarian path between Deism and orthodoxy. "These two, faith and repentance, i.e., believing Jesus to be the Messiah and a good life, are the indispensable conditions of the new covenant, to be performed by all those who would obtain eternal life"; p. 128, cf. also pp. 123ff, 134f passim.

8. The climactic argument against the credibility of miracles in general is, by common consent, David Hume's Essay 10, "Of Miracles," in *An Enquiry Concerning Human Understanding* (1758).

9. The argument over the credibility of New Testament miracles began with their complete allegorization by Thomas Woolston, *Six Discourses on the Miracles of Our Saviour* (1727–30). The most elaborate defense of the apostles' veracity in claiming the resurrection of Jesus was written by Thomas Sherlock, *Trial of the Witnesses* (1729).

10. This remarkable story is told with great skill by C. C. Gillispie, *Genesis and Geology* (New York: Harper Torchbook, 1959), e.g. chs. 4, 5.

11. William Chillingworth, *The Religion of Protestants* (1638), quoted in *The Cambridge History of the Bible* (Cambridge: Cambridge Univ. Press, 1963), vol. 3, p. 175.

12. The standard early nineteenth-century review of the history of biblical interpretation is Gottlob Wilhelm Meyer, *Geschichte der Schrifterklärung seit der Wiederherstellung der Wissenschaften*, 5 vols., 1802–09. For contemporary bibliographical reference see K. G. Bretschneider, *Systematische Entwicklung aller in der Dogmatik vorkommenden Begriffe* (3rd ed., 1826), esp. pp. 106ff, 284ff. For twentieth-century reviews of the history of modern biblical scholarship, see H.-J. Kraus, *Geschichte der historisch-kritischen Erforschung des Alten Testaments* (2nd ed., Neukirchen-Vluyn: Neukirchener Verlag, 1969); H.-J. Kraus, *Die biblische Theologie* (Neukirchen-Vluyn: Neukirchener Verlag, 1970); W. G. Kümmel, *Das Neue Testament: Geschichte der Erforschung seiner Probleme* (Freiburg/Munich: Alber, 1958); *The Cambridge History of the Bible* (Cambridge: Cambridge Univ. Press, 1963–70).

13. For a useful analysis of positivity in Kant and the early German Idealists (1790–1800) I am indebted to the unpublished Yale Ph.D. dissertation of Garrett Green, "Positive Religion in the Early Philosophy of the German Idealists" (1971).

14. See C. Hartlich and W. Sachs, *Der Ursprung des Mythosbegriffes in der modernen Bibelwissenschaft* (Tübingen: Mohr, 1952), pp. 15, 59, 135 passim.

15. For a discussion of the theory and Semler's use of it see G. Hornig, *Die Anfänge der historisch-kritischen Theologie*, Forschungen zur systematischen Theologie und Religionsphilosophie (Göttingen: Vandenhoeck and Ruprecht, 1961), vol. 8, ch. 8.

16. This was Semler's position in his *Beantwortung der Fragmente eines Ungenannten insbesondere vom Zweck Jesu und seiner Jünger* (1779) and *Antwort auf das Bahrdische Glaubensbekenntnis* (1779).

17. See "Accommodation" in *Realencyclopädie für protestantische Theologie und Kirche* (hereafter RE) (3rd ed., Leipzig, 1896), vol. 1, p. 129.

18. "Heilsgeschichte" and "heilsgeschichtliche Schule" came to designate a particular perspective or technical school of thought concerning the unity and continuity of the Bible, prominent in the nineteenth and twentieth centuries. The concept, and sometimes the word, can be traced back to the seventeenth century.

See the article on "Heilsgeschichte" in *Die Religion in Geschichte und Gegenwart* (hereafter RGG) (3rd ed., Tübingen, 1959), vol. 3, pp. 187f; also H.-J. Kraus, *Die biblische Theologie*, pp. 17ff, 240ff passim.

In the late eighteenth and early nineteenth centuries, the phrase "die heilige Geschichte" was used in a much less technical sense to characterize the supernatural, historical narrative of both testaments. D. F. Strauss, for instance, uses it this way in *Das Leben Jesus*, ¶10 (all reference to this work will be to the 2nd German ed., Tübingen, 1837).

CHAPTER 4

1. Anthony Collins, *A Discourse of the Grounds and Reasons of the Christian Religion* (London, 1737), pp. 35f.

2. Ibid., pp. 54, 55.

3. Thomas Sherlock, *The Use and Intent of Prophecy in the Several Ages of the World* (London, 1728), Discourse 3, passim.

4. Anthony Collins, *The Scheme of Literal Prophecy Considered* (London, 1727), p. 358.

5. Stephen, *English Thought in the Eighteenth Century*, vol. 1, pp. 186f.

6. Edward Chandler, *A Defence of Christianity from Prophecies of the Old Testament* (1725). Collins wrote *The Scheme of Literal Prophecy Considered* chiefly with Chandler's book as his target.

7. John Locke, *An Essay Concerning Human Understanding*, Book 4, ch. 16, nos. 10–11.

8. Joseph Butler, *Analogy of Religion*, pt. 2, ch. 7.

9. Calvin, *Institutes*, Book 1, ch. 7, p. 1.

10. Collins, *Scheme*, p. 366.

11. For these guidelines see Locke, *Essay*, Book 3, ch. 11, no. 24; Book 4, ch. 4, nos. 12–13; and ch 5, nos. 5ff passim.

12. Ibid., Book 4, ch. 18, no. 3.

13. Collins, *Grounds and Reasons*, pp. 45f.

CHAPTER 5

1. See E. Hirsch, *Geschichte der neuern . . . Theologie*, vol. 2, ch. 24.

2. S. J. Baumgarten, *Untersuchung theologischer Streitigkeiten*, ed. J. S. Semler (1764), vol. 3, p. 14; see also S. J. Baumgarten, *Evangelische Glaubenslehre*, ed. J. S. Semler (1760), vol. 3, pp. 55f, 72f, and §7 (pp. 104–51). These two posthumously edited works, taken from Baumgarten's lectures, are arranged in tandem, so that every locus in the dogmatic theology corresponds by number to the same topic in the polemical work.

3. Baumgarten, *Evangelische Glaubenslehre*, p. 37.

4. Hirsch, *Geschichte der neuern . . . Theologie*, vol. 2, p. 378.

5. "Sapere aude" Kant had proclaimed in the famous opening paragraph of his

essay, "Beantwortung der Frage: Was ist Aufklärung?" (1784). See I. Kant, *Was ist Aufklärung?* ed. J. Zehbe (Göttingen: Vandenhoeck und Ruprecht, 1967), p. 55.

6. Gottlob Wilhelm Meyer, *Geschichte der Schrifterklärung*, vol. 5, pp. 490f.

7. See Carl Friedrich Stäudlin, "Ueber die blos historische Auslegung der Bücher des neuen Testaments," *Kritisches Journal der neuesten theologischen Literatur*, no. 4, 1813; nos. 1 and 2, 1814.

8. Christian Wolff, Gesammelte Werke, eds. J. Ecole, J. E. Hofmann, M. Thomann, and H. W. Arndt, pt. 1, vol. 1, *Vernünftige Gedanken von den Kräften des menschlichen Verstandes* (*Deutsche Logik*) (Hildesheim: Olms, 1965), ch. 2, §3, p. 151; ch. 1, §4, p. 123.

9. Ibid., ch. 1, §48, p. 147; for his full discussion of the nature of explanation see ch. 1, §§40–57; ch. 1, §41, p. 144.

10. Quoted by the editor from the *Latin Logic*, ibid., p. 258 (ch. 1, n. 3): "If all things are to be demonstrated in logic, the principles must be sought for from ontology and psychology."

11. Ibid., ch. 2, §8, p. 153.

12. Ibid., p. 258 (editor's note).

13. Ibid., ch. 11, §5, p. 227; ch. 10, §1, p. 219.

14. Meyer, *Geschichte der Schrifterklärung*, vol. 5, p. 498.

15. See S. J. Baumgarten, *Biblische Hermeneutik*, ed. J. C. Bertram (1769), section 7.

16. See editor's introduction to Wolff, *Vernünftige Gedanken von den Kräften*, pp. 74f.

17. Ibid., ch. 10, §1, p. 219; also editor's note to this section, p. 272.

18. First edition, 1730.

19. See Wolff, *Vernünftige Gedanken von Gott, der Welt und der Seele des Menschen* (9th ed., 1743), §245; also Joachim Birke, "Christian Wolffs Metaphysik und die zeitgenössische Literatur- und Musiktheorie: Gottsched, Scheibe, Mizler," *Quellen und Forschungen zur Sprach- und Kulturgeschichte der germanischen Völker*, n.s. 21 (145), 1966, 14, 32.

20. Translated as *Lectures on the Sacred Poetry of the Hebrews* (new ed., 1829).

21. See René Wellek, *A History of Modern Criticism: 1750–1950* (New Haven: Yale Univ. Press, 1955), vol. 1, pp. 99f.

CHAPTER 6

1. "Interpretation therefore comprises two things, the proper perception of the meaning of words, and their proper explanation," J. A. Ernesti, *Institutio interpretis Novi Testamenti* (5th ed., 1809), p. 8. Large and crucial portions of this book were translated by Moses Stuart under the title *Elements of Interpretation* (1824). Stuart, who was also the first American translator of Schleiermacher, added excerpts from authors identified with Ernesti's school of interpretation. Despite its incompleteness, Stuart's translation is more useful for a comprehensive insight into Ernesti's

distinctive hermeneutical position than the complete translation by C. H. Terrot (vol. 1, 1843; vol. 2, 1848) under the title *Principles of Biblical Interpretation*.

2. J. S. Semler, *Vorbereitung zur theologischen Hermeneutik* (1760), vol. 1, pp. 160f. See also Wilhelm Dilthey, *Leben Schleiermachers*, vol. XIV, 2 in *Gesammelte Schriften*, (Göttingen: Vandenhoeck und Ruprecht, 1966), pp. 638f.

3. Ludwig Wittgenstein, *Philosophical Investigations*, trans. by G. E. M. Anscombe (2nd ed., Oxford: Blackwell, 1963), §117.

4. G. W. Meyer, *Geschichte der Schrifterklärung*, vol. 1, p. 13.

5. See E. Hirsch, *Geschichte der neuern . . . Theologie*, vol. 4, p. 55.

6. J. S. Semler, *Abhandlung von freier Untersuchung des Kanons* (1771), vol. 1, reprinted in *Texte zur Kirchen- und Theologiegeschichte* (1967), vol. 5, §§10, 11.

7. See *Allgemeine Bibliothek der biblischen Litteratur* (1793), vol. 5, no. 1, p. 89. Semler's theological outlook has been the subject of a small but ongoing discussion involving considerable disagreement. For a summary of the arguments see G. Hornig, *Die Anfänge der . . . Theologie*, ch. 1.

8. "Vom Zwecke Jesu und seiner Jünger" (1778). See A. C. Lundsteen, *Hermann Samuel Reimarus und die Anfänge der Leben-Jesu Forschung* (Copenhagen: Olsen, 1939). For recent English translations of and comments on this, the most important of the *Fragments* from Reimarus which Lessing edited, see *Reimarus: Fragments*, ed. C. H. Talbert, trans. by R. S. Fraser (Philadelphia: Fortress Press, 1970); and *The Goal of Jesus and His Disciples*, ed. and introd. by G. W. Buchanan (Leiden: Brill, 1971). A complete German text of Reimarus's anti-Christian and antibiblical polemic is contained in H. S. Reimarus, *Apologie oder Schutzschrift für die vernünftigen Verehrer Gottes*, ed. Gerhard Alexander (Frankfurt a.M.: Insel Verlag, 1972), 2 vols. For the broader context of the German Enlightenment and its religious thought, see E. Hirsch, *Geschichte der neuern evangelischen Theologie*, vol. 4; Karl Aner, *Die Theologie der Lessingzeit* (Halle a.S.: Niemeyer, 1929); Henry Allison, *Lessing and the Enlightenment* (Ann Arbor: Univ. of Michigan Press, 1966).

9. D. F. Strauss, *Hermann Samuel Reimarus und seine Schutzschrift für die vernünftigen Verehrer Gottes* (2nd ed., Bonn: Strauss, 1877), §40.

10. "Gegensätze des Herausgebers." G. E. Lessing, *Gesammelte Werke*, ed. Paul Rilla (Berlin: Aufbau-Verlag, 1954–58), vol. 7, p. 813.

11. "Axiomata," 1(3), ibid., vol. 8, p. 168.

12. For a survey of contemporary responses to the Wolfenbüttel *Fragments*, see G. W. Buchanan (n. 8 above), Introduction, pp. 15–26.

13. Quoted by G. R. Cragg, *Reason and Authority*, p. 32.

14. Conyers Middleton, "An Essay on the Allegorical and Literal Interpretation of the Creation and Fall of Man," *Miscellaneous Works* (1752), vol. 2, p. 131.

15. Ibid.

CHAPTER 7

1. Pages 1–9, 165f passim.

2. W. K. Wimsatt, Jr., and Cleanth Brooks, *Literary Criticism: A Short History* (New York: Knopf, 1957), pp. 308–09.

3. Armand Nivelle, *Kunst- und Dichtungstheorien zwischen Aufklärung und Klassik* (Berlin: De Gruyter, 1960), p. 184.

4. Robert Lowth, *Lectures on the Sacred Poetry of the Hebrews* (1829), p. 29.

5. Ibid., Lectures 32–34.

6. Clara Reeve, *The Progress of Romance* (2 vols. in 1, 1785), vol. 1, p. 111.

7. Ibid., vol. 2, pp. 77ff, 92ff.

8. Hume, "Of the Study of History," in *Of the Standard of Taste and Other Essays*, ed. S. W. Lenz (Indianapolis: Bobbs Merrill, 1965), p. 96.

9. See Leo Braudy, *Narrative Form in History and Fiction: Hume, Fielding, Gibbon* (Princeton: Princeton Univ. Press, 1970), p. 85: "Hume's *History* purported at its outset to be a repository of political and moral philosophy. But in Hume's final state of mind the precepts for direct action that can be drawn from his work are few indeed."

10. See James William Johnson, *The Formation of English Neo-Classical Thought* (Princeton: Princeton Univ. Press, 1967), ch. 2, esp. pp. 43ff.

11. Bruce Wardropper, quoted by Keith Stewart, "History, Poetry, and the Terms of Fiction in the Eighteenth Century," *Modern Philology 66* (2), Nov. 1968, 111, n. 7.

12. Ibid., p. 111. See A. D. McKillop, *The Early Masters of English Fiction* (Lawrence: Univ. of Kansas Press, 1956), p. 42.

13. Henry Fielding, *The History of Tom Jones* (New York: New American Library, 1963), Book 8, ch. 1, p. 338.

14. McKillop, p. 42.

15. See R. A. Donovan, *The Shaping Vision: Imagination in the English Novel from Defoe to Dickens* (Ithaca: Cornell Univ. Press, 1966), pp. 245f; also Braudy, ch. 4, who contrasts Fielding favorably with Hume because the latter in his *History* does not speak enough in his own voice.

16. Fielding, p. 338.

17. Donovan, p. 248.

18. See S. T. Coleridge, "Biographia Literaria," ch. 17 in *The Portable Coleridge*, ed. I. A. Richards (New York: Viking Press, 1961), pp. 535ff.

19. Auerbach, *Mimesis*, pp. 491f.

20. Ibid., pp. 44.

21. "Strauss is concerned not with the criticism of the writing but only with the criticism of the history." F. C. Baur, *Kritische Untersuchungen über die kanonischen Evangelien* (Tübingen: Fues, 1847), p. 40. (See Baur's discussion of Strauss, ibid., pp. 40–76.)

22. See *The Cambridge History of the Bible*, vol. 3, ch. 8; W. Neil, "Critical and Theological Use of the Bible 1700–1950," pp. 271f.

23. For a survey of religious practice including biblical preaching in the evangelical revival, see Horton Davies, *Worship and Theology in England from Watts*

and Wesley to Maurice, 1690–1850 (Princeton: Princeton Univ. Press, 1961), pt. 2, pp. 143–240.

CHAPTER 8

1. See Andrew Brown, "John Locke and the Religious 'Aufklärung,'" *Review of Religion 13*, 1949, 126–54.

2. *Johann Gottfried Eichhorns Urgeschichte*, ed., introd., and annotated by D. Johann Philipp Gabler (1790–93). See Hartlich and Sachs, *Der Ursprung der Mythosbegriffes*, ch. 3.

3. See W. G. Kümmel, *Das Neue Testament*, pp. 81ff.

4. Gabler, *Eichhorns Urgeschichte*, pt. 1 (1790), p. xv; see also Hartlich and Sachs, p. 24.

5. Four volumes, 1771–75.

CHAPTER 9

1. For "biblical theology," the history and systematic study of the concept, see Martin Kähler, "Biblische Theologie" RE 3, pp. 192ff; Gerhard Ebeling, "The Meaning of 'Biblical Theology,'" *Journal of Theological Studies 6*, 1955, 210–25; H.-J. Kraus, *Die biblische Theologie*, esp. pts. 1, 2(I), 4(I); Brevard S. Childs, *Biblical Theology in Crisis* (Philadelphia: Westminster Press, 1970), pt. 1.

2. A partial German translation of this essay, which some historians of modern biblical scholarship regard as epoch-making, may be found in Kümmel, *Das Neue Testament*, pp. 115–18.

3. For a more detailed examination of this important notion, *die Sache*, and the tendency to identify textual meaning with it, see chapter 13.

4. See n.7, ch. 5. Excerpts from Stäudlin's essay may be found in Kümmel, *Das Neue Testament*, pp. 135–38. The discussion between Stäudlin and Kell is described in detail in Joachim Wach, *Das Verstehen* (Tübingen: Mohr, 1926–33), vol. 2, ch. 1. It is well to take Wach's work with caution. For all its erudition it was a product of his youth and is frequently marred by misleading generalizations, if not downright errors. Thus he connects Stäudlin's claim that to combine into one totality the interpretation of individual passages is already to move beyond historical interpretation with the *analogia fidei* of the orthodox Protestant tradition (ibid., p. 150). Neither the passage on which he bases this comment nor Stäudlin's general position, which was that of a conservative Rationalist, justifies linking him with this typically Protestant scholastic doctrine. Similarly mistaken is Wach's estimate of the Hegelian background of D. F. Strauss's theory of myth. (See Hartlich and Sachs, *Der Ursprung des Mythosbegriffes*, pp. 121ff.)

5. Part 1 (2nd ed., 1775), pp. LXVIf, 5f.

6. Ibid., pp. VI, 62–123 (§§28–35).

7. Ibid., pt. 2 (1st ed., 1772), pp. 270ff.

8. Ibid., e.g., pt. 1, Preface, pp. 2f.

9. For a useful discussion of this school of thought, see H.-J. Kraus, *Die biblische Theologie*, pt. 1, chs. 2, 3, 5.

10. J. A. Bengel, *Gnomon of the New Testament* (Edinburgh: Clark, 1860), vol. 1, author's preface, §14.

11. Ibid., 8, 14, 21.

CHAPTER 10

1. See for instance Herder, *Briefe, das Studium der Theologie betreffend*, pt. 1, in *Sämmtliche Werke*, ed. Bernhard Suphan (Berlin: Weidmann, 1877–1913), vol. 10, p. 30 (letter no. 2); pt. 4, vol. 11, pp. 10–14 (letter no. 39). (This work will be cited as *Briefe*.)

2. Friedrich Meinecke, *Die Entstehung des Historismus*, in *Werke*, ed. and introd. by Carl Hinrichs (Munich: Oldenbourg, 1959), vol. 3, p. 361. The standard biography of Herder, also a massive intellectual history of his time, is still *Herder*, the great work by Rudolf Haym, concluded in 1885 (repub. with introd. by Wolfgang Harich; Berlin: Aufbau-Verlag, 1954).

3. Meinecke, p. 362.

4. J. W. Goethe, *Aus meinem Leben: Dichtung und Wahrheit*, in *Gedenkausgabe*, ed. E. Beutler (Zürich: Artemis-Verlag, 1948), vol. 10, p. 448.

5. Herder, *Briefe*, vol. 10, p. 7.

6. *Vom Geist der ebräischen Poesie* (1825), pt. 1, author's outline (emphasis added). See also *Briefe*, vol. 10, pp. 15, 30f.

7. Meinecke, *Entstehung des Historismus*, p. 357.

8. See for instance René Wellek, *History of Modern Criticism: 1750–1950*, vol. 1, p. 184.

9. *Briefe*, vol. 10 p. 14, no. 2.

10. See for example *Briefe*, vol. 10, pp. 139ff, 163ff.

11. *Der Ursprung des Mythosbegriffes*, pp. 48ff.

12. See W. G. Kümmel, *Das Neue Testament*, pp. 88–99.

13. E. Hirsch, *Geschichte der neuern . . . Theologie*, vol. 4, pp. 224f.

14. See Hirsch, vol. 4, p. 227.

15. Hirsch, vol. 4, p. 233.

16. Meinecke, *Entstehung des Historismus*, pp. 356f.

17. Thomas Willi, *Herders Beitrag zum Verstehen des Alten Testaments*, Beiträge zur Geschichte der biblischen Hermeneutik, no. 8 (Tübingen: Mohr, 1971), pp. 44f. Willi rightly corrects and modifies Rudolf Smend's view that Herder "archaizingly guides man into the past" in contrast to the Rationalists' modernizing use of the Bible. See ibid., p. 45, n. 38.

18. In his devastating criticism of the tradition which argues that Hebrew semantics are governed by a particular and unique Hebrew mental structure, James Barr cites Herder as an early propagator of this point of view. See *The Semantics of Biblical Language* (Oxford: Oxford Univ. Press, 1961), pp. 14, 85f.

CHAPTER 11

1. Goethe, *Dichtung und Wahrheit*, vol. 10, p. 681.

2. Meinecke, *Entstehung des Historismus*, pp. 463ff.

3. Goethe, *Gespräche mit Eckermann*, in *Gedenkausgabe*, ed. E. Beutler, vol. 24, p. 635; see also Goethe's earliest conversations with Schiller as reported by Goethe, *Annalen*, in *Sämtliche Werke* (Jubilee ed., Stuttgart and Berlin: Cotta, 1902–07), vol. 30, pp. 388–92.

4. Meinecke, pp. 366f.

5. "Of the Study of History," pp. 97f.

6. Meinecke, pp. 220ff.

7. *Das Theater des Herrn Diderot*, trans. from the French (1760), pt. 2; translator's preface and p. 231.

8. From a letter by Lessing to his brother Karl, Oct. 20, 1778. Quoted in Peter Demetz, *Gotthold Ephraim Lessing: Nathan der Weise* (Frankfurt a.M./Berlin: Ullstein, 1966), p. 183.

9. See *Das Theater des Herrn Diderot*, pp. 236ff.

10. Quoted in Demetz, p. 123.

11. Goethe, *Dichtung und Wahrheit*, p. 310.

12. See Demetz, p. 143.

13. Act 3, scene 7.

14. *Wesley's Standard Sermons* (London: Epworth Press, 1921), vol. 2; pp. 309ff (Sermon 44).

15. Auerbach, *Mimesis*, pp. 441–42.

16. *Versuch über den Roman*. Facsimile of the original edition of 1774 with an epilogue by Eberhard Lämmert (Stuttgart: Metzler, 1965), p. 392; and Epilogue, pp. 557, 573.

17. See the section entitled "Brief über den Roman" in "Gespräch über die Poesie" (1800); F. Schlegel, *Kritische Schriften*, ed. Wolfdietrich Rasch (Munich: Hanser, 1964), pp. 508–18.

18. *Kritische Schriften*, p. 517. René Wellek's brief summary statement is completely justified: "He condemns the realistic novel of the English, including even Fielding" (*A History of Modern Criticism: 1750–1950*, vol. 2, p. 19; cf. p. 29).

19. F. Schlegel, *Geschichte der alten und neuen Literatur*, in *Kritische Friedrich-Schlegel-Ausgabe*, ed. H. Eichner (Paderborn: Schöningh, 1961), vol. 6, p. 331.

20. Meinecke, *Entstehung des Historismus*, pp. 592f.

21. See Hajo Holborn, *A History of Modern Germany, 1648–1840* (New York: Knopf, 1966), p. 306.

22. Auerbach, *Mimesis*, p. 445.

23. For a brilliant but finally unconvincing contrary view of *Faust* as moving toward contemporary realism, see Georg Lukács, "Faust Studies," in *Goethe and His Age* (New York: Grosset and Dunlap, 1969), pp. 157–253, esp. pp. 175ff.

24. Auerbach, p. 451.

25. Introduction to "Contribution to the Critique of Hegel's Philosophy of Right," in *Deutsch-Französische Jahrbücher*, 1844, trans. in *Marx and Engels on Religion*, introd. by Reinhold Niebuhr (New York: Schocken Books, 1964), p. 41.

26. Ibid.

27. Marx, "Theses on Feuerbach," ibid., p. 72.

28. Fifth printing, New York: Macmillan, 1956, p. 1.

CHAPTER 12

1. In a letter to his friend Christian Märklin, dated July 22, 1846. See Strauss, *Ausgewählte Briefe*, ed. Eduard Zeller (Bonn: Strauss, 1895), p. 183.

2. Strauss, *Gesammelte Schriften*, vol. 5, p. 4.

3. Georg Lorenz Bauer (1755–1806), professor in Altdorf and colleague of Johann Philipp Gabler, was a consistent defender of the "mythophile" argument. See Kümmel, *Das Neue Testament*, pp. 124–26, 132–35; Hartlich and Sachs, *Der Ursprung des Mythosbegriffes*, pp. 69–87.

4. Right from the beginning, historically oriented critics were accused of having no way to appreciate the "inner" or "religious" meaning of the biblical texts. This protest was leveled against them from a variety of theological standpoints. In addition to Stäudlin, one may mention the same judgment on the part of Schleiermacher's friend and follower, Friedrich Lücke, in his *Grundriss der neutestamentlichen Hermeneutik und ihrer Geschichte* (1817), pp. 72f. The mythophiles were regarded as epitomizing this lack.

5. See Strauss, "Die Halben und die Ganzen," in *Gesammelte Schriften*, vol. 5, pp. 149ff; "Literarische Denkwürdigkeiten," in *Kleine Schriften* (Bonn: Strauss, 1895), p. 14; above all Strauss, *Streitschriften zur Vertheidigung meiner Schrift über das Leben Jesu* (new ed., Tübingen, 1841), part 3, pp. 57–126, which is devoted to an analysis of the relation between his book and Hegel and his school. *Gesammelte Schriften*, vol. 5, p. 177: "My whole critique of the life of Jesus grew out of Hegel's thesis that religion and philosophy have the same content, the first in representational [*Vorstellung*] the second in conceptual [*Begriff*] form. Here is how Hegel's school understood their master's words: The historical credibility of the gospel accounts is demonstrated by the fact that they convey, in representational form, true philosophical ideas. The actuality of history is understood to be derived from the truth of ideas. The whole critical part of my *Life of Jesus* was directed against this position. . . . From the truths of ideas, said I, nothing can be derived concerning historical reliability. The latter must be judged solely in the light of its own laws, in accordance with the rules of events and the nature of the accounts. But I did not doubt at the time that the same ideas were on the one hand represented in the religious accounts, even if they were unhistorical, and on the other hand grasped conceptually by philosophy." For an exemplary account distinguishing Strauss's use of "myth" as a historical-critical explanatory category from its Hegelian-philosophical use, and ranging Strauss into the eighteenth-century critical tradition derived from C. G. Heyne, see Hartlich and Sachs, ch. 5.

6. Strauss, *Das Leben Jesu*, vol. 1, pp. 90ff.

7. Ibid., vol. 1, pp. 471, 472.

8. Ibid., vol. 1, p. 111.

9. Ibid., vol. 1, pp. 54f.

10. Until the constructive conclusion of the work (vol. 2, §§143–51), this remains Strauss's utilization of the category "myth." It is and remains (except for that final section) a notion used to explain the historical origins of the gospels. It goes without saying, therefore, that Strauss's emphasis is wholly different from Rudolf Bultmann's "demythologization" project, in which myth is a form in which abiding existential meaning is rendered in the original writings, so that it is not to be done away with but interpreted. This comes close to what Strauss suggests in the final section of his work, but it is obviously not the use to which he puts "myth" in the body of the essay. For a comparison between Strauss and Bultmann, see Gunther Backhaus, *Kerygma und Mythos bei David Friedrich Strauss und Rudolf Bultmann*, in *Theologische Forschung; Wissenschaftliche Beiträge zur kirchlich-evangelischen Lehre*, no. 12 (Hamburg-Bergstedt: Reich Verlag, 1956).

11. Strauss, *Das Leben Jesu*, vol. 1, p. 66.

12. A terminological ambiguity should be cleared up at this point. Strauss speaks of external and internal "grounds" for estimating the reliability of the gospel reports. It should be noted that the terms grounds and evidence do not coincide precisely. For one of the *internal grounds* by means of which Strauss established the nonhistorical character of much of the gospel writings actually involved use of *external evidence*, though of course of a literary kind. It is the argument from literary parallels, which became one of the hallmarks of the *religionsgeschichtliche Schule*'s procedure. Strauss found parallels to supernatural stories and concepts, etc., applied to Jesus in the gospels, in the Old Testament, and in nonbiblical writings of the biblical period, though he did not make extensive use of the last material. The rationale of his argument is that whenever such literary parallels can be found outside, either without specific application or applied to somebody other than Jesus, the case for the reliability of the gospels is weakened decisively. First of all the uniqueness of the story of Jesus and the claim that he is the divinely ordained culminating point of much ancient history, especially of the Old Testament, are both completely attenuated. The latter, in fact, is turned on its head. What the writers have done, of course, is to fit available material to Jesus at their will. Second, if we believe, as we obviously do, that the same content used outside the Bible is mythical in character, why should we decline to do so when we see it in the Bible? Third, parallel or similar stories in the same geographical, cultural context involve a common source, and it is not a supernatural one but the general and completely natural, mythical consciousness of the time and area. In other words, the argument from religious syncretism, toward which the whole mythical school pointed the way, weakens the case for the uniqueness as well as the factual reliability of the Christian story. But even without the hypothesis of syncretism, one may argue the parallel structure of myths in

diverse areas and times, and therefore a common primitive consciousness. This precludes elevating one of its instances in honor above the others. This was the usual procedure of the mythical school when comparing biblical with classical Greek and Roman myths. Cf. Georg Lorenz Bauer, *Hebräische Mythologie des Alten und Neuen Testamentes* (1802), vol. 1, p. 49.

13. The most spirited and persuasive recent defense of the integrity of a procedure like that of Strauss and its pertinence to theological truth claims (against theologians of the neo-orthodox school of the twentieth century) is Van A. Harvey, *The Historian and the Believer* (New York: Macmillan, 1966).

14. *Der Ursprung des Mythosbegriffes*, chs. 2, 3.

15. Strauss himself had already drawn attention to this situation in the third of his *Streitschriften* (see n. 5 above). But the contrary, erroneous impression has persisted as, e.g., in Joachim Wach, *Das Verstehen*, vol. 2, pp. 272f (see above, n. 3, ch. 9).

16. F. D. E. Schleiermacher, *Hermeneutik*, ed. and introd. by Heinz Kimmerle (Heidelberg: Winter, Universitätsverlag, 1959), p. 87.

17. Transitional figures of great importance were men like Herder and the early Schelling, whose discussions were influenced by rationalist and historical-critical spirits like Heyne and Eichhorn, while they themselves furthered romantic notions of myth and historical understanding. For Herder, see the discussions in Meinecke, *Die Entstehung des Historismus*, ch. 9; Fritz Strich, *Die Mythologie in der deutschen Literatur von Klopstock bis Wagner* (Halle a.S.: Niemeyer, 1910), vol. 1, ch. 2; Ernst Cassirer (whose brief but wise remarks set Herder's historical views in chronological and developmental context), *The Philosophy of the Enlightenment* (Boston: Beacon Press, 1955), ch. 5, "The Conquest of the Historical World". For Schelling, see his early essay, "Ueber Mythen, historische Sagen und Philosopheme der ältesten Welt" (1793), in *Sämmtliche Werke* (Stuttgart and Augsburg: Cotta, 1856), vol. 1, pt. 1, pp. 43–83.

18. *Der Ursprung des Mythosbegriffes*, pp. 50f.

19. In this respect, as in so many others, it was Hegel who "mediated" and transcended the difference between Rationalists and Romantics.

CHAPTER 13

1. By 1846 Strauss could say concerning "Hegel's system" that it was like a loose tooth in his mouth, on which he would no longer risk biting down (letter to Friedrich Vischer, June 3, 1846) *Ausgewählte Briefe*, p. 177.

2. So both J. P. Gabler and G. L. Bauer. Strauss was by no means the first to derive amusement from H. E. G. Paulus's contorted efforts, postulating possible natural events on the basis of the gospels' miracle reports. Gabler among others had done so thirty-four years earlier in a review of Paulus's *Kommentar über das neue Testament*, pt. 1, in his *Neuestes theologisches Journal* (vol. 7(1), 1801), pp. 363–413, esp. 384ff. In contrast to Paulus, he had made a strong plea for treating such miracles

as those connected with Jesus' birth as philosophical rather than historical myths, so that there could be no use in looking for the "facts" to these stories, or treating them as the stories' meaning. It is all the more surprising to see Gabler claiming historical facts (historical myths he called them generally) whenever possible, e.g. in an essay to which we shall recur directly on the explanation of the story of Jesus' temptation. There he postulated a psychic event on Jesus' part as the origin, explanation, and meaning of the text. (Cf. *Kleinere theologische Schriften*, 1831, vol. 1, pp. 201–14).

Even more surprising is the case of G. L. Bauer. He had fulfilled Gabler's plea for a *mythologia sacra* in his *Hebräische Mythologie des Alten und Neuen Testamentes* (1802). Even earlier he had provided the hermeneutical foundation for this enterprise in *Entwurf einer Hermeneutik des Alten und Neuen Testamentes* (1799). (See the highly laudatory exposition of these works in Hartlich and Sachs, *Der Ursprung des Mythosbegriffes*, pp. 70–87.) However, in his *Biblische Theologie des Neuen Testaments* (vol. 1, 1800), he has recourse not only to well-nigh constant naturalistic explanation of miracles, but in the case of the resurrection of Jesus, at any rate, also to the affirmation of the historicity of miracle (ibid. §53). Small wonder that Strauss protested that these men, and others like them, used the category of myth both confusedly and timidly (*Das Leben Jesu*, vol. 1, §§10, 11).

3. Gabler, once again, e.g. in the preface to his edition of Eichhorn's *Urgeschichte* (1790), pt. 1, pp. 30f; (1793), pt. 2, vol. 2, pp. CXIIff.

4. J. S. Semler, *Vorbereitung zur theologischen Hermeneutik* (1760), vol. 1, pp. 160f.

5. The influence of Ernesti (*Institutio interpretis Novi Testamenti*) and of his school—including such men as S. F. N. Morus, K. A. G. Keil, Friedrich von Ammon—was considerable, but it was mainly confined to the shaping of "lower" or textual in contrast to "higher" or historical criticism. However, as the conflict between Keil and Stäudlin was to make clear, for a follower of Ernesti like Keil the boundary between grammatical historical and historical-critical procedures was extremely vague, far more so than it had been for Ernesti himself.

6. See his essay, "Ob es Mythen auch im neuen Testament gäbe" (*Kleinere theologische Schriften*, 1831, vol. 1), and above all his strong advocacy of the mythical point of view in his edition of Eichhorn's *Urgeschichte*.

7. "Ueber den Unterschied zwischen Auslegung und Erklärung, erläutert durch die verschiedene Behandlungsart der Versuchungsgeschichte Jesu," in *Kleinere theologische Schriften*, vol. 1, pp. 201–14. The quotations in the following paragraphs are from the same essay.

8. "Ob es Mythen auch im neuen Testament gäbe."

9. See Ernesti's disagreement with Semler, evoked by Semler's discussion of the notion of the demonic in the New Testament and then expanded to a debate over general principles of interpretation. A fragmentary but nonetheless brilliant and penetrating discussion of the issues may be found in Dilthey, *Leben Schleiermachers*, XIV, 2, pp. 635–49 (see n. 2, ch. 6 above).

10. Hirsch, *Geschichte der neuern . . . Theologie*, vol. 4, p. 11.

11. See J. A. Ernesti, *Elements of Interpretation*, trans. by Moses Stuart (1824), esp. introduction and pt. 1, ch. 1. (Cf. n. 1, ch. 6 above.)

Although Ernesti seems to confine meaning to conventional use, this does not necessarily involve him in a denial of the natural life and growth of a language. Nor on the other hand does he confirm it. A modern reader may be startled by apparent similarities between Ernesti and the later work of Ludwig Wittgenstein on matters of use, rules, and language as a "form of life." But a comparison would be difficult, though tempting on the face of things. Ernesti was, after all, a straightforward Rationalist of the eighteenth century, for whom "sense" is generally unvarying and set within a specific period of time and a given lectionary structure, and words have a chiefly signifying use. (See §§27, 30, 105.)

12. Ibid., §25.

13. Ibid., §33.

14. For general accounts of Hess, see RE 7, pp. 793ff; Hirsch, vol. 4, pp. 192-203.

15. In Hess (ed.), *Bibliothek der heiligen Geschichte* (1791, 1792), pt. 2, pp. 153ff.

16. Hartlich and Sachs, p. 59.

17. Cf. the article "Hermeneutik" by G. Heinrici, RE 7, pp. 737f.

18. New York: Harper Torchbooks, 1960.

19. Dilthey, pp. 651f.

20. Kant, *Religion Within . . . Reason*, pp. 65-70.

21. But from another perspective this claim has to be qualified, for hermeneutically, as in so many ways, Kant was the one great Enlightenment figure to peer toward the horizons of Romanticism and Idealism. Though he allegorized scripture, his use of it tended toward symbolism, if by symbolizing we mean that certain fact-like descriptions, while not making literal sense, nevertheless are indispensable in the representation of a complex of meaning known apart from them. The doctrine of vicarious atonement for example serves Kant in just such fashion: it is an outward representation of the inward continuity of the single personhood of any human being who has turned from evil to good, when there is no other way (and certainly no direct way) of setting forth both this continuity and the radical change the person has undergone.

CHAPTER 14

1. Hartlich and Sachs, *Der Ursprung des Mythosbegriffes*, p. 59.

2. Strauss, *Das Leben Jesu*, vol. 1, pp. 8off; p. 2; p. 31.

3. Ibid., p. 31. In this section of his presentation, Strauss is heavily dependent on the first seven sections of G. L. Bauer's *Hebräische Mythologie des Alten und Neuen Testamentes*, pp. 3-58.

4. On the question of myth as interpretive category, especially in Old Testament study, see Brevard S. Childs, *Myth and Reality in the Old Testament*, Studies in Biblical Theology no. 27 (Naperville, Ill.: Allenson, 1960). Chapter 1 includes a brief but

telling criticism of Hartlich and Sachs, similar to that made of the mythophiles in the present essay.

5. Gabler, introduction to Eichhorn's *Urgeschichte*, pt. 1, pp. 30f.

6. Bauer, *Hebräische Mythologie*, vol. 1, pp. 40, 56.

7. Strauss, *Das Leben Jesu*, vol. 1, p. 78.

8. Ibid., pp. 79f. Some theologians of our day to whom Strauss's historical-critical views are by and large quite congenial, would disagree with him over this matter: God's being affected by time and change in the world is, they say, no myth at all but a right and proper metaphysical affirmation of the nature of Deity. It goes to show that one man's myth is another man's reason.

9. *The Concept of Mind* (New York: Barnes and Noble, 1949), p. 40.

CHAPTER 15

1. The bibliography is too vast to mention here. However, there is broad agreement especially from the retrospective glance of the twentieth century, that Schleiermacher's hermeneutics represents a watershed in the study of the subject. From principles and rules for exegesis, it is generally said, hermeneutics now becomes a coherent and unified inquiry into the operations involved in understanding. Thus, Gerhard Ebeling—in a fine article that has become standard reference not only for its informativeness but also for the point of view it represents—says: "Coming from Ernesti and Semler, Schleiermacher, utilizing those impulses that went beyond the Enlightenment, was the first to develop a general hermeneutics systematically from the analysis of the understanding." (Ebeling, "Hermeneutik"; RGG 3, cols. 242-62; see col. 255.) The point is well stated in one of Schleiermacher's own earliest aphorisms on hermeneutics, which the latest editor of this work puts at the beginning of the whole text: "Actually only that belongs to hermeneutics which Ernesti called *subtilitas intelligendi*. For [*subtilitas*] *explicandi*, as soon as it is more than the external side of understanding, is once again an object of hermeneutics and belongs to the art of presentation" (Schleiermacher, *Hermeneutik*, ed. Heinz Kimmerle; Heidelberg: Winter Universitätsverlag, 1959 [Abh. Heidelberger Akad. Wissenschaften, Phil.-hist. Kl., 1959, pt. 2, p. 31]). One of the commentators to recognize the enormous change which Schleiermacher had introduced into the topic was Wilhelm Dilthey in a well-known essay, "Die Entstehung der Hermeneutik" (*Gesammelte Schriften*, vol. V, pp. 317ff). (The reader must be warned that Dilthey's own analysis of Schleiermacher's hermeneutics was far more complex and balanced than his rather one-sided emphasis on Schleiermacher's "psychological" interpretation in this article.)

Fully recognizing the crucial novel development which Schleiermacher introduced into reflections on the nature of hermeneutics, some modern authors fault him for what they regard as his "subjectivism," "psychologism," and "individualism" in the later statements of his theory of how we understand discourse. Among authors who tend in this direction one may mention James M. Robinson and John B. Cobb, Jr., *The New Hermeneutic* (New Frontiers in Theology, vol. 2) (New York: Harper, 1964), especially the essay by J. M. Robinson, "Hermeneutic since Barth" (pp. 1–77). The most enthusiastic statement in English of a point of view agreeing with Robinson and favoring M. Heidegger's and H.-G. Gadamer's view on language-and-being over the hermeneutics of Schleiermacher, Dilthey, and Emilio Betti, but especially over the formalism (presumably the realism) of "Anglo-American literary criticism," is Richard Palmer, *Hermeneutics* (Evanston, Ill.: Northwestern Univ. Press, 1969).

In German, in addition to the older historical survey already mentioned, Joachim Wach, *Das Verstehen* (esp. vols. 1, 2), one may cite Emerich Coreth, *Grundfragen der Hermeneutik* (Freiburg: Herder, 1969) as a useful introduction to philosophical and theological issues of interpretation since Schleiermacher. Most commentators except those influenced by the later work of Ludwig Wittgenstein are persuaded of the soundness of Schleiermacher's new departure because it is governed by the question: What is it to understand discourse, spoken or written? This is true even of those who think that finally the question has to be changed to the less methodological and more ontological issue: How is it *possible* to understand? Thus Richard Palmer (*Hermeneutics*, p. 86), despite his enthusiasm for the hermeneutics of H.-G. Gadamer, who in turn regards himself more in the tradition of Hegel than Schleiermacher, gives the following ringing endorsement to Schleiermacher's basic formulation of hermeneutical issues: "In the conditions of dialogue, it is one operation to formulate something and bring it to speech; it is quite another and distinct operation to understand what is spoken. Hermeneutics, Schleiermacher contended, dealt with the latter. This fundamental distinction of speaking and understanding formed the basis for a new direction in hermeneutics, and it opened the way to a systematic basis for hermeneutics in the theory of understanding. If hermeneutics is no longer basically devoted to clarifying the vexing practical problems in interpreting different kinds of texts, then it can take the act of understanding as its true starting point: Hermeneutics becomes in Schleiermacher truly the 'art of understanding.' " Whether or not these are the only alternatives, and whether moving from one ("practical problems") to the other ("the act of understanding") is progress or, instead, an instance of Hobson's choice, the point is clear. (For a brilliant critique of the hermeneutical tradition from Schleiermacher to Gadamer on the basis of Ludwig Wittgenstein's later writings I am indebted to the unpublished Ph.D. dissertation [Yale, 1972] of Charles M. Wood, *Theory and Religious Understanding: A Critique of the Hermeneutics of Joachim Wach.*) (See also n. 30, below.)

2. A useful analysis, if one accepts this nineteenth-century perspectival procedure as normative, is that of Peter C. Hodgson *The Formation of Historical Theology* (New York: Harper and Row, 1966), pp. 271ff. Hodgson tries to schematize the variety of ways in which "faith" and "historical knowledge" have been related, once these two seemingly inexorable and authoritative methodological entities had come to be juxtaposed.

3. See W. G. Kümmel, *Das Neue Testament*, pp. 88–104.

4. The story of the discussion, from Reimarus to the author's own day, is told by Albert Schweitzer, *The Quest of the Historical Jesus*.

5. See M. Kähler, *Der sogenannte historische Jesus und der geschichtliche, biblische Christus* (2nd ed., Leipzig: Deichert, 1896).

6. The issue is complex and worth a special examination. Schleiermacher did of course reflect on their connection, but his thoughts on the matter remained indecisive. He seemed to think that the relation between historical understanding and hermeneutical art is similar to the relation between grammatical and psychological interpretation within hermeneutics itself. Of the two disciplines, hermeneutics and historical criticism, he regarded the first as basic. Its operation is required both before and after the work of criticism is done. But there are also indications that he thought of historical understanding (in a wider sense, including but not confined to criticism) and hermeneutics as overlapping in a way similar to the "part–whole" relation within the operation of understanding itself. In this sense their relation overlaps with the operation which he, following Friedrich Ast, termed the "hermeneutical circle." See Schleiermacher, *Brief Outline of the Study of Theology*, trans. by T. N. Tice (Richmond, Va.: Knox, 1966), §§110–48; *Hermeneutik und Kritik*, in *Sämmtliche Werke* (Berlin: Reimer, 1838), pt. 1, vol. 7, pp. 3, 272 passim; *Hermeneutik* (ed. Kimmerle), pp. 83f, 88f.

7. Strauss said little about Schleiermacher's hermeneutics, but he never tired of asserting that Schleiermacher's christology was an unworkable compromise between traditional ecclesiastical claims and modern historical-critical investigation, and failed to do justice to the integrity of each. See Strauss, *Das Leben Jesu*, vol. 2, §147; *Die christliche Glaubenslehre*, vol. 2, §65; *Der Christus des Glaubens und der Jesus der Geschichte* (reprinted in Texte zur Kirchen- und Theologiegeschichte, no. 14; Gütersloh: Mohn, 1971).

8. See Dilthey's exposition of the contrast between "pragmatic" and "genetic" procedures at the beginning of the era of Idealism in philosophy, *Gesammelte Schriften*, XIV, 1, p. 661.

9. So for example Ernst Bloch, *Subjekt–Objekt. Erläuterungen zu Hegel* (Berlin: Aufbau-Verlag, 1952), p. 69.

10. Quite apart from Hegel's aesthetic judgments on the proper modes of artistic expression to fit the day—he thought the novel appropriate for "so prosaic" a time—his *Phenomenology* is a gold mine of speculation on the possible and impossible implications of an aesthetic and literary sort he may have had in mind. See for example E. Hirsch's essay, "Die Beisetzung der Romantiker in Hegels Phänomenologie," in his *Die idealistische Philosophie und das Christentum* (Gütersloh: Werner, 1926), pp. 117–39, in which Hirsch speculatively applies Hegel's use of the famous literary category "the beautiful soul" to Friedrich Schlegel, Novalis, and Hölderlin—all of whom he thinks Hegel had in mind in this section of *Phenomenology*.

11. *Hermeneutik*, pp. 79, 127 passim; *Brief Outline*, §132.

12. *Hermeneutik*, p. 32: "If one regards understanding alone as the task of hermeneutics and remains faithful to the view of treating thoughts not as something objective, as subject matter, but as facts, one will not get to all the false dialectical distinctions of different senses."

13. G. W. F. Hegel, *Phänomenologie des Geistes*, ed. J. Hoffmeister (Hamburg: Meiner, 1952), pp. 66, 564.

14. In the *Hermeneutik* Schleiermacher occasionally uses *wissen* as synonymous or at least generically similar to *verstehen*. However, he goes on to refer *wissen* as a concept to the examination of dialectical procedure. And it is of course in his *Dialektik* that this term with all it connotes becomes the major preoccupation. In the latter work (*Sämmtliche Werke*, pt. 3, vol. 4/2, pp. 39ff) he distinguishes sharply between *denken* and *wissen*, giving the former an abstract status to which Hegel, for whom thinking was inexorably reality-oriented except in its distorted uses, would never have agreed.

15. See "Brouillon zur Ethik 1805/06" in *Schleiermachers Werke*, ed. Otto Braun (Leipzig: Meiner, 1913), vol. 2, p. 101.

16. *Phänomenologie*, pp. 70–74.

17. Ibid., pp. 74f. In contrast to Schleiermacher, Hegel was extraordinarily skillful in the art of the imaginative depiction of phenomena of the historical, cultural world, a fact that is noted by some of his earliest commentators, for example Rudolf Haym. It is of course by no means adventitious to his philosophical enterprise. On the other hand, Schleiermacher was undoubtedly Hegel's superior for subtlety and precision of dialectical connections.

18. Ibid., pp. 558f.

19. Ibid., p. 564.

20. H.-G. Gadamer, *Wahrheit und Methode* (Tübingen: Mohr, 1960), p. 158.

21. *Hermeneutik*, pp. 86, 130.

22. Richard R. Niebuhr rightly says about Schleiermacher's hermeneutics: "Schleiermacher's style is not one of indirectness in antithesis but directness in polarity." "The original situation of the rational self is . . . a dialogical one": *Schleiermacher on Christ and Religion* (New York: Scribner, 1964), pp. 74, 81. See also H.-G. Gadamer: "Schleiermacher's problem is not that of a mysterious history, but that of the mysterious thou" (*Wahrheit und Methode*, p. 179).

23. *Hermeneutik*, p. 109. The task is quite similar to that proposed by Friedrich von Blanckenburg in *Versuch über den Roman* as the proper aim of the novel. The distinctive inner spiritual life of the hero must be distinguished from others and portrayed by the novelist. This was a striking overlap between the views of the late Enlightenment and the Romantics.

24. "All that is to be presupposed in hermeneutics is language alone, and all that is to be found, including the other objective and subjective presuppositions, must be found from language" (*Hermeneutik*, p. 38).

25. "Just as every discourse has a dual relation, to the totality of the language and to the total thought of the speaker: so also all understanding consists of the

two moments of understanding the discourse as taken from the language and understanding it as a fact in the thinker" (*Hermeneutik*, p. 80).

26. *Hermeneutik*, p. 56.

27. *Hermeneutik*, p. 82.

28. *Hermeneutik*, pp. 80, 128.

29. *Zusammengehörigkeit, Gleichstellung*, are the words Schleiermacher uses (*Hermeneutik*, pp. 80, 88).

30. *Hermeneutik*, pp. 135, 138. To this aspect of Schleiermacher's hermeneutical views Wilhelm Dilthey gave one-sided but profound expression in his great, short expository essay, "Die Entstehung der Hermeneutik" in *Gesammelte Schriften*, vol. V, pp. 317-38, esp. pp. 329f. This partiality was vigorously criticized by Heinz Kimmerle, the latest editor of the *Hermeneutik*, and others (e.g. Gadamer), who have claimed on the one hand that Dilthey overemphasized the "psychologistic" elements in Schleiermacher's hermeneutics through most of the latter's life, and on the other, that Dilthey ignored a final stage in Schleiermacher's views in which thought and speech tend to get even more sharply (and hence psychologistically and subjectivistically) separated than Dilthey allows. (See *Hermeneutik*, editor's introduction, pp. 14-24.) The correctness of this view of both Dilthey's understanding of Schleiermacher and of Schleiermacher himself has in turn been vigorously challenged by Martin Redeker, editor of the second part of Dilthey's *Leben Schleiermachers* (Dilthey, *Gesammelte Schriften*, XIV, 1, 2; see XIV, 1, pp. LVff.) and commentator on Schleiermacher (*Friedrich Schleiermacher. Leben und Werk*; Berlin: de Gruyter, 1968). The publication of Redeker's edition of Dilthey's lengthy exposition of Schleiermacher's thought caused Kimmerle to modify, though by no means to abandon, his criticism of Dilthey (see H. Kimmerle, *Nachbericht zur Ausgabe Fr. D. E. Schleiermacher: Hermeneutik*, Heidelberg: Winter Universitätsverlag, 1968, p. 5).

31. See the academy lectures of 1829 on hermeneutics, *Hermeneutik*, pp. 123-56, esp. pp. 140f.

32. *Hermeneutik*, p. 87; see also pp. 50, 91, 138. The last passage represents a subtle and significant modification: "better than he can render account of himself." For some notes on the genesis of this remark, see Gadamer, *Wahrheit und Methode*, pp. 182f. To Professor Victor Gourevitch I owe the information that Kant, who had used the expression, probably got it from Fielding. It must be remembered that Kant used it in a different sense from Schleiermacher. For Kant it referred to the interpreter's critical and logical understanding of the subject matter; for Schleiermacher to the interpreter's understanding of the process of creation and the author's thought.

33. *Hermeneutik*, p. 88.

34. "System des transcendentalen Idealismus" (1800), in *Schellings Werke* (from the original edition; new arrangement), ed. M. Schröter (Munich: Beck, 1958), vol. 2, pp. 327-634, esp. pp. 612-29. "If aesthetic intuition is only transcendental [intuition which has] become objective, then it is self-evident that art is the only

true and eternal organ and document of philosophy that authenticates always and ever anew what philosophy cannot depict externally, viz., the unconscious in action and production and its original identity with the conscious. Art is highest for the philosopher because it (as it were) opens up to him the holy of holies, where in eternal and original unity there . . . burns in one flame what is separated in nature and history, and what must ever remain fugitive in life and action, as in thought" (pp. 627f).

35. While not explicitly stated in this essay, this view is clearly implied by his focus on *Dichtungsvermögen* as the "original intuition" ("System . . . ," p. 626).

36. In making this claim I follow Dilthey's powerful description of the common development of Schelling and Hegel in 1801, which still seems to me correct despite considerable later criticism. Dilthey sees the heart of their common view in an "intellectual intuition" which is a conscious knowing of a transcendence of all subject–object differentiation, a grasp of an original "divine connectedness of things" which overcomes the contrast and even the heterogeneity between the universal and the particular, the finite and the infinite. (See Dilthey, *Gesammelte Schriften*, vol. IV, p. 206.) For Schelling, the most immed\ently relevant essays for the development of this stage of his philosophizing are "Darstellung meines Systems der Philosophie" (1801) and "Bruno oder über das göttliche und natürliche Prinzip der Dinge: Ein Gespräch" (1802). Both are to be found in *Schellings Werke*, vol. 3.

37. Schleiermacher is always firm and clear on this point. For instance in the *Dialektik*: "Intuition of God never becomes actually executed but remains merely an indirect schematism" (*Sämmtliche Werke*, pt. 3, 4/2. p. 152).

38. For the latter term, see *Hermeneutik*, p. 119 passim. For a clear coordination of "immediate intuition" and "divination," and the contrast between both of them and the "comparative method," compare pp. 109 and 119.

39. For example in his description of feeling as steadily accompanying both intuition and action, as well as being the point of transition and unity between them. See for instance *Sämmtliche Werke*, pt. 3, 4/2, pp. 429f. In *On Religion: Speeches to Its Cultured Despisers* (New York: Harper Torchbook, 1958) the early Schleiermacher speaks of a preconscious, immediate union of intuition and feeling (see the second speech, e.g. pp. 40, 44). It was a claim he did not repeat explicitly in his later writings.

40. H.-G. Gadamer, *Wahrheit und Methode*, p. 179.

41. See *Hermeneutik*, pp. 50, 61, 79, 91, 95.

42. "Vorlesungen über die Aesthetik," in *Sämmtliche Werke*, pt. 3, vol. 7. A short overview of Schleiermacher's aesthetics may be found in René Wellek, *A History of Modern Criticism: 1750–1950*, vol. 2, pp. 303–08.

43. Schleiermacher makes this perfectly clear in his exposition of the saying in the academy lectures of 1829. See *Hermeneutik*, pp. 138f., and Gadamer, pp. 180–85.

44. *Hermeneutik*, pp. 50, 81, 87, 91, 138.

45. Friedrich Ast, *Grundlinien der Grammatik, Hermeneutik und Kritik* (1808). See Dilthey, XIV/2, pp. 657ff, 708.

46. For Schleiermacher's only extensive exposition of the notion, see *Hermeneutik*, pp. 141ff.

47. *Hermeneutik*, pp. 93, 149f.

48. *Hermeneutik*, pp. 163ff.

49. *Hermeneutik*, pp. 117f.

50. See *Hermeneutik*, pp. 133–35.

51. For this distinction between the individual life-moment of inception and the subsequent development of thought and presentation, and the corresponding distinction between psychological and technical aspects of interpretation, see Schleiermacher's extensive marginal notes of 1832/33 to his lectures of 1820 and 1829 on the second (i.e. the technical in contrast to the grammatical) part of hermeneutics: *Hermeneutik*, pp. 163f. See also pp. 108, 116f, 133ff.

52. *Hermeneutik*, p. 141.

53. *Hermeneutik*, p. 154.

CHAPTER 16

1. Contrary to Kimmerle, *Hermeneutik* (editor's introduction), pp. 20ff.

2. *Hermeneutik*, pp. 163ff.

3. Schleiermacher, "Einleitung ins neue Testament," in *Sämmtliche Werke*, pt. 1, vol. 8, pp. 218ff.

4. Dilthey, XIV, 2, p. 777.

5. Dilthey, XIV, 2, p. 787.

6. See *inter alia* Schleiermacher's lectures on the life of Jesus in *Sämmtliche Werke*, pt. 1, vol. 6 (e.g. pp. 461, 463f).

7. See the comment on Schlegel, in notes 17 and 18, ch. 11.

8. In this connection Schleiermacher asserts repeatedly that the really important matter is the actual physical contact between Jesus and his disciples after his crucifixion. It is as real as the fully natural and human relation between them before his death. See *Sämmtliche Werke*, pt. 1, vol. 6 (e.g. pp. 463f, 471, 473f, 493, 495f, 498–511).

9. In his account of the contact between Jesus and his disciples after Jesus' crucifixion, Schleiermacher makes much of the confusion of individual details. But it does not, he says, detract from the likelihood of the historical basis of the story of this sequence as a whole.

10. Schleiermacher, *Sämmtliche Werke*, pt. 1, vol. 2, pp. 614ff. passim.

11. Schleiermacher, *The Christian Faith* (Edinburgh: Clark, 1928), ¶99. Compare this also with such remarks as the disavowal that a spiritual act such as the fulfillment of divine righteousness needs a physical event such as total death for its completion. (See *Sämmtliche Werke*, pt. 1, vol. 6, p. 443.)

12. See the end of the section on the "realm of the Son" and the section on the "realm of the Spirit" in Hegel's *Philosophy of Religion*, in *Sämmtliche Werke*, ed. H. Glockner (Stuttgart: Frommann, 1959), vol. 16, esp. pp. 300–33.

Index